D1081617

INSTEAD OF EDUCATION

INSTEAD
OF EDUCATION

Ways to Help People Do Things Better

JOHN HOLT

E. P. DUTTON & CO., INC.   NEW YORK

Copyright © 1976 by John Holt

All rights reserved. Printed in the U.S.A.

FIRST EDITION

10   9   8   7   6   5   4   3   2

No part of this publication may be reproduced or transmitted
in any form or by any means, electronic or mechanical, including
photocopy, recording, or any information storage and retrieval
system now known or to be invented, without permission in writing
from the publisher, except by a reviewer who wishes to quote brief
passages in connection with a review written for inclusion in a
magazine, newspaper or broadcast.

Published simultaneously in Canada by Clarke, Irwin & Company
Limited, Toronto and Vancouver

ISBN: 0-525-13437-9

Library of Congress Cataloging in Publication Data
Holt, John Caldwell, 1923–
 Instead of education.

 1. Education—Philosophy.   2. Holt, John Caldwell,
1923–   3. Education, Compulsory.   I. Title.
LB885.H6396   1976   370.1   75-30783

Contents

INSTEAD OF EDUCATION

I

Doing, Not "Education"

This is a book in favor of *doing*—self-directed, purposeful, meaningful life and work—and *against* "education"—learning cut off from active life and done under pressure of bribe or threat, greed and fear.

It is a book about people doing things, and doing them better; about the conditions under which we may be able to do things better; about some of the ways in which, *given those conditions*, other people may be able to help us (or we them) to do things better; and about the reasons why these conditions do not exist and *cannot be made to exist* within compulsory, coercive, competitive schools.

Not all persons will give the word "education" the meaning I give it here. Some may think of it, as I once described it, as "something a person gets for himself, not that which someone else gives or does to him." But I choose to define it here as most people do, something that some people do to others for their own good, molding and shaping them, and trying to make them learn what they think they ought to know. Today, everywhere in the world, that is what "education" has become, and I am wholly against it. People still spend a great deal of time—as for years I did myself—talking about how to make "education" more effective and efficient, or how to do it or give it to more people, or how to reform or humanize it.

But to make it more effective and efficient will only be to make it worse, and to help it do even more harm. It cannot be reformed, cannot be carried out wisely or humanely, because its purpose is neither wise nor humane.

Next to the right to life itself, the most fundamental of all human rights is the right to control our own minds and thoughts. That means, the right to decide for ourselves how we will explore the world around us, think about our own and other persons' experiences, and find and make the meaning of our own lives. Whoever takes that right away from us, as the educators do, attacks the very center of our being and does us a most profound and lasting injury. He tells us, in effect, that we cannot be trusted even to think, that for all our lives we must depend on others to tell us the meaning of our world and our lives, and that any meaning we may make for ourselves, out of our own experience, has no value.

Education, with its supporting system of compulsory and competitive schooling, all its carrots and sticks, its grades, diplomas, and credentials, now seems to me perhaps the most authoritarian and dangerous of all the social inventions of mankind. It is the deepest foundation of the modern and worldwide slave state, in which most people feel themselves to be nothing but producers, consumers, spectators, and "fans," driven more and more, in all parts of their lives, by greed, envy, and fear. My concern is not to improve "education" but to do away with it, to end the ugly and antihuman business of people-shaping and let people shape themselves.

This does not mean that no one should ever influence or try to influence what others think and feel. We all touch and change (and are changed by) those we live and work with. We are by instinct talkative and social creatures, and naturally share with those around us our view of reality. Both in my work as writer and lecturer, and among my friends, I do this all the time. But I refuse to put these others in a position where they feel they have no choice but to agree with me, or seem to agree. I want them to have the right, if they wish, to reject absolutely any and all of my ideas, as I would want and demand for myself the right to reject theirs. Also, I have learned that no one can truly say Yes to an idea, mine or anyone else's, unless he can freely say No to it. This is why, except as an occasional visitor, I will no longer do my teaching in compulsory and competitive schools.

I do not mean to say, either, that no one should ever have the right to ask another to show what he knows or can do. Clearly, if someone wants to drive a car, fly a plane, or do something that might directly affect the lives or health of other people, then society, through some agent, has the right to demand that he show that he is able to do what he wants to be allowed to do. Indeed, even where health and safety are not involved, a person can often rightly be asked to show his competence. If he wants to play in an orchestra, sing in a chorus, act in a play, or join other people in any work they are doing, whether for money, pleasure, or other reasons, they have a right to ask him to show that he can do it well enough to help and not hinder them. But these demands are specific in time and place. They are not at all the same thing as saying to someone that just to be allowed to live in the world at all he must be able to show that he knows this or that.

By "doing" I do not mean only things done with the body, the muscles, with hands and tools, rather than with the mind alone. I am not trying to separate or put in opposition what many might call the "physical" and the "intellectual." Such distinctions are unreal and harmful. Only in words can the mind and body be separated. In reality they are one; they act together. So by "doing" I include such actions as talking, listening, writing, reading, thinking, even dreaming.

The point is that it is the do-er, not someone else, who has decided what he will say, hear, read, write, or think or dream about. He is at the center of his own actions. He plans, directs, controls, and judges them. He does them for his own purposes—which may of course include a common purpose with others. His actions are not ordered and controlled from outside. They belong to him and are a part of him.

The best and only really good place for do-ers would be a society that does not yet exist. In that society all people, of whatever age, sex, race, etc., could have work to do which was varied and interesting, which challenged and rewarded their skill and intelligence, which they could do well and take pride in doing well, over which they could exercise some control, and whose ends and purposes they could understand and respect. Today, very few people feel this way about their work—only a small number of artists, artisans, skilled craftsmen, specialists, professionals, and a few others. Beyond this, all people would feel—as very few people do now—that what they thought, wanted, said, and did would make a real difference in their lives and the lives of people around them. Their politics, like their work, would be meaningful. Their elected officials would be public servants, not petty kings and emperors. They would shape and control the society they lived in, instead of being shaped and controlled by it. In such a society no one would worry about "education." People would be busy *doing interesting things that mattered*, and they would grow more informed, competent, and wise in doing them. They would learn about the world from living in it, working in it, and changing it, and from knowing a wide variety of people who were doing the same. But nowhere in the world does such a society exist, nor is there one in the making. Except perhaps in societies too small and primitive to be helpful, we have no models to go on; we must invent and design such a society for ourselves. Neither in the United States, nor any other countries I know of, are there more than a handful of people thinking and talking seriously about what such a society might be like, or how we might make it. What people talk and argue about instead is growth, efficiency, and progress, and how human beings may best be selected and shaped ("educated") and used for those ends.

This is not a book about such a doing society, or what it might be like. Enough to say that it would be a society whose tools and institutions would be much smaller in scale, serving human beings rather than being served by them; a society modest and sparing in

its use of energy and materials, and reverent and loving in its attitudes toward nature and the natural world. This is a book about
how we might make the societies we have slightly more useful and
livable for do-ers, about the resources that might help some people,
at least, to lead more active and interesting lives—and, perhaps, to
make some of the beginnings, or very small models, of a doing society. It is not a book about how to solve or deal with such urgent
problems as poverty, idleness, discrimination, exploitation, waste,
and suffering. These are not educational problems or school problems. They have not been and cannot and will not be solved by
things done in compulsory schools, and they will not be solved by
changing these schools (or even by doing away with them altogether). The most that may happen is that, once freed of the
delusion that schools *can* solve these problems, we might begin to
confront them directly, realistically, and intelligently.

In this book I feel myself speaking mostly to that minority of
people, including parents, teachers, would-be teachers, and students themselves, who believe that children (like all people) will
live better, learn more, and grow more able to cope with the world
if they are not constantly bribed, wheedled, bullied, threatened,
humiliated, and hurt; if they are not set endlessly against each
other in a race which all but a few must lose; if they are not constantly made to feel incompetent, stupid, untrustworthy, guilty,
fearful, and ashamed; if their interests, concerns, and enthusiasms
are not ignored or scorned; and if instead they are allowed, encouraged, and (if they wish) helped to work with and help each
other, to learn from each other, and to think, talk, write, and read
about the things that most excite and interest them. In short, if
they are able to explore the world in their own way, and in as
many areas as possible direct and control their own lives. In a very
interesting and important new book, *The Self-Respecting Child*
(Thames and Hudson, London), Alison Stallibrass describes in the
most precise detail (see quotes in Appendix), how this exploring
takes place, and *from the earliest days of a baby's life.* Even then, he
knows what he needs and wants to know. Children do not need to

be made to learn about the world, or shown how. They want to, and they know how.

For the time being, my message to this minority is this: The chances are we will have universal compulsory education and compulsory schools for at least another generation. Do not waste your energy trying to reform all these schools. They cannot be reformed. It may be possible for a few of you, in a few places, to make a place called a school which will be a humane and useful doing place for the young. If so, by all means do it. In most places, not even this much will be possible. The most we will be able to do may be to find ways to help some children escape education and schooling, and to help some others, who cannot escape, to be less damaged by it than they are now. That is, we may be able to help some children to find ways to prevent school from killing the curiosity, energy, resourcefulness, and confidence with which they explore the world, and to find ways outside of school to nourish and encourage these qualities, so that even if they learn little or nothing worthwhile in school, they can continue the learning they were doing so well before they went to school.

Along with this, what we can do and should do right now is attack the legitimacy of compulsory education and schooling. As the CIA would put it, we need to "destroy its cover." That is, as we are beginning to do for the CIA, we need to show what education and schooling really do. We need to reveal as untrue—as myths, illusions, and lies—the stories and alibis the schools and the educators tell us (and often themselves) to justify themselves and explain their repeated failures. We need to say to people, "If you want to have compulsory education and compulsory schooling, you can have them. But don't be fooled by the advertising and the label on the package! Understand what it is you're getting." Perhaps within a generation or so most people will indeed understand, and decide they want no more of it.

But perhaps not. In that case, this book might be considered as a warning to any people or society which takes human freedom and dignity seriously and values them highly. You cannot have human liberty, and the sense of all persons' uniqueness, dignity, and worth on which it must rest, if you give to some people the right to tell other people what they must learn or know, or the right to say officially and "objectively" that some people are more able and worthy than others. Let any who want to make such judgments make them privately and in the understanding that such judgments can only be personal and subjective. But do not give them any permanent or official sanction, or the liberty and dignity of your citizens will soon be gone.

2

The Myth of "Learning"

Some may wonder why I speak of "doing," or "doing things better," instead of "learning." For one thing, the word "learning" implies (as most people now seem to believe) that learning is separate from the rest of life, that we only do it or do it best when we are not doing anything else, and best of all in a place where nothing else is done. Almost everyone who goes through S-chools comes out believing (1) if I want to learn anything important, I have to go to a place called a school and get someone called a teacher to teach it to me; (2) the process will be boring and painful; and (3) I probably won't learn it.

The idea that everything important must be learned in school is very new. Until quite recently, most people understood very well that while some things might be learned best in school, others could be learned as well or better out of school, and many could not be learned in school at all. They would have laughed at the idea that all knowledge and wisdom could be found or put in classrooms and books. Even now, most of the people who think everything must be learned in school did not themselves learn there most of what they know.

Not only did I not learn in school most of what I know, but I did not learn it in what people call "learning situations," that is, from experiences that I went into in order to learn something. I do not do any of the things I do "in order to learn something." I have learned much about music and music-making by going to rehearsals and concerts. But I do not go to them to "learn about" music, but because I love what I see and hear there. In my short visits to other countries, or other parts of my own country, I have learned many things about those places. But I did not go there "to learn," but to see people and do things. In the last year or two I have done some work with other citizens in my home town of Boston to defeat or at least delay a bad and crooked so-called urban-development scheme. From this I have learned much about the law, politics, and economics of the city, and about the workings of the state and city governments. But I did not go into the work to learn all this, but to try to prevent my city from being robbed and ruined. I read many magazines and books, not to "learn" what is in them, but because I think they may be interesting, or helpful, or exciting. I may now and then read to find out something, but whether I learn, i.e., remember it, depends on whether it helps me to do my work and live and enjoy my life.

I must repeat here what I have written before: The best learning community I have ever seen or been part of was not called, or meant to be, a learning community at all. It was a submarine—the USS *Barbero*—in World War II. We were not on it to "learn," but to help fight the war. Like millions of other people at the time, we did not talk or think about "learning"; we learned from the demanding work we did together, and we shared our experience and skill as widely as we could. In a truly healthy and vital society, all people would feel this way. No one would want other people to be ignorant, unskilled, or stupid, so that he could more easily trick them or control them or get rich at their expense. In *Brave New World*, Aldous Huxley makes his World Controller, Mustapha Mond, say that a society made up entirely of Alphas, intelligent people, had once been organized as an experiment, but that it did not and never could work. Huxley was mistaken. Our submarine was such a society (one of many), *and it could not have worked any other way.* The tragedy is that for many people it is only in time of war that they have a chance to live in such a society.

The trouble with talk about "learning experiences" is that it implies that all experiences can be divided into two kinds, those from which we learn something, and those from which we learn nothing. But there are no experiences from which we learn nothing. We learn something from everything we do, and everything that happens to us or is done to us. What we learn may make us more informed or more ignorant, wiser or stupider, stronger or weaker, but we always learn something. What it is depends on the experience, and above all, on how we feel about it. A central point of this book is that we are very unlikely to learn anything good from experiences which do not seem *to us* closely connected with what is interesting and important in the rest of our lives. Curiosity is never idle; it grows out of real concerns and real needs. Even more important, we are even less likely to learn anything good from coerced experiences, things that others have bribed, threatened, bullied, wheedled, or tricked us into doing. From such we learn mostly anger, resentment, and above all self-contempt and self-hatred for having allowed ourselves to be pushed around or used by others, for not having been smart enough or strong enough to resist and refuse. Some would claim that most people in their daily lives do a great many things—dull, repetitious, and meaningless work, driving a car for hours in traffic, watching television—from which they learn nothing. But of course they learn something. The people doing moronic work learn to hate that work, and themselves for having to do it—and in time, all those who do not have to do it. The people driving cars in traffic learn to think of all the other people they see, driving or walking, as nuisances, obstructions, even as enemies, preventing them from getting where they want to go. And people watching television learn over and over again that the people they see on the screen, "real" or imaginary, are in every way better than they are—younger, handsomer, sexier, smarter, stronger, faster, braver, richer, happier, more successful and respected. When the time finally comes to come back from Dreamland to reality, and get up wearily and turn off the set, the thought is even more strongly in their minds, "Why couldn't I have been more like them?"

It is the quality of our experiences, the satisfaction, excitement, or joy that we get or fail to get from them, that will determine how those experiences change us—in short, what we learn. This is why, as I wrote in *How Children Fail*, a child in a situation that *he experiences* as humiliating, threatening, and painful, cannot and will not learn what the teacher is trying to teach him, or if he does, will forget it in a day or two. This is why the kids in Jim Herndon's Dumb Class (see *How to Survive in Your Native Land*) could not learn to do in school *even those things which they did very well out of school*. This is why people can learn only when they come boldly, confidently, and eagerly to the learning.

Doing Is Learning

Another common and mistaken idea hidden in the word "learning" is that learning and doing are different kinds of acts. Thus, not many years ago I began to play the cello. I love the instrument, spend many hours a day playing it, work hard at it, and mean someday to play it well. Most people would say that what I am doing is "learning to play the cello." Our language gives us no other words to say it. But these words carry into our minds the strange idea that there exist two very different processes: (1) learning to play the cello; and (2) playing the cello. They imply that I will do the first until I have completed it, at which point I will stop the first process and begin the second; in short, that I will go on "learning to play" until I "have learned to play," and that then I will begin "to play."

Of course, this is nonsense. There are not two processes, but one. We learn to do something by doing it. There is no other way. When we first do something, we probably will not do it well. But if we keep on doing it, have good models to follow and helpful advice if and when we feel we need it, and always do it as well as we

can, we will do it better. In time, we may do it very well. This
process never ends. The finest musicians, dancers, athletes,
surgeons, pilots, or whatever they may be, must constantly practice
their art or craft. Every day the musicians do their scales, the
dancers exercise at the barre, and so on. A surgeon I knew would
from time to time, when not otherwise busy, tie knots in fine
surgical gut with one hand, without looking, just to keep in practice. In that sense, people never stop "learning to do" what they
know how to do, no matter how well they do it. They must "learn"
every day to do it as well as they can, or they will soon do it less
well. The principal flutist of the Boston Symphony under Kous-
sevitsky used to say, "If I miss a day's practice, I hear the difference; if I miss two days', the conductor hears the difference; if I
miss three days', the audience hears the difference."

The Baby Is Not "Getting Ready"

Educators talk all the time about "skills": reading skills, writing
skills, communication skills, even listening skills. It may be true, at
the level of words, to say that anyone doing a difficult thing well is
using a variety of skills. But this does not mean that the best way
to teach a difficult act is to break it into as many separate skills as
possible and teach them one by one. As Whitehead said years ago,
we cannot separate an act from the skills involved in the act. The
baby does not learn to speak by learning the skills of speech and
then using them to speak with, or to walk by learning the skills of
walking and then using them to walk with. He learns to speak by
speaking, to walk by walking. When he takes his first hesitant steps
he is not *practicing*. He is not getting ready. He is not learning how
to walk so that later he may walk somewhere. He is walking because he wants to walk, *right now*. He has thought about it, worked
it out in his mind, convinced himself that he knows how to do it
and can do it. And now he is going to do it.

We cannot separate skills and acts, and we make a disastrous
error when we try. Talking is not a skill, or a collection of skills,

but an act, a doing. Behind the act there is a purpose; whether at two or ninety-two, we talk because we have something we want to say, and someone we want to say it to, and because we think or hope our words will make a difference. The baby who begins to talk, long before he makes any sounds that we hear as words, or even understands words, has learned from sharp observation that the sounds that bigger people make with their mouths affect the other things they do. *Their talk makes things happen.* He may not know exactly what, or how. But he wants to be a part of that talking group of bigger people, wants to make things happen with *his* voice. In the same way, walking is not a skill, but an act, with a purpose; the baby wants to move as he sees the bigger people moving, and quickly and skillfully, like them. Reading is not a skill, but an act. The child sees written words all around him; he sees that the older people look at those words, use them, get meaning from them. Those words make things happen. One day (if we give him a chance) he decides that he wants to find out what those words say and mean, and that he can and will find out. *At that instant, and with that decision, he begins to read.* Not to "learn to read," but to read. Of course, at first, he doesn't do it well. He may not even be able to read one word. But if he is allowed (as few children are) to continue to *do* it, to seek out *in his own way and for his own reasons* the meaning of written words, with only as much help as he may ask for; if this task which he has set himself isn't taken from him and replaced with a lot of fragmented and meaningless tasks invented by someone else and done on their command; if he is not convinced by adults (as many children are) that he is not able to do this task he has set for himself, to figure out what written words say, but must "get" reading from a teacher as a patient gets a shot from a doctor; if he is very lucky, and none of these bad things happen, he will be reading well in a short time, perhaps even in a matter of months.

Not long ago I wrote to a number of people who work in reading and reading instruction in various schools of education, to ask if they knew of any research to find out how many children teach themselves to read, and beyond that, how they may have done it. Only one person answered, to say that he had never heard of any such research. Nor have any of the hundreds of educators and reading experts I have asked since. At first it seems strange that reading experts have not asked this question. One might think it would be the first question they would ask. On second thought, it is not strange at all; the answer to this question might be dangerous. It might show once again that our most rapid, efficient, far-reaching, useful, and permanent learning comes from our doing things that *we ourselves* have decided to do, and that in doing such things we often need very little help or none at all.

Knowledge Is Action

Beyond this, we would do very well to understand that what we have mistakenly come to think of as "bodies of knowledge" or "fields of learning" or "academic disciplines" or "school subjects" are not nouns but *verbs*, not things that exist independently somewhere out there, but things that people *do*. No one can say, *"Here* is Biology, *here* Mathematics, *here* Philosophy." No one can *point* to Physics, or show us Chemistry. In reality no dotted lines divide History from Geography or Physics from Chemistry, or Philosophy from Linguistics, and so on. These are simply different ways in which we look at parts of the wholeness of reality and human experience and ask certain kinds of questions about them. History is the *act* of asking questions about certain aspects of the past. So are Geology and Paleontology, but the questions are different. Physics and Chemistry are ways of asking different questions about the nonliving world about us. And so on. All of these are, of course, collective acts; we do them with other people, and many people have done them over many years. Thus each one of these human activities has its own history, and at least a part of Mathematics or Physics or Philosophy is the account of what other mathematicians or physicists or philosophers have done. But our "knowledge" of these things is a record of what these people *did;* what questions they asked, how they went about getting their answers, what answers they got, what conclusions they drew from their answers. Whatever we do in these fields is added to, and therefore part of, what others did before. As Ivan Illich says, there is no knowledge in the world; the world is as it is. Knowledge is a process in the minds of living people. It is what we do as we try to find out who and where we are, and what is going on about us.

3

Do-er Schools vs. Educator Schools

Of the places we name "schools," some are *doing* places—typing schools, driving schools, cooking schools, dance schools, karate schools, ski schools, and so on. Many other resources for do-ers, such as libraries, museums, or theaters, are not called schools at all. The Berlitz language schools are good examples of schools that are resources for do-ers rather than for educators. First of all, they do not try to compel us by law to study another language, or say that if we do we will get good jobs, be successful and rich, or that if we don't we'll be failures and poor. They make no such promises or threats. They only imply that if we speak another language we will get more pleasure out of life.

In the Harvard Square subway station in Cambridge is a poster for a language school called Academia. On it is a pen-and-ink drawing of a man and woman talking to each other. The poster is headed, "Whatever It Is, It Sounds Better in French." Then this dialogue: Woman: "Cheri, veux-tu sortir les poubelles?" Man: "Oui, mon amour." Translated, Woman: "Lover, don't forget to take out the garbage," Man: "Oh yes, indeed."

Not all schools for do-ers make so lighthearted an appeal. A subway ad for a technical school begins bluntly, "Education Is

Useless Unless You Profit from It." Perhaps it is because the language schools appeal to people who can afford to travel to foreign countries that they don't feel they have to make such big promises. They do not say, either, that if we would like to speak another language, we must learn it in a school, let alone their school. They only say that if for our own reasons we would like to speak another language, they have resources—people who speak the language, tapes, records, other learners—which may help us and which (usually for a fee) we are welcome to use if we want.

The Berlitz and other schools do not give us an exam to see whether we are smart enough to get in, whether we are "Berlitz material" or "Up to the Berlitz experience." Nor do they say that their schools are best because they are the hardest to get into. Once in the school, we study only the language we want. We do not have to study German in order to be allowed to study French. We stay only as long as we want; when we have had enough, we leave. They do not test us at the end to see how much we have learned, nor give us a diploma or any other kind of job ticket. They keep no records about us and our work for other people to see. They do not put a label on us to tell the world that we were good or bad students, or make any other public judgments about us.

By contrast, the great majority of what we call schools are educator schools. They include all elementary, secondary, and other schools that people are required by law to attend. They also include virtually all junior colleges, colleges, universities, and graduate and professional schools, which give out the tickets which most people need to live and work in society and which they cannot get in any other way.

The schools for do-ers, which help people explore the world as they choose, I now call "small 's' schools" (written *s-chools*). The schools for educators, which get and hold their students by the threat of jail or uselessness or poverty, I now call "capital 'S' schools," (written *S-chools*). There is very little we can do to make these S-chools better, and they are almost certain to get worse.

Nothing to Do with Gerbils

The difference between s-chools and S-chools has nothing whatever to do with pedagogy, with philosophies of education, ways of teaching, curricula, materials, and so forth. Of course, the more choice, movement, action, freedom, cooperation, talk, variety, energy, excitement, and joy there is in a classroom, and the less invidious comparison, testing, gold-starring, grading, pecking-ordering, humiliation, coercion, threat, punishment, and fear, the better it will be for the children—and for the teachers, too. But how nice a school is or whether or not it has gerbils (or other animals) has nothing to do with whether it is a s-chool or a S-chool.

Much as I admired and loved A. S. Neill and approved of Summerhill (the school he started and led), it was still a S-chool, because the students who were there could only choose to go to Summerhill or *some other S-chool* (almost certainly worse). They could not choose not to go to school at all. Once, at the end of a long conversation when I first came to Summerhill in 1965, Neill, between puffs on his pipe, said to me, "You know, it's a paradise for kids to be able to do what they like." True, and thanks to Neill's courage and wisdom, the kids there could do much more of what they liked than they could anywhere else. But London was then full of things that many of the children were interested in, and it was only an hour and a half away by train. Yet they could not go there. Nor—because of the law, not Neill—could they work, or travel, or live alone or with friends of their choosing, or in any way live actively and responsibly as human beings. The only choice society offered them was, go to this school or some other school. Any school which is part of such a system of coercion is a S-chool.

Why did the kids in Jim Herndon's class (see *How to Survive in Your Native Land*) like to do "all that creative stuff" in class? Because it was better than the regular stuff. But when he and a colleague set up a special Creative Arts class, and told the kids they could do what they wanted, hoping they would spend all their time doing creative stuff, they found that none of them wanted to do *any* of it. They had previously only done it as the best of a bad bunch of choices. Would all the teen-agers now at Summerhill, or schools like it, be there if the law gave them the choice of working, traveling, living alone or with friends? Almost certainly not. When the law gives them such a choice, then Summerhill (and other schools) will become s-chools. Not before.

After all, if the government told convicted criminals they could choose which prison they would go to, the prisons might in time become slightly better. But they would still be prisons.

Nothing to Do with Rules

By contrast, many s-chools are very tightly and rigidly structured. Any school of dance or the martial arts puts the students under the most intense and inflexible discipline. Watch students in a ballet or karate class at their work. As long as they stay in the class, they have no choices at all. Now, the instructor tells them, move like this. Arms move, legs move, all together. Go when I say go. Stop when I say stop. In a ski school the instructor says, now we do a turn to the right, all follow me. No, your shoulder is here, your knee here, it should be there, try it again. A friend in his late twenties is studying gymnastics for the first time. No one has told him to. Being able to do it is not going to get him a job or a raise. He does it only because he wants to. But the discipline is exact and intense.

Another example, in some ways less physical, is language—though language is probably the most difficult muscular coordination that most people ever learn. The institution called CIDOC, in Cuernavaca, Mexico, where Ivan Illich and many others often give seminars, runs among its other activities a Spanish-language school. The school is very demanding, intensive, formal, and tightly organized. The students use an enormous textbook written for the U.S. Foreign Service. Every day they memorize a large list of words and sentences. Then in their classes, usually two students per class, they spend hours in conversational drill with a native language speaker, using in many ways the words and sentence forms they have learned, the instructor correcting them rigorously at every mistake. Students must attend all classes. A student who misses even one or two must persuade the director to allow him to continue in the school.

Some of the young Americans who come to CIDOC, having heard my distinction between s-chools and S-chools, cannot understand why I call this language school a s-chool. The reasons are plain. The language school does not tell people that they must learn Spanish, nor offer prizes for learning Spanish or penalties for not learning it. They are not part of any structure which offers such prizes or makes such threats. Nor does the school say that people can learn Spanish only in a school, or only in their school, or better in their school than in any other. There are hundreds of ways to learn Spanish, or help others to learn it. One can learn Spanish by walking the streets of Cuernavaca (or some other town) talking to people. Most of the people who speak Spanish (or any other language) learned it this way. But this takes time, has some disadvantages, and is difficult for those who are shy. Still, says the school, if you want to do it that way, fine. All we say is that if you come here, and do what we ask you to do, at the end of three months you will speak fluent and correct Spanish. This has happened often enough so that we feel confident that we can offer you an agreement. If you enter into this agreement we will undertake to do certain things for you, make certain resources available to you. You on your hand will undertake certain things for us—among others, to attend classes regularly, and to do for each class the preparation we ask you to do. It is altogether up to the student whether he makes that bargain. But if he makes it, the school will hold him to it. They say, in effect, we cannot and will not try to keep our end of the bargain unless you keep yours. Which is fair enough.

t-eachers and T-eachers

As places called "schools" are on both sides of the line between doing and education, so are people called "teachers" doing work called "teaching." On the doing side, people are helping do-ers do what they have freely decided what they want to do. On the education side, people are trying to make others learn what others have decided they ought to learn. I call the former action "t-eaching," the latter "T-eaching." These two actions once seemed to me one and the same; the differences between them made no difference. A teacher was simply a person trying to get a student to learn something. If the student was eager, so much the better for the teacher. Usually the student was indifferent, unwilling, or resisting. But in either case the work seemed the same. Now these two tasks seem so different that they ought not to have the same name. Perhaps there should be a new word for helping people do what they want to do. But the words "teach" and "teacher" are old and honorable, and I will not surrender them up to the T-eachers.

Like the distinction between s-chools and S-chools, this distinction between t-eacher and T-eacher is hard to make clear. Some think that by a t-eacher I mean a kind and sympathetic teacher who gives the children much liberty and many choices. But anyone teaching in a S-chool is bound to be a T-eacher, except perhaps when leading an extracurricular activity that is completely voluntary and for which no grade or credit is given. Thus, the leader of a school drama group, or of a sport not recognized as a school sport, or of some art or craft activity, or hobby or discussion group, might be working as a t-eacher.[1] But even the most pleasant or interesting classes in a S-chool are part of a system of compulsion and coercion, bribe and threat, and therefore anyone leading such classes is a T-eacher, just as I was during the fourteen or fifteen years I worked in S-chools.

As with S-chools and s-chools, the difference between T-eachers and t-eachers has nothing to do with philosophy, methods, or personality, whether the teacher is easy or demanding, kindly or harsh, interesting or dull, friendly or cold. It has to do

---

[1] For a very lively, funny, unsentimental and perceptive account of the work of one t-eacher (a poet) in a New York City S-chool, see Phillip Lopate's *Being with Children* (Doubleday).

with the degree to which the students *are free to choose* to spend their time with him or not, do what he is doing, use his help, listen to and accept or reject his ideas. As I prefer classrooms without desks to classrooms with desks in a row, so I prefer teachers who are kindly, interesting, sensitive, tactful, sympathetic, and generally fond of their students. But a person could be all of these, and still be a T-eacher, or be none of them, and yet be a t-eacher. If the latter, he might not have many students. But if the understanding or skill which he offered to share was hard to find, or if he was exceptionally skillful at sharing it, some people might still come freely to him.

Power against Truth

This distinction between T-eachers and t-eachers is important for many reasons. One has to do with what George Dennison, in *The Lives of Children*, called "reality of encounter." He rightly said that one reason why schooling is so seldom helpful to children, and almost always deeply harmful, is that they have no reality of encounter with their teachers. The teachers are not themselves, but players of roles. They do not talk about what is real to them, what they know, are interested in, and love, but about what the curriculum, the teachers' manual, and the lesson plan says they must talk about. "Start a discussion about. . . ." They do not respond naturally and honestly to the acts and needs of the children, but only as the rules tell them to respond. They ask themselves all the time, "If I do this or say this, or let the students do this or say this, will I get into trouble?" and act according to the answer. Not that their fears are groundless, or these dangers imaginary. Far from it. The newspapers often tell of teachers who were fired for saying things the community did not like. No one is fired for hiding the truth from children, but many are fired for telling the truth.

In one year I spent much time working with one first-grade class, where I came to know the children well. One day two six-year-old girls came up to me and furtively showed me a picture that one or both of them had drawn. It was a (technically) crude drawing of a person defecating, the feces being fired backwards like bullets. My reaction to being shown this picture was about 10% amusement and 90% anxiety. I imagined angry teachers, parents, perhaps even judges saying, "Do you mean to say that you allowed children in your class to draw pictures like this? What had you done to make them think that it would be all right for them to draw, *and show you*, such a disgusting picture? And what did you say to them to make sure they would never draw such a picture again?" And so on.

I don't remember exactly what I said to the children, but I did not pretend to be shocked or indignant. I probably said that they had better hide or tear up the picture, since if many people saw it they would be in trouble. Maybe I even hinted that I would also be in trouble. What I did not do, but wish I had done, was express my non-T-eacherish, human response to the picture, both amuse-ment and amazement. Or, perhaps ask the girls why they showed me the picture. Perhaps they wanted me to talk about a mystery that other adults had hidden from them. Or they may simply have wanted to see how I would react, perhaps shrewdly guessing that seeing the picture might startle me, as it did. And yet I can imag-ine in some schools, or outside of school, talking with the children about the picture, and about defecating, or whatever else they wanted to talk about. From such talk the children might have learned a great deal. They want to learn about the world from us. What they learn, most of the time, is only that we adults pretend, keep secrets, and tell lies.

There can *never* be reality of encounter, truthfulness, honesty, when one person holds power over another. I recall talking to an old friend, then a senior at Harvard, who had enjoyed his years at college and had done very well there. I asked him one day whether he and his classmates very often disagreed with their professors. He laughed and said, "They all *tell* you they want you to." But, he then said, he and his fellow students had learned that anyone want-ing or needing an A in a course (and they all did) had better not argue with the professor. In tests, papers, even discussions, the way to get A's was to stick close to the professor's opinions, changing the language just enough so that he wouldn't think his own words were being thrown back in his face.

Years later I said to a group of teachers in Toronto that when one person holds power over others there is not likely to be very honest conversation between them. After the meeting, a young woman teacher came up, indignant and angry. She did not at all like the distinctions I had made between doing and education, S-chools and s-chools, T-eacher and t-eacher. She insisted that the fact that she could give her students grades or punishments did not prevent them from having honest talks together and that they were in no way afraid to tell her what they thought. She resented my implying that her class was fearful or dishonest. In my turn I made such points as I could. She did not waver, and if anything, grew more angry, told me the things I was saying were untrue and harmful. After ten minutes or so, I asked her, "Are there people in your school or school system who have power over you, the power to fire you, to give or deny raises, promotion, and the like?" She said there were. I said, "Would you talk to one of them as you have been talking to me for the past ten minutes?" As she considered it, her expression changed. After a while, she said softly, "No, I wouldn't." I said, "Neither would I. That's my point." And that is the point.

4

Resources for Do-ers

What resources for do-ers do we now have, but need more of? Or don't have, but should? Resources that people of all ages could use, to lead more active, varied, and interesting lives, places young people might go to if they could spend less time in school, places in which adults might use more of the leisure they have but do not know what to do with.

The list of these is long, and readers will easily think of things to add to it. Some existing resources I will describe are examples which people in other communities could very easily follow, often for very little money. Of these, one I know well is the Beacon Hill Free School, in my own neighborhood in Boston. It is an excellent example of a s-chool. Some excerpts from the Summer 1974 catalog of the school will give an idea of how it works:

> We are beginning our fifth year of free courses with this term, and to now have offered over 300 courses to thousands of people of all ages, at no cost. We continue to thrive because instructors are willing to volunteer their time and services, and because neighbors and neighborhood organizations are willing to donate unused space in the evenings. What small costs accrue for printing, mailing, and the like, are met by donations from kind friends and an occasional benefit. There are no requirements, tests, grades, credits, or degrees. Catalogs are shaped at the General Meetings held every three

months, where anyone is free to offer a course, and anyone free to take what is offered. What administration there is is performed by a few people.

The school was begun by Jack Powers, with the help and inspiration of many others. . . . The purpose of the school is to get people of all ages together, using the resources of the community, human and material, and we thank all those who have made it possible.

The school has four sessions a year. Each session begins with a General Meeting, most of which have been held at the Charles Street Meeting House. People come to the meeting either to offer a course or an activity, or to learn more about what is being offered. After Jack Powers, the coordinator of the meeting, has said a few words about the school, for anyone who may not know how it works, all those who want to offer a course tell the others there what they are offering. Anyone may offer a course, and on any subject he or she wants. No t-eacher has to show proof of competence. If he can attract and hold students, that is enough. If a t-eacher offers a course, and people don't come, or come only a few times, he gets the message. If people like the course, the t-eacher will probably offer it again. Of the thirty-seven courses offered in the Summer '74 catalog, seventeen were continued.

As the following excerpt from the catalog shows, there is no school building:

Our Hosts: BEACON HILL FRIENDS HOUSE,
　　　　　　　6 Chestnut St., Beacon Hill
　　　　　　　BOSTON CENTER FOR THE ARTS,
　　　　　　　551 Tremont St., South End
　　　　　　　CHARLES ST. MEETING HOUSE,
　　　　　　　70 Charles St., Beacon Hill
　　　　　　　HILL HOUSE, INC., 74 Joy St., Beacon Hill
　　　　　　　HIPPOCRATES HEALTH INSTITUTE,
　　　　　　　25 Exeter St., Back Bay
　　　　　　　HOLT ASSOCIATES, INC., 308 Boylston St., Boston
　　　　　　　KING'S CHAPEL PARISH HOUSE, 64 Beacon St., Boston
　　　　　　　ST. JOHN THE EVANGELIST CHURCH,
　　　　　　　33 Bowdoin St., Boston

STONE SOUP GALLERY, 313 Cambridge St., West End and the instructors and friends who have offered their homes. IMPORTANT NOTES: YOU MUST CONTACT INSTRUCTOR BEFORE ATTENDING ANY CLASS FOR THE FIRST TIME. DATES LISTED AT START OF LISTINGS ARE STARTING DATES OF COURSES. *Continuing* MEANS THAT THE COURSE IS CARRIED OVER FROM THE LAST TERM. YOU MUST STILL CALL INSTRUCTORS BEFORE ATTENDING A *Continuing* COURSE FOR THE FIRST TIME. TBA MEANS THAT DAY, TIME, ETC., WILL BE ARRANGED WITH INSTRUCTOR & INTERESTED STUDENTS. CALL INSTRUCTOR! THERE ARE ALWAYS UNAVOIDABLE CHANGES!

The Free School, where it can, finds space in the community for its t-eachers to hold classes. If it can't, teachers and students find their own space. The catalog actually serves as the only administrative tool for letting students know when and where classes will meet. Instructors list an address and/or phone number where students can reach them. After that, it's up to them to decide where and when to meet. The following course entries show what kind of information instructors give to students:

BICYCLE CLINIC
TUES. 6–7:30 PM
Hill House

Continuing. How to maintain your own bicycle, i.e., fixing flats, adjusting gears, etc. Lv. ms. for George Berry at XXX–XXXX. Will take place in the game room, 1st floor. Bring your bike for small repairs.

CREATIVE WRITING
THUR. 7–9 PM
Hill House, 1st fl.,
Sr. Lounge

Continuing. Newcomers welcome. Writing as a creative medium with emphasis on problems of communication & social change. This includes fiction. The use of photography & investigative journalism as a focal point. Instructor, Frank Anthony, XXX–XXXX, days.

MODERN POETRY FORUM
MON. 8–9 PM
TBA

Continuing. Newcomers welcome. An exploration into the American idiom in contemporary poetry, starting with traditions emanating from Pound, Whitman, W. C. Williams, & Charles Olson. Will attempt to meet outdoors, Beacon Hill area. Leaders, info: Joe & Rose Dunn, XXX–XXXX.

BASIC ELECTRONICS   *Continuing.* Newcomers welcome. A course
MON. 5:30 PM   for people who have little or no experience in
Hill House   electronics, but are interested in kit-building,
                      repair, & understanding basic principles.
                      Some experiments. Class leader, Peter Grif-
                      fin, XXX–XXXX.

Here is a list of all courses offered in the Summer '74 session:
Life Drawing; Bicycle Clinic; Creative Writing; Modern Poetry
Forum; Basic Electronics; Exploring Our Sexuality; Portuguese;
Dynamics of Human Communication; Spanish; Hatha Yoga; Sen-
sitivity Training; Conversational Russian II; Creative Movement;
Beethoven; Topics in Western Philosophy; Welfare Advocacy
Training; Are You Considering Suicide?; Getting Thought
Together; Yoga; Living Foods: Indoor Gardening, Organic Nutri-
tion; Lecture: Survival into the 21st Century; Zone Therapy; Kun-
dalini Yoga; Poetry Read-In, Rap-In; Poetry Workshop; Tiddly-
winks; Novels of F. Scott Fitzgerald; General Mathematics, with
Application; Physics Related to Life Sciences; Industrial Design;
Reading Improvement; Jobs, Work, and Identity; Music; Iran: Peo-
ple, Arts, and Land; Acupressure and Swedish Massage; Woodwork; Individualism & Parenthood; Ecology: Interrelationships on
Our Earth; Recycling and Materials Composition; Alternate
Sources of Energy; A Study of the Belle Isle Salt Marsh.

Over the years people have offered more craft or
dance/movement/yoga or encounter/discussion/sensitivity courses
than such S-school-type courses as languages, math, etc. But there
is always a varied and interesting mixture. These courses are about
the kinds of things that people in this area are interested in. Other
areas of the country, or even the city, with different interests,
might have very different offerings.

The school guesses—since it keeps no records on its students, it
can only guess—that in its first four years, about two thousand
people took its courses. In any one session, three or four hundred
people may be involved. At first, almost all the students and
teachers seemed to be people who had been to college or even grad-

uate school and were doing more or less academic or artistic work. But as time has gone by and the school has become better known, some people have offered or attended courses who didn't have much schooling and ordinarily would have little to do with any place that called itself a "school."

In many respects, the Free School is like more traditional centers of adult education, of which we have one in Boston and one in Cambridge, or like some of the Free Universities that students organized in the last ten years or so on many of our college campuses. There are, though, some important differences, one of which may make the Beacon Hill Free School a much easier model for others to copy. As Jane Lichtman wrote, in her *National Directory of Free U's*, "The Beacon Hill Free School has the least administrative structure and the most diversity. . . . For all its simplicity it operates beautifully."

It does, and mostly because it is simple. It has no building, and hence does not have to worry about paying for it, or keeping it up, or losing it. Since it charges no money, it does not need to guarantee anything to its students, and hence does not have to worry about the credentials or even the competence of its teachers. Since students don't pay, and teachers aren't paid, the school does not have to keep elaborate books, records of money received, and so on. It has almost no budget; its only expense is the quarterly catalog, which is very inexpensively produced and printed. Copies of the catalog are shown and distributed in many parts of the neighborhood, but anyone who wants one has only to write in, sending a self-addressed, stamped envelope. All told, the school probably spends less than $100 a year. Since at any time there are well over two hundred people making use of it, we could say that its per-pupil cost was *less than fifty cents a year!* This compares remarkably well with the $600 + per pupil per year that our public S-chools spend (about $1700 in Boston). Granted, its students use the Beacon Hill Free School for only an hour or so a week, instead of the thirty to thirty-five hours a week that most children spend in school. But on the same per-hour basis, the S-chools would spend less than $20 per student per year. This is certainly a resource for human growth and learning that poor communities, or poor nations, would do well to study and imitate.

Another important difference between the BHFS and most of the campus-based Free Universities I have heard of is that it is not built around a political ideology. This has given it a broader base in the community, and drawn in, as teachers and students, people who might feel threatened or angered by much of what they might see in a campus Free University catalog, i.e., much writing about "revolution," "the oppressed." "capitalism," along with pictures of clenched fists, bearded guerrillas, and Mao. Also, these campus-based s-chools are very vulnerable. The students who care about them and put work into them eventually graduate and leave, often without having found successors. Also, they depend for their facilities on the university, which will cut them down if they become too radical—or too popular.

It is worth noting that the BHFS, small as it is, already has trouble finding space for its courses. Most of the people in the area, at least those who use the school, live in small apartments, too small for many of the kinds of classes or activities they want to offer. Institutions in the area, especially churches, have been generous with space, but they don't have much, and they need some for their own programs. This lack of meeting space makes some kinds of activities difficult or impossible—such as, perhaps, a neighborhood chorus or musical group. Even if many more people wanted to take part in the school, as teachers or students, the school could hardly find a place for them. And yet, only a few blocks up the hill, there is a public S-chool building, full of rooms that would be ideal for these purposes. But, like almost all public S-chool buildings, outside of school hours this one is tightly locked. We need to find ways, as people have in a few communities, to make these buildings, often expensive and lavishly equipped, available for all people to use.

Another very important resource for do-ers, and a model which has already been copied in forty or more communities, is The

Learning Exchange, in Evanston, Illinois, a small suburban city just north of Chicago. The Exchange was started in May 1971 by Dennis Detzel and Robert Lewis, then graduate students at Northwestern University. The idea for The Exchange grew out of conversations Detzel had with Ivan Illich and others at CIDOC in Mexico, and follows very closely one of the proposals in Illich's book *Deschooling Society*. The founding group believed, as they say in their 1974 catalog,

> that there were a great many people in greater Chicago with skills, talents, and knowledge to share. Craftsmen, professionals, laborers, housewives, retired people, students—virtually every member of society could teach something to someone else. We also believed that many places could serve as "classrooms"—people's homes, offices, libraries, community centers, churches, and parks. Even a telephone could serve as a "meeting place"—people could answer questions about a subject or have discussions over the phone. . . . To fill this need, we set out to design a service that was simple to use and available to anyone in metropolitan Chicago who wanted to teach, learn, or share their interests. The organization would have no entrance requirements, and degrees or certificates would not be issued or required of people wishing to teach through the service.

The Exchange works like this. A person phones or writes if he (1) wants to learn or find out something, (2) has some knowledge or skill that he would like to teach others, or (3) wants to meet other people who share a particular interest. His name, address, phone, field of interest, and what he wants to do (i.e., learn, teach, share interests) go on a card and into a file—or fairly soon, if The Exchange keeps growing as it has, into a computer.[1] Also, his field of interest is added to The Exchange's list of interests. If The Exchange has in its files names of other people who want to teach, or learn, or share whatever this caller is interested in, he is given this information. It is then up to him to get in touch with the others,

[1] A recent New York *Times* story said that the telephone company in Des Moines, Iowa, has made up a list, which they will give to any who ask for it, of all the people in the area who speak, write, or read foreign languages. Perhaps in time they, or some other phone company, will extend this to cover other kinds of skill and information.

and decide with them if, how, when, where, and on what basis they want to get together. If The Exchange knows of no people who want to teach, etc., what this caller is interested in, they put his name on file. If, later, others call in who can teach what he wants to learn, The Exchange will tell him about them. As the catalog says, "The Learning Exchange is a way to do what you want, where you want, when you want, for as long as you want, with people you like." Or, at least, like well enough to want to go on meeting with them.

The Exchange began its work in a borrowed office, with a borrowed phone, a small file box and some 3 x 5 cards, and $25 from Northwestern University. Six months and $27 later it had built up a file of two hundred and ninety topics. By the end of 1973 The Exchange had its own office, a staff of four, and the names of fifteen thousand persons interested in two thousand topics. The topics are listed in their 1974 catalog. They make interesting reading, and say something about the extraordinary range of human experience and interests. Also, that there is no way in which a conventional S-chool, with its buildings, departments, paid and credentialed staff, could deal with more than a tiny part of this wealth of human knowledge or satisfy more than a tiny part of this human curiosity. Here are the first twenty topics listed under "A":

A.C.T. Test
Abortion—Pro & Con
Abstracting
Accordion
Accounting
Acrobatics
Acting
Acupuncture
Adler, Alfred
Adlerian Lecture Series, Speakers
Adlerian Life Style & Interpretation
Adoption, Single Parenthood
Adult Education
Adventures in Attitudes
Advertising

Advertising Agency Management
Aerialist
Africa
African Culture
African Culture & Art

A steelworker named Mike LaVelle (see Studs Terkel's *Working*) writes a regular column for the Chicago *Tribune*. The following quote, from his November 28, 1972, column, shows us something of how The Exchange works in practice:

> The old man, a retired welder, is teaching a group of teenagers how to weld. He becomes exuberantly young in these new uses of his age and knowledge, and they become just a bit older and wiser in the discovery of new muscles and the magic of their own hands.
>
> A middle-aged computer programmer living in a Mexican neighborhood learns Spanish from a young Mexican-American high school dropout, and, in exchange, teaches the dropout computer programming.
>
> A 14-year-old girl who loves to play the violin teaches it to a 23-year-old college professor and a 33-year-old housewife and the sounds of these enchanting strings she loves are tripled.
>
> Teaching? Learning? Sure, but more than that goes on at The Learning Exchange in Evanston. Like or want to learn poetry? Meet a poet. Writing? Meet a writer. Carpentry? Meet a carpenter. Electricity? Meet an electrician. That's what The Learning Exchange is all about.
>
> A working thesis of The Exchange goes something like this: What you don't know you can learn and what you know you can teach. This teaching and learning can be done without the tuition of programmed institutions and the degrees they dispense. It's all up to you, your life, your experience; in essence, it's your cumulative knowledge. You are a living university whether you work with your head or your hands.
>
> There are no ego trippers at The Learning Exchange—a Ph.D. means as little or as much as a welder's torch, a carpenter's saw, a housewife's skillet, or an assembly line worker's hands. Male, female, black, white, old, young, collegiate, hardhat—you are what The Learning Exchange is all about.

The February 1973 progress report of The Exchange tells us some other things that happened, including the following:

A Chinese woman is improving her English and learning business economics through The Learning Exchange. She is also teaching Chinese to three people.

A low-budgeted Catholic grammar school in a small Chicago suburb wanted to broaden their curriculum to include photography. The Learning Exchange found them a student photographer who later taught a four-week course on the basics of photography.

A 78-year-old woman in a nursing home taught German to a college student and also met several people who shared her interest in German classics. She registered to proofread theses and dissertations for graduate students, but has not had any matches thus far.

An insurance investigator with a Ph.D. in philosophy used The Learning Exchange to keep alive his interest in Philosophy & taught a small class on Ethics & Values in his home.

A blind woman was helped toward her college degree because of music theory tutoring she obtained through The Learning Exchange. She also taught Braille to an older man who was losing his sight.

A 25-year-old community worker in the Uptown Area noticed that many unemployed youths were interested in auto mechanics. The Learning Exchange helped him find another mechanic to assist him in starting an auto mechanics workshop and referred several students to them. The Learning Exchange also helped them find a heated garage and is currently assisting them in obtaining a small grant for an extra set of tools.

A college student was having some difficulty grasping some of the theories presented in her psychology class. From The Learning Exchange she obtained the name and phone number of a person who indicated he was well-read in psychology. She had a 45-minute telephone conversation with him that helped her get through her course.

I have the Fall 1974 catalog of The Learning Exchange in De Kalb, Illinois. I don't know when it started; probably a year or more after the one in Evanston. Its catalog lists about 450 topics of interest. The mix is very much like that of The Exchange in Evanston. Under "Music" alone there are 43 instruments or musical activities. What a wealth of human resources and human potential we have in our society, and how little of it is used and satisfied!

All of these learning exchanges share a problem. Success may kill them. When small, they can use borrowed offices and phones and volunteer help and so work for almost no money. As they grow bigger, and reach and serve more people, they begin to need their own space, and some full-time help; their costs per person served become greater rather than less, and they need a lot more money. The Exchange in Evanston believes, as I tend to, that the cost of this kind of service should, if possible, be borne by the people who use it. This makes the exchange more secure; politicians or foundation officers can't bring it to a stop by deciding to cut its budget. Also, it tends to make it more responsible. With this in mind, The Learning Exchange in Evanston is now sending to all people calling for the first time a one-page description of its work and a membership form. To be a member costs $15 for one year, $25 for two years, $30 for three years. Members receive a card, a quarterly newspaper about new offerings and developments, a copy of the annual catalog, and a special "Members Only" phone number to ensure faster service. There is also a $5-per-year Limited Income membership for senior citizens and other low-income persons, which carries the same privileges. The membership form also says that one does not have to be a member of The Exchange to use its listing and referral services. As I write, The Exchange tells me it is getting about half its expenses paid from memberships; whether this figure will rise, hold steady, or fall, time will tell. But such a process may make it very difficult to make these exchanges self-supporting in places where they are most needed, among poor people who have least access to S-chools and other expensive sources of information. Why should not these exchanges, or the people making use of them, get a part of the 90+ billion dollars a year spent, most of it badly, by the S-chools?

5

More Resources for Do-ers

Libraries–Resource Centers for Do-ers

A very good model for resources for do-ers is the public library. Unlike S-chools, it does not say we must use it, or that bad things will happen to us if we don't, or wonderful things if we do. It is simply there, for us to use if, when, and how we want. If we want to use it, it does not test us at the door to see if we are smart enough, or claim it is better than other libraries because only the smartest are let in. It does not tell us what to do once we are in. It does not test, grade, rank, or keep files on us.

Right now the number of things that libraries can help us do is fairly limited. This is partly because libraries don't have enough money—though they serve all the people of a community, they have only a tiny fraction of the money given to S-chools, who serve only a few. Also, until recently most librarians took a rather traditional and limited view of their work. Libraries were a place to store books and other written records. They were an adjunct to S-chools, a place where people, mostly T-eachers and students, could go to look things up. Most people, having learned to dislike the things (including reading) they were made to do in S-chools don't do them any more after they leave school, and so don't use the library. But this is beginning to change. Libraries are doing more than they used to, and some librarians are beginning to say that there are many more things that they could and should do.

One such librarian, Murray L. Bob, director of the Chautauqua-Cattaraugus Library System in Jamestown, N.Y., not long ago sent me a copy of an article he had written called "New Directions for Public Libraries." In it he proposes, among other things, that there should be a library outlet, a deposit station, and book-mail service in every state, county, and city residential institution, on every Indian reservation, in every migrant camp, and so on; that the library should collect, store, catalogue, and make available all kinds of audio-visual materials, such as tapes, records, films, slide films, film loops, videotapes, and the like; that libraries should put branches where people work—something already being done in parts of Scandinavia; that libraries can and should "help increase the commerce in ideas by . . . freely lending or allowing to be used in the library, at no cost, small printing presses, cameras for filming, tape recorders for recording—duplicators of all kinds for duplicating of all kinds." He goes on to say:

> I am not talking of duplication which infringes on copyright— duplication of what is already published. I am talking about the duplication of works of "Mute Miltons"; of making the presses available at no cost to organizations and individuals of every kind. The right of free speech means very little if people outside of immediate earshot can't hear, read, view, that speech. The means to disseminate and to decentralize opinion is one of the overriding needs in our monopolized mass media culture.

I could not agree more strongly. We have learned or been taught to think that Freedom of the Press means the right of multimillionaire owners of newspapers or radio or TV stations to print and say whatever they like. Even this right is well worth defending, as the Nixon affair showed us. But that isn't what Freedom of the Press was first supposed to mean. It meant freedom *to run a press*, that is, to print and spread out one's own ideas.

Murray Bob goes on to say, in part:

In the same measure as the federal government is withdrawing support from public libraries, it is providing support to arts institutions. Q.E.D. let libraries become arts institutions. . . .

In rural areas and in small towns of, say, under 30,000 (not
graced by the presence of a college) or in new suburbs, there is virtually no way to support a multiplicity of cultural institutions. . . .
Therefore, a single house of culture might indeed make sense. The
libraries with their tradition of tax support are the logical recipients
of additional public funds for additional cultural purposes. . . . Of
course, if the library is going to maintain an arts gallery and performing arts auditorium, it has to be staffed not only by librarians,
but by curator "impresario" types.

Finally, he proposes, very sensibly, that libraries be the centers
for the kinds of learning exchanges about which I have already
written.

We could extend even further than Murray Bob the list of what
a library keeps and lends, and the things which it does, or helps
people to do. In *Freedom and Beyond* I suggested that libraries should
make available not just books and a few audio-visual materials, but
musical instruments, music-practice rooms for both individuals and
groups, and the equipment needed to do a wide range of arts and
crafts. Many more people might do these things if they had conve-
nient and inexpensive places to do them. Most people haven't space
where they live to practice musical instruments, or to paint, or
make things out of wood or metal, or work in ceramics, let alone
the money to buy the needed equipment. In very large cities there
may be a few places where, usually for a fee, these things can be
done. But they are too far from where most people live, and cost
too much, for many people to be able to use them. Smaller towns
or suburbs have no such resources at all. Small wonder so many
people are forced into the passive amusement of watching TV.
There is very little else for them to do.

Libraries might also keep and lend toys, games, elementary scientific equipment, chemistry and electronic kits, sports equipment,
skates, rackets, and so on. Children of middle-class or rich parents
learn a lot through their toys and games. Poorer kids have few or

none of these. Most well-off kids have more toys than they need; their closets bulge with stuff they never use. Why not have in libraries a place where this could be collected and lent out, along with the stuff the libraries bought themselves? So many things are wasted in our modern societies. Why not expand libraries into places where these things are kept and used? And why not have libraries keep and lend not only tools for arts and crafts, but tools people use to repair or build their own dwellings, or furniture or cars, or appliances, or other things they use? Who would do the work? We have millions of people (many of them teachers) looking for work, and this work, unlike much of the work people do, would not use up energy or raw materials, would not pollute, and would be well worth doing. Where would we find the space? We already have it, in all those S-chool buildings we built at such expense. In one S-chool of about five hundred students, in a city of half a million, I saw more tools and equipment for arts and crafts than were available to the entire adult population of the city. In another, even smaller city, the lab S-chool of a college of education was almost as well and lavishly equipped. Why should this stuff not be available to any people, young or old, in or out of S-chool, who wanted to use it? A friend writes, from a small town, that the S-chools in his area are terrible, and that his kids and all the kids he knows hate them and would like to get out of them. But, he asks, where else in this community are these kids going to have access to a $50,000 shop, or musical instruments, or athletic facilities? As things stand, nowhere. But why should kids have to go full time to a S-chool just to be able to use the S-chool shop? Why shouldn't they be able to go to the S-chool only when they want to use the shop? And why shouldn't adults be able to use it, as well? The whole public paid for these facilities, with tax money, and the whole public should be able to use them.

Here is another project for libraries, and one very close to their traditional task. In *Freedom and Beyond* I proposed a reading program which for little or no money might help children, above all poor children, read better than they do. Let me insist here that reading better is not going to make most poor kids rich, or even richer. Poverty is not a reading problem and better reading won't solve it, and it is a cruel lie to pretend that it could or will. But even if it doesn't bring success and money, reading is worth doing for the immediate understanding and pleasure it can bring.

I proposed that we have what we might call "reading guides." They would be volunteers. College or high school students, or even younger children, if they could read, could be reading guides; or housewives, or older and retired people; or librarians; or parking-lot attendants; or anyone else who in his daily life might come into contact with children or other nonreaders. The guides would wear some kind of identifying armband, hat, button, etc., so that people wanting information could easily spot them. The understanding would be that when a guide was wearing his sign, anyone who wanted could ask either one of two kinds of questions. He could show him a written word and ask, "What does this say?" and the guide would tell him. Or he could say to the guide, "How do you write such and such a word?" and the guide would write it for him. Nothing else; that's all the guide would have to do.

It should cost almost nothing to get such a program going. What about testing the guides? No need for it. There is no reason why a guide should be able to read or write every word he might be asked. Most of the words he will be asked will be fairly easy, anyway. If he is asked a word he doesn't know, he can say, "I don't know that one, you'll have to ask another guide." A school, a church, a group of parents, or students themselves could start such a program. So far, no one that I know of has taken up my suggestion to start such a program. Perhaps in time, as S-chool reading programs continue to cost more and fail worse, someone will. If they do, such a program will need a base, a place where people could hear about it, find out how to take part in it, get whatever badge or button or ribbon they needed, perhaps discuss the work of the program, how they could improve it and reach more people with it. A library, or branch library, would be a natural place to do this.

Murray Bob talked, as surely many library people do, about having more branch libraries. This is a good idea, but we need more than branch libraries if we are to put at least some reading matter close to most of our low-income and poor people. Even the smallest branch libraries, as we now understand them, are too expensive to scatter thickly throughout a city. What we need, and most of all in the crowded areas where most poor people live, are what we have not had, mini-libraries, stocked with newspapers, magazines, and paperback books, but without the expensive reference materials and elaborate files of more formal libraries. These could be in very small spaces—in a storefront, in the basement of a church. Perhaps we could put them in the back of old trucks or buses, and have them go on a regular schedule from block to block through a neighborhood. Thus people would know that on certain days of the week or month the mini-library would be right on their block, easy for them and their children to use.

There have been for some time such mobile libraries, usually called bookmobiles. But these are usually so elaborate and expensive that no library system could afford to spread them thickly throughout a city. Some bookmobiles I have asked about cost more than $15,000. The job can be done for much less. A few years ago a resourceful and imaginative woman I know, Darlene Ertha, living in a rural area where there were very few libraries, and so where most people had little available to read, decided to do something about it. She was given an old school bus (it would have cost about $800 to buy). For another $500 or so, she made needed mechanical repairs. Then, with about $100 worth of materials, and doing most of the work herself or with friends, she took out the seats and fitted out the bus as a combination library and paperback bookstore. She called the bus The Bookworm, and down both sides of the bus painted a large green worm, whose eye was the bus headlight. For several years, until she moved away, she drove this bookworm, on a regular schedule, to a number of the villages in the area.

Once we get past the idea that everything has to be brand new and specially built, we could do something like this, for not much money, on a very large scale, both in the country and in the cities. There are plenty of old trucks and buses around that could be converted. As I write, the Post Office in Boston is announcing a sale of its old trucks; many of these would be ideal for mini-libraries. Many people could do the work and would like to do it. Again, such programs are not going to make many poor people richer, or even give them jobs. But they might make their lives more interesting, might even given them ideas for other kinds of cooperative action that would make their communities and neighborhoods better to live in.

Perhaps the most exciting of the ideas that Murray Bob wrote about is the idea of a popular press. This is an idea I have been thinking about and, in a small way, doing, for some time. In my office we have for some years now been reprinting, often in reduced size, and sending out, free or at cost, large numbers of articles about education and other things that we thought people might find useful. Of one piece, we have sent out more than 50,000 copies. We use commercial printers for this. Here technology, for a change, has made some machines that ordinary people can use for their own purposes. A commercial copy and printing place just down the street, of a kind fairly common in cities, has among other things a copying machine that will in one operation copy a text and reduce it in size, 15, 23, or 35 percent. This puts publishing within the reach of a great many people. Look at these figures. An 8½ x 11 sheet of paper, well filled, can hold a little over a thousand words of typed text. With this machine, we can reduce it in size enough to more than double the words we can put on a page. To do it costs, for 10 copies, 7.4¢ a sheet; for 100 copies, 2.64¢ a sheet; for 1000 copies, 1.6¢ a sheet. On both sides of one sheet we can get about four thousand words, as long as most magazine articles, at a cost of from 15¢ down to 4¢ a copy, depending on how many we want. On both sides of twenty sheets we can get eighty thousand words, as long as a good sized book, for between 80¢ and $3.00. Today even the cheapest paperback book costs more than 80¢, and most cost much more. This means that people with something to say can, even using a commercial printer, publish their own books for the price, or less than the price, of a paperback. It won't look very elegant, and they must then find a way to get it into the hands of readers, but that is a problem which they can probably find many ways to solve.

Some such service might be made available in libraries, for people to use free. They might also have some electric typewriters or composing machines, on which people could make up their original copy. The commercial publishers would aim, as they do now, at a larger market. Perhaps now and then a writer, having published his own article or book, might persuade a commercial publisher to publish it, if he could show that many people had already bought it.

Such a free press might in time be very useful to poor or low-income communities. These communities are on the whole shut out of the mass print media, and are not large or rich enough to support a commercial press of their own. Hence they have no voice with which to speak to each other or the world outside. This helps make and keep them isolated, fragmented, and politically weak. If they had ways to speak to each other about their common concerns, and make these known to people outside, they might be much more unified in spirit, and politically and economically more effective. Also, people in these communities often rightly complain that their children in school have to use texts that speak of a Dick-and-Jane, middle-class, Anglo-Saxon, suburban life and culture that none of the children know. With access to a popular free press, people in these communities could, with their children, write many texts for their schools, or simply books to use outside of schools, that their children would find meaningful, interesting, and useful. Some of these texts might at first not be much good. In that case, the people using them could stop using them, and could tell the writers of these texts what was wrong with them, and how they had to be changed to make them more useful. Once people grasped the idea that anyone could write down his thoughts for other people to read, it might make great changes in modern society. And such a popular press would do more to increase people's interest in reading and writing than any number of S-chool courses.

Other Resources

Many commercial publications are to a greater or lesser degree a resource for do-ers. The classified ad section of newspapers is one example. Magazines such as *Popular Science, Popular Mechanics*, etc. have for years had do-it-yourself sections, about how to fix a car, or build toys or furniture or boats, or remodel a house. Cookbooks are, or can be, a resource for do-ers. A number of companies publish a whole series of manuals on how to make or fix things. The Rodale press, in its magazine *Organic Gardening* and in many books, has helped people raise more and better food in their gardens. To these examples we could easily add a great many others.

The last ten years or so have been hard ones for magazines. Many large and famous ones—*Collier's, Life, Look*, and others—have folded; others are struggling to hang on. But in these years there have been some outstanding successes. Two of these I want to mention here, because they were meant to be, and are, resources for do-ers. The first is, of course, the *Whole Earth Catalog*, which must by now be well known to a large part of the English-speaking world. Newer and smaller, but also growing very rapidly, is *Mother Earth News*. Both are written by and for a large and various group of people, mostly under forty, who are trying to discover, perfect, and perhaps spread new ways of living and working in a civilization that seems to them (and to me) to be falling apart and destroying itself. What was perhaps most radical and new about these magazines was that they broke down the usual barrier between, on the one hand, the Writers and Experts, and on the other, the Readers. In these publications the readers *were* the writers. They were not one small group of insiders talking to another larger group of outsiders, but people sharing with each other ideas, information, as the *Whole Earth Catalog* puts it, "access to tools," which might help them make for themselves the new kinds of life and work they wanted. Conventional magazines had for some time been trying to change people's opinions and politics. These two were among the first concerned with helping them change their lives, and above all, helping them not by telling them what to do, but by putting them in touch with each other. They were and are good examples of what Illich has called a network, a kind of Learning Exchange in print. They were unconventional in some other ways; they used very cheap paper, they packed a lot of words and information on a page, and they used inexpensive and in the case of *Whole Earth* very unconventional kinds of layout and format. Also, they were supported by their readers, not by advertisers; *Mother Earth News* carries a very small amount of advertising and *Whole Earth Catalog* none at all.

Using the model of the *Whole Earth Catalog*, people in many cities have published directories in which people with not much money and perhaps unconventional ways of living and working might find tools and resources they needed. In Boston, much of this information can now be found in two newspapers, somewhat radical, somewhat muckraking, in any case aimed mostly at young people, the *Phoenix* and the *Real Paper*, though the more established and conventional daily *Boston Globe* also supplies some of this information. Other descendents of the *Whole Earth* can be found here and there in the commercial press. *MS*, the (or at least a) magazine of the women's movement, though not at all like *Whole Earth* or *Mother Earth* in format, or their interest in going back to the land, is like them in this respect: it is a resource, and an information exchange, for women who are trying both to break free of old patterns of living in a society largely controlled by men, and to gain legal, social, and personal equality.

The latest (#36) issue of *Mother Earth News* tells of the work of the Institute for Local Self Reliance, a nonprofit, tax-deductible foundation to help establish economically self-sustaining and ecologically sound urban communities, ruled by the individuals and families who live in them. The ILSR's work has—so far—included experiments with new ways to produce, process, and distribute food, to recycle waste, and to use solar energy, in inner-city neighborhoods. Much of this work is going on right now in the Adams-Morgan area of Washington, D.C. For more information see *Mother*

Earth News, or write ILSR (send self-addressed, stamped envelope) at 1717 18th St., N.W., Washington, D.C. 20009.

In India there is now growing, and with little or no help or co-operation from the big institutions of government and the universities, an information exchange network, in which very ordinary, poor, and in some cases illiterate farmers and villagers can share ideas about better ways of growing food, building shelters, getting water, and in general solving the day-to-day problems of their lives. Since many of the people in this network cannot read, the materials they send each other show with very clear and easy-to-understand line drawings what they also write about with words.

In the U.S., and probably in other countries, people are finding new ways, outside the commercial and money economy, to share their skills and meet their needs. In many cities there are food buying cooperatives, whose members are able to save 20 or 30 percent on their food. There are also cooperative garages, where people can go to fix their own cars, using the tools of the garage and perhaps getting some advice and help when they need it. The Women's Movement has set up a number of health centers, where women can get and share information about medical and health needs not well met, or met at all, by a medical profession dominated by men. In Cambridge, Mass., there is a shop called Frameworks, where people can go to frame their own prints and pictures, use the tools of the shop, and the help of professionals if they need it.

Since housing, or rather shelter, is one of the greatest unmet human needs in most modern countries, rich or poor, one of the most exciting resources for do-ers I know of is Shelter Institute (72 Front St., Bath, Maine 04530), where people can go to find out, in theory *and practice,* how to build their own homes—or barns, garages, etc. The Institute has a library and bookstore, with books on all aspects of home construction. More important, it offers two courses to would-be builders, a basic course of forty-five hours over three weeks, a shorter design workshop, and a chance to get some practical experience working on a house that someone is already building. Their bulletin describes the basic course and design workshop as follows:

BASIC COURSE: 45 hours. No prior knowledge expected. Enrollment limited for individual attention. This course teaches engineering and physics of building materials, soil climate, and solar effects so that the student can make original designs which will meet his needs and take most advantage of natural surroundings. Focus on long range perspective to assure long range success: is a flush toilet appropriate if the water table is falling? Will your income rise proportionately with the cost of oil, or will a solar-wood heat design better provide long-term security? All common framing, wiring, and plumbing methods are studied as well as alternatives to free the student from standardized, restricting and expensive commercial practices. Codes are carefully considered. All mathematics, such as use of fiber stress values to determine bending moments for proper load resistance calculations, are presented in a step by step order. Course structure follows the building sequence from site selection and road building through water and utility source, psychology of design, the various house systems to leach field and alternative waste systems. $200, $300/couple.

DESIGN WORKSHOP: Ordinarily but not necessarily taken after the basic course. Its purpose is the support and guidance of the student through the evolution of his shelter design. The one-time fee permits unlimited attendance at once/week design sessions. Seminar format will be: 1) student presentation of design progress for discussion by the group, 2) raising of specific problems for suggestions from the group, 3) presentation of ideas of general interest such as how to build a sauna, portable pig shelter, etc. At the end of seminar attendance the student should have developed blueprints, a scale model and building cost estimate. Participating, in addition to the Tute staff will be guest architects, materialsmen, bankers and other professionals. Weekly, no time limit. $100/house.

By such means it may soon be possible for many people who cannot now afford commercially produced housing either to build, or rebuild and upgrade, their own.[1] Not just in the country and suburbs, either; in time, by such means, the people who live in our central cities may be able to make for themselves the decent housing that society, industry, and government have never been able to make, and probably never will be able to make for them.

[1] An important book on the subject is *Freedom to Build*, by John Turner and Robert Fichter (Macmillan).

6

Sports Resources

Some of the resources we need are in the area of sports. We humans are active, playful, game-loving creatures. In games and sports we find many of our peak experiences, moments or hours of great excitement, aliveness, exaltation. More amateur and informal sports would help many people live happier lives.

Much has been said about running making us more fit. But it can also be a great pleasure, and a great relaxer, an aid to thought and meditation. Many more people might run and enjoy running if they could find places to do it. Some city parks have walking and running paths and trails. In Boston, along the edge of the Charles River, one can run three miles or more. A few people can run on a nearby school track. But most people don't have a good place to run. If they try to run in a city they will be stopped constantly by lights and traffic. In some areas they may worry about their safety. In the suburbs, where there are few sidewalks, they must watch out for cars, not to say dogs. In most places they may worry about looking like a fool, which is enough to stop most people. They need more running tracks, both indoors and out, and running paths, wherever room can be found for them.

Bicycling is another good exercise, and a good way of getting around in or near cities. For several years in Boston we had commuter races between bicyclists and people who regularly drove their cars into the city. Bicyclist and car owner would meet at the latter's house, and leave together for the city, meeting again at the door of the car owner's office. In almost all such contests, the bicyclists won. But bike riding is often difficult and dangerous in this country. Few automobile drivers are careful of cyclists and give them a little room; many treat them as if they had no right to be on the road, and some even deliberately try to run them off the road. In Denmark, at the edge of many auto roads is a small road or path, three to six feet wide, especially reserved for bicycles (sometimes motor assisted). We need more bikeways, more bike lanes in regular streets, and laws which, at least on certain streets and at certain hours of the day, will give the bicycle right of way over cars.

Skating, both ice and roller, is a very good exercise, and figure skating a vigorous and beautiful sport. For this we need many more rinks, indoors and out, some artificial, others simply flat spaces flooded in cold weather. In Boston the Swan Pond in the Public Garden freezes over quickly in cold weather, and many people skate on it. But the city does nothing to keep the ice in good condition, so that after a snowfall, or a few thaws and freezes, people can no longer skate on it. Concrete outdoor roller-skating rinks could be much cheaper than ice rinks and would need little or no maintenance.

Swimming or playing in water is another great exercise and pleasure, certainly for children. Many of our big cities are near the ocean, lakes, or rivers, and if we had not polluted them so badly, or could ever get them clean again, many people would be able to swim in them, as Chicagoans now swim in Lake Michigan. Meanwhile, we also need many more swimming pools. More Pools, Less Schools. They need not always be deep, elaborate, or expensive. In central Boston I know of only two pools where the general public may swim in winter, but in England some cities much smaller than Boston have one or more large public pools, often open nearly twenty-four hours a day. The city of Reykjavik, in Iceland, with only 100,000 people, has many public pools.

One great summer resource in Boston is the Frog Pond, in the Boston Common. This is a large—perhaps two hundred feet long—kidney-shaped wading pool (without frogs), less than three feet deep at its deepest point, and sloping so gradually from its edges that even tiny infants can play safely in it. Since they have to go many steps to get into deep water, they cannot accidentally tumble into it. The water itself tells them how far they may explore in it, so they don't need careful watching. At one end is a big fountain that throws a heavy circular spray of water into the air. All around are benches. On any summer day one can see many dozens of children, aged one to twelve or more, playing, splashing, shouting, in the deepest parts even swimming, while mothers or relatives sit around the edge and talk, knit, read the paper, and so on, not having to worry about what is going on in the water. It would probably not cost much to build other pools like this. The only equipment is the motor and pump that run the fountain. Maintenance is very low. We could surely have many more like this than we do.

Fountains alone, even without pools, can be great places for people to gather, talk, and play. A new one in Portland, Oregon, has become a social center, bringing much life into the heart of the city. Many young people go to the fountain to meet friends, or to play in it, and many other people go there to watch them. Our Boston fountains, one in Copley Square, one near City Hall, are less imaginative (and less expensive), but they liven up what would otherwise be rather cold and ugly public spaces. This afternoon, as I write, at the ring-shaped fountain at the Christian Science Center development (the only lively thing in it), a couple of small children are running around inside the charmed circle of water, knowing that their fully dressed parents will not follow them in there. Perhaps next summer many more children will play there.

One of the pleasant sights of Boston is the sailboats on the Charles River. Some of these are from college boat clubs. Most are owned by a low-cost boating club called Community Boating. The sailing program there, and in other parts of Boston, is described in an article in the "Calendar" section (a good resource) of the July 17 *Boston Globe*. The story says, in part:

> More than 9000 children and adults are sailing or learning to sail free or nearly free this summer at four city, Metropolitan District Commission and private nonprofit boathouses. The oldest and largest of these is Community Boathouse. . . . The private, nonprofit club is open to anyone. It has 30 staff members, 82 13-to-24-foot sailboats, five rowboats and four motor launches.
>
> . . . At the MDC [Metropolitan District Commission] Boathouse on the Mystic River or the Pleasure Bay boathouse. . . . Any resident of Massachusetts who can swim can sail free at both boathouses. If you can't sail, an instructor will teach you—free.
>
> . . . At Pleasure Bay . . . more than 900 children and adults signed up to sail in the first two weeks of the program. By the time it closes, a week or so before school reopens, 1400 people will have used its 44 boats, if it's as popular this year as it was last year.
>
> You have to be 10 to sail in the MDC Mystic program on Shore Drive in Somerville. About half the boathouse's 1400 users were adults last year. . . .
>
> . . . Boston children have been sailing free on Jamaica Pond since 1951; and since 1971, adults have been sailing there free, too. . . . About 600 children and 400 adults sailed free at Jamaica Pond last year.

We need more such resources, and also places, as in the lakes in some city parks, or the Thames River above London, where people can rent or borrow sturdy rowboats, or tough metal or Fiberglas canoes. Many of our waterfront cities have elaborate facilities for those few people who can afford to buy boats. Most people have no way to get out on the water.

We need many more playing fields. Soccer has become a much more popular sport in Boston, but as of not long ago there were only two or three full-sized and marked public soccer fields in the city. Not all fields need to be full-sized, or to be lined and have goals; soccer players, like touch-football and softball players, are used to playing in odd-shaped spaces and marking their own lines and goals with shirts and the like. But they need more space.

People are beginning to develop a four-wall version of soccer which in time might become even more widely played than the original. In the four-wall game, the ball can be played off the wall like the puck in hockey, and thus kept in play all the time, making the action continuous and much faster. This form of the game needs much less space than the original and is even more strenuous, so that players can get all the exercise they need (or can stand) in a much shorter time. According to one report, even professional soccer players can play the four-wall game for only about three minutes at a stretch before needing a rest. Spaces for such games could be cheaply built; the floor and walls would not need to be as carefully finished as in handball or racketball courts. In any case, almost any four-wall court, or enclosed space, could be used for such purposes.

As we know, basketball has become the favorite sport of most city boys. They don't need entire courts; given a post or a wall with a backboard and some space around it, they can make up games to fit—two-on-two, three-on-three, or whatever. Any facilities there may be in a city neighborhood will be used all day and if lighted much of the night. But there are not enough, and many or most are in school yards which, for fear of vandalism, are locked up outside of school hours. For very little money and space used, more basketball backboards would give much exercise and pleasure to many young people, many of whom can't afford any other kind. Now that tennis has become so popular, we need many more outdoor public courts, and, to help people learn the game, backboards. Paddle tennis courts take up little space and can be used in any season and any weather. Volleyball, too, can be played in almost any kind of weather, and doesn't take up much space, though it does need tall net posts and a large net. Outdoor handball courts (now used for racketball), and concrete rinks for roller-skate hockey, are much used around New York.

As for indoor resources, we could certainly use much more space and equipment for gymnastics and tumbling, which more and more people want to do, but cannot find a place to do. Another game that doesn't take up much room, and from which people can get much excitement and exercise in as little as half an hour, is squash rackets. Squash courts used to be very expensive to build, but a recent article in *Sports Illustrated* said that some people have designed a court which is not only inexpensive to build, but which can be folded up and rolled away when not in use. Or, like the Chinese, we might play more table tennis; it can be played by people of any size and age, and when played well it can be very good exercise.

I would put in a plug for more facilities for weight training. When I first began to do it, just before I went into the Navy, almost all coaches used to say that it would make people "muscle-bound." By now most coaches and athletes, in almost every serious competitive sport, use it to build strength, flexibility, quickness, coordination, and condition. In this respect, it is at least as good as any exercise or sport I have ever done, and is also physically and mentally relaxing. It takes little space, and the weights do not wear out. But even in large cities it is not easy to find a place to do it.

Finally, we need much more indoor space for people doing work in movement, yoga, martial arts, and every kind of dance. In most cities, even serious and well-established dance companies and groups have trouble finding proper space in which to work. As more people begin to want to do these things, they will need more space to do them in. Some will ask, what will all this cost? Many of the facilities I have suggested, enough for the active recreation of tens of thousands of people, could be built for much less than the cost of one of the giant domes and stadiums being built everywhere, almost always with public money, so that people can watch twenty to thirty professional athletes perform. In a society of doers, many more would be playing than watching.

Of all such resources of which I have ever heard, by far the finest is described at length in a book called *The Peckham Experiment*, by Innes H. Pearse and Lucy H. Crocker (Allen and Unwin, London, 1943). The book, long out of print, but which we urgently need to have back in print, is about a health, sports, and recreational facility, organized as a club for families, which was built in

1935 in the Peckham district of London and ran until 1939, when the war dispersed all its families and staff and ended its operation. No institution that I know of expresses so well in action what I have come to believe about the needs of children and adults in society. To describe the center, the ideas behind it, its purpose, its operation, the things adults and children did there, and the ways in which doing these things helped them to grow, I have quoted extensively from the book in Appendix B. Please read it; it is at least as important as anything else in this book.

7

Do-ers and their t-eachers

No one can act or learn for another. The do-er must do the work himself. The task, the choice, the purpose must be his. But a t-eacher may be able to help in many ways. Here is a good statement of some of these ways, taken from a letter written by a young man to a mutual friend. He says, in part:

> Also took ballet lessons all winter, which was a very high experience in a number of ways.
> First, I got strong very fast and, somewhat more slowly, very flexible.
> Second, finding myself doing a peculiar thing that couldn't be justified in any sensible way to others or myself—finally giving up attempts at justification, just doing it.
> Third, it was the first time I had ever been in an esoteric school, i.e., an exceedingly formal study of a formal discipline, which cannot be explained in words (or only in mystical, incomprehensible French terms).
>
> Demonstation by the master.
> I respond with an approximation, which the master shapes to a finer and finer tolerance (the same exercises getting progressively harder and more demanding of attention as I learn how to do them). Eventually, "instructions" start coming from my own nervous system: I learn about the equipment and about the expectations of the discipline.

The information is very rich: breaking of muscle restrictions; cultivation of attentiveness; the simultaneous-and-independent movement of diverse limbs (i.e., turn yourself into a machine); healing of injuries and previous physical trauma; balance, center of gravity, posture, spatial orientation; lifting, jumping, spinning.

Well, I've never learned anything in this manner before. In fact, I think it is probably the first new thing I've learned in *years*. It draws out of me more interest/concentration/energy than anything except music ever did. Learning how I learn.

Here we see some of what the true t-eacher, the master, does for the student. He breaks down the large task so that whatever he may ask the student to do, the student, with effort, will be able to do, and from doing it will get greater powers, with which to do the next task. He gives a model, shows what is to be done. He may say something that will make it easier for the student to know and do what is to be done. He gives feedback, makes the student see and feel what in fact he did. He makes a correction, shows the student the difference between what he did and what he was supposed to do, and shows how to close that difference. Most important, by doing this, he tries to give the student (or help him make for himself) standards, criteria, a heightened awareness, a model in his own mind/body, from which he will in time get his own instructions, feedback, and correction. Thus, as he sharpens the student's movements, he sharpens the criteria by which the student will later judge and correct his own movements. The true master does not want to make the student into a slave or puppet, but into a new master. He is not a behavior modifier. He does not move the student by imperceptible steps toward an end which only he, the master, can see. He seeks instead to give the student greater control of his own behavior, so that he may move himself toward his own ends—in this case, the end of dancing—"lifting, jumping, spinning."

Some may sense a contradiction between these words and criticisms I have made of reading (and other) T-eachers. If it is right for this master to divide the task of dancing into a closely controlled sequence of exercises and movements, why is it wrong for the reading T-eacher to do what seems to be the same? In the first place, reading, unlike dancing, is not a muscular act, and it is a serious mistake to treat it like one. The dance master must stretch and strengthen the student's muscles so that the student may make the next movement, and without injury. But one cannot injure oneself with a difficult thought. There is a reason for the sequences in dance training. The experience of tens of thousands of dancers has shown that the student cannot make certain movements safely and well unless he can make other movements first. This is not true of reading. As no two children learn to speak in the same way, no two of the many children who teach themselves to read do that in the same way. They may learn the meaning of written words in any order they wish, and they very often learn "hard" words first. But there are not an infinite number of ways to learn to do ballet; such differences as there may be between one school and another, or one teacher and another, are slight.

Also, the tasks that the dancing master gives the student make sense. The student can see, and feel in his body, the connection between these beginning movements and the full skill and art he wants to master. Indeed, the greatest dancers begin their work every day with the same simple movements the student is trying to learn to do. Not so for the T-eaching of reading. The child cannot see any connection between the things he is told to do, and the goal he at first wanted to reach—making sense of print. The T-eacher's orders only turn him from his task and purpose. The things the T-eacher tells him to do are usually absurd. No skillful reader does them or ever did them. The people who read well do not read that way and did not learn to read that way. Methods of T-eaching reading have been made not out of the experience of good readers, but out of theory—like the pet theory of a tennis coach who years ago told me to approach every ball as if doing a waltz, and as I did so to hum a little waltz tune to myself.

Professor David Hawkins, in his article "What It Means To Teach," (*Teacher's College Record,* September 1973) said some good words about teaching. He might not admit the distinction that I make between t-eacher and T-eacher. But the people he talks about sound to me like t-eachers. He says, in part:

> I should like to begin by observing that the teacher-learner relationship is at least as old as our human species, and that its formal institutional framework, though much more recent in origin, is only a stylized and often stilted version of something which goes on all the time among us, especially between the older and the younger. I want to underline the antiquity of this honorable relationship if only to remind you of the obvious, that it is a key link in the chain of human history and culture, and that without it we would perish immediately. Also, to remind you that it is not something on which anyone has a patent.
>
> . . . A reasonable general account of the relationship is, therefore, that the teacher is one who acquires authority through *a compact of trust* [italics mine], in which the teacher seeks to extend the powers of the learner and promises to abridge them only transiently and to the end of extending them. The teacher offers the learner some kind of loan of himself or herself, some kind of auxiliary equipment which will enable the learner to make transitions and consolidations he could not otherwise have made. And if this equipment is of the kind to be itself internalized, the learner not only learns, but begins, in the process, to be his own teacher—and that is how the loan is repaid. . . .

"A compact of trust." Yes—but how can there be a compact of trust when the student is not free to choose what he shall learn, or when, or how, or with how much and what kind of help? How can there be a compact of trust when the student is not free to choose or to change his teacher? How can there be a compact of trust when the teacher may be obliged (as I once was), in order to keep his job, to do things that he *knows* will harm the student, destroy his confidence and ability to learn? Or when the teacher is obliged, if the student does something poorly, to tell the whole world, to put it into a record which will follow the student all his life?

To return to t-eaching, the man who taught me to drive was an old man, unschooled, not a good driver himself, and with no other great talent or skill that I knew of. But he was a great teacher of driving, and ordered the task perfectly. He had seen that many drivers, particularly beginners, were nervous and prone to panic because they did not understand the relationship between engine, gears, clutch, the nature of the road, and the acceleration or speed of the car. He decided that before he would let me on the road I must master these relationships. Master them in action, that is; he probably could not have put them into words, and I would not have understood if he had. He drove the car up a little-used road on a quite steep hill, pulled it to the side, put on the hand brake, and told me to get in the driver's seat and drive away, slowly, smoothly, with no jerks and no slipping back. He showed me once or twice how to do this; then it was my turn. After many hours on that hill I was eventually able to pull away smoothly every time, as often as he wanted. Clutch, gears, and throttle have never troubled me since; indeed, using the gears well is one of the things I enjoy most about driving.

The task was ideal for still another reason. The car itself gave me the feedback and correction I needed. For a few times he had to say, "You gave it too much (or not enough) gas," or "You let the clutch pedal out too fast." After that I could tell from what the car did what I had done wrong and how I needed to change. I had the criteria I needed to correct my actions. He had no need to say anything, and left me to do the task without interference. Later, on the highway, when seeing other cars coming I began like all beginners to twitch the wheel this way and that, he would say in a deep slow voice, "Just stay on your side, and don't pay any attention to them." This is another task of the teacher, to give the student moral support until his new-found skills become automatic and he no longer has to think or worry about them. All in all he was a splendid teacher.

Another time, I was the teacher. At the start of one school year I was driving with my friend Sam Piel, one of the students, from New York City to the Colorado Rocky Mountain School. On the last day of the trip he told me that he loved music and wanted more than anything to be able to make music, but could not, because he was tone deaf. I suddenly remembered that years before when I was at school, Arthur Landers, the musical director, had told us at a chorus rehearsal that there was no such thing as tone-deafness, that with very rare exceptions people called tone-deaf merely had not learned to coordinate ear and voice, to match the sounds they heard with the sounds they were making, but that this was easy to learn and that anyone with a little patience could quickly teach it to them. One had only to play a note on the piano and ask the "tone-deaf" person to match it, guiding him up and down until he did. I asked Sam if he would like to try it, using my voice instead of a piano. He said he would, so we began. I would sing a note and ask him to match it. He would sing a note, I would match his, then sing mine again, and tell him to come up or down to mine. When he matched it, we would sing the note together so that he could get used to the sound and feel of it. Then I would sing a new note and we would start again. After a while he could match any note I sang. Then I began having him sing the first interval of the scale, the do-re. By three hours later, when we arrived at school, he was able to match any note I sang, and starting with that note, to sing the first four notes of the diatonic scale—do-re-mi-fa. In that year in school he sang folk songs, in the next, sang in the chorus and took up guitar, and in the next began the cello, where he showed such promise that his teacher told him that if he wanted, he could probably be a professional musician.

Here are all the elements of t-eaching—the task suited to the student's strength, the feedback and correction, the internalizing of standards and criteria, and with all this, the vital element of support. It helped that we were good friends; he would probably not have been willing to try the experiment with someone he knew less well. The car, too, was a shelter, shut off from the world outside, almost from the rest of life. It was old and rackety; we had lived in it for four days; it had been a home. In it we might do things and face risks we might not dream of doing or facing anywhere else.

The Nature of Feedback

The word "feedback" is well known to people who work with electronics, computers, and the like. An example we all know is the thermostat. We set it at, say, sixty-five degrees Fahrenheit. If the room is colder than sixty-five, an electric signal goes to the furnace or heater saying, "Turn on" or perhaps "Send more hot air or hot water." If the room is warmer than sixty-five, the thermostat sends an opposite signal. But there has to be a thermometer attached; the furnace can't "know" whether to send more hot air or less unless it "knows" how hot the room is already.

The feedback we use in learning physical movements and skills is much the same. The dancing master, the gymnastics coach, the ski instructor, or whatever, says to the student, "Make this motion, take this position." The student looks at the model, and tells his own muscles to do the same thing. If the student is an excellent athlete, his muscles do what he wants, and his motion or position is very like that of the model. But many people do not have that control, and their motion or position is not quite the same. If they know exactly what their motion or position is, they may know (but may not) how to correct it. But if they think they are doing what the instructor told them, but in fact are doing something quite different, no change, correction, or improvement can take place. They need something to tell them what in fact they have done.

For dancers this may sometimes be a mirror. Often that is not enough. The master will say, "No, you are doing this," and will imitate the student. Then, "I want this," and another demonstration. Perhaps he will touch or move the student to show him what to do. The ski instructor, having no mirror (though now in some places they wisely use videotape), must imitate the student. Those who teach beginners to ski, or do other sports, find that many people are extraordinarily out of touch with their bodies, muscles, and limbs. When asked to bend this knee, bring this shoulder forward, the students try to do it, think they *are* doing it, but often do something quite different. The teacher must show them what they *are* doing, and what he would like them to do instead. Often they cannot make the needed correction, and he must bring their shoulder or knee to the proper position. They look at him, see his position, get the feeling of their own muscles, think, "When I feel like this, I look like that." They are slowly developing a better feedback mechanism in their own bodies.

An example of a bad feedback mechanism: On large ships the rudder is turned by a steering engine. Whoever controls the rudder does not hold something connected to it as the steering wheel of a car is connected to the front wheels. He can only give one of three orders to the steering engine: "move the rudder right," "move it left," or "don't move it." So he needs something to tell him how far to the right or left it has moved. If this mechanism is out of order, and says that the rudder is left when in fact it is right, he will not be able to control that ship.

This is the situation of people who are clumsy, unathletic, uncoordinated. They may send the right messages, orders, to their muscles and limbs. But their limbs and muscles don't carry out the orders, but do something else instead. Worse yet, these people don't know what those muscles and limbs are doing. They think they are carrying out the orders when they are not, like some golfers who swear they don't move their heads when in fact they sway like trees in the wind. Coaches and others who try to teach other people muscular skills have faced for years the fact of good or bad coordination. They tend to think of it as a mysterious natural gift, something people have or don't have, like blond hair or brown eyes, but in any case, not something a coach can do anything about. This is not so; there are ways to give people more awareness of their body and limbs, a better feedback system. Training in dance is surely one. My own experience, both as do-er and t-eacher, has shown that intelligent exercising with weights is another, since by working many different groups of muscles against strong resistance one finds out, so to speak, where those muscles are, what they are doing, and how they feel while doing it.

Indeed, a friend once told me of a young woman therapist who used exercises with weights to improve the body control and coordination of people we used to call "spastics." Such people, for whatever reason, have a very bad communication system with their muscles. The system is noisy; all sorts of unintended random messages go out over it, making muscles twitch and jerk; the intended messages often get lost in the static. It is rather like trying to talk over a very bad phone connection. This young woman reasoned that if a spastic was trying to do a particular exercise against the resistance of a weight, the muscles involved in that exercise *could not* twitch; their tension would be steady, because the weight would make it so. Thus the person would begin to be aware of that muscle group, like hearing a steady tone through random noise, and so would gradually develop better communication with and from it. I was told that this method had been very helpful to this therapist's patients. Whether such a method is much used now, I do not know.

Feedback without a Teacher

In January 1974 *Sports Illustrated* ran a remarkable story about the Japanese baseball player and later figure skater Sushiki. It said in part:

> One day a base runner . . . permanently injured (Sushiki's) throwing arm. . . . Sushiki was despondent . . . until a friend took him to an exhibition by Dick Button, the Olympic skater. . . . Sushiki had never been on skates in his life, he could not afford lessons, and there were very few rinks in Japan. But he obtained movies of Button and taught himself to skate just by studying the films. In 1958 he was Japan's national skating champion, and is now in his 11th year as a star of the Ice Capades.

This story has much to tell us about teaching and learning difficult tasks, and above all, how the learning of such tasks might be made much less expensive and so available to more people.

Sushiki must have been, and still be, an unusually well-trained, intelligent, and coordinated athlete. The skills, movements, and muscular requirements of baseball and figure skating are very different. The skater, like the dancer, must develop new muscles, and stretch and use them in new ways. Watching Dick Button on film and then imitating him is not something that just anyone can do. Sushiki had to make himself his own skating teacher. He had to work out for himself a series of graded tasks, do them, and make the needed corrections, like the young man in ballet school described earlier. But he is a splendid example, the best I have heard, of an important principle. The student, the do-er, can only learn a difficult action insofar *as he can put the teacher inside himself.* He must be student and teacher at the same time. He must, more and more, grade his own tasks, get his own feedback, make his own corrections, and develop his own criteria, standards, for doing these things. Only as he is able to depend less and less on the teacher outside, and use more and more the teacher inside, will he be able to do well what he wants to do. A music student who never knows whether he is playing a note right or wrong except when his teacher tells him so, can't and won't improve from one lesson to the next. In fact, he will forget between lessons most of the few things he may learn there. And so it must always be the first and central task of any teacher to help the student become independent of him, to learn to be his own teacher. The true teacher must always be trying to work himself out of a job.

Few understand this. Most think the opposite, that the only way to help a person do a difficult task well is always to tell him when he is doing it wrong. Not long ago someone asked me if I was taking regular cello lessons. At the time I was not. He asked, with some irritation, "Then where do you get your standards from?" By this he meant "Who shows you how to do it right, and tells you when you are doing it wrong?" I replied that I got my standards from the cellists—Casals, Rostropovich, Starker, Rose, DuPre, etc.—whose playing I hear on recordings, and from the cellists whom I both see and hear play in Boston—Jules Eskin and others in the Boston Symphony, and guest artists when they come here. At concerts I watch the cellists carefully, sometimes even with binoculars, to see what they do with their fingers, hands, arms. From these great players I get a very clear model of what good cello playing looks like and sounds like. These are my standards. This is not to say that one can learn nothing by working with a skilled player on a more personal level, which indeed I intend to do. But what I need from such a t-eacher is not "standards," but ideas about how I may come closer to the standards I already have.

Where and how does the learner get his feedback, if not from a teacher? If he is doing a physical movement, he can get it from a mirror, as dancers do. When I was ten years old or so, just learning to play golf, and years before I ever heard of feedback, I used to watch the club pro giving lessons, or hitting balls from the practice tee. Later, outside my house, I practiced my own swing in front of a window, trying to make it look like the pro's swing, and to remember what it felt like when it did. What they used to call grooving the swing. Later, learning to play tennis, I did the same thing with forehand, backhand, and serve. Here my models—the best players where I played—were not quite good enough. They were fairly skilled, but, as I only learned later, they had some bad habits, which I copied, and then could not get rid of for years. Not until I saw Pancho Gonzales (who incidentally was almost entirely self-taught) at Forest Hills, the first year he won there, did I see how a tennis ball should be hit.

Today, since sports are big business, and winning at sports very important for many people, we have learned a great deal about models and feedback. One can now get and see quite easily films of champion athletes in many sports. The catalog of the Wolverine Sports Supply Co., Ann Arbor, Michigan, lists a large number of 8 mm. film loops of top athletes doing a great variety of movements and skills. For feedback, more and more teachers of sports use videotape, far better then words or even imitation in helping the student see what he is doing.

Such ways of giving models and feedback might be useful to beginning string players, pianists, and drummers and percussionists, who use their arms and shoulders very much in playing, and for whom the proper kinds of motions are very important. Thus it has helped me to get from top cellists a model, not just of what good cello playing sounds like, but what it looks like. When I practice I often play in front of a mirror, so that I can make my hand and arm movements more like theirs. And, just as I did learning to play golf, I try to remember in my muscles how these arm movements *feel* when they look right, so that I can get some of this feedback from inside, without even having to look in the mirror.

In time, this happens. Not long ago I talked with a woman who had played the piano quite well when young, but stopped for about thirty years, and only recently started to play seriously again. Describing some of her feelings doing this, she said with surprise and delight, "I can feel my hands getting *intelligent*. They know where to go, what to do. Often they seem to know how to do things I cannot remember having taught them, so that I think to myself, When did I learn to do that?" A wonderful sensation. The body plays the piano or cello without always having to be told how. It knows when it is doing well or badly. The same is true of typing. My fingers tell me, by the way they feel, when I make a mistake on the typewriter, hit the Z instead of the A. In the same way, serving in tennis, I often know, almost the instant the ball leaves the racket, whether the serve will be in, short, or long.

A tape recorder can help a music student know what his playing sounds like. Of course, he can hear what he does as he does it. But this may not give him all the feedback he needs, and a tape recorder may tell him things about his playing he might otherwise not know. For one thing, the player is much closer to the instrument than the listener, and the sounds he hears is thus a different sound. Because it is different, he can't very well compare it with what he hears when others play. Beyond that is this problem, that the player, even though he hears as he plays, cannot give all of his attention to the hearing; he must think mostly about the music he is making, the notes under his fingers, and the notes coming up. He hears only with part of his mind. Finally, the player, especially if a novice, is likely to be so caught up in the excitement of playing that he cannot hear objectively what he is doing. If I play a piece on my cello somewhat better than I have played it before, it feels so good and I am so pleased and excited that I may be tempted to think it sounds much better than it really is.

The tape recorder helps solve these problems. In my office, where I practice, I set up a microphone across the room. This feeds into the tape recorder, to which I can listen through headphones. Thus even as I play I can hear what my cello would sound like to someone else out in front. From time to time I record a scale or exercise, or one of the pieces I am playing, and later play it back, so that I can listen critically and with full attention. So doing, I hear many faults that I missed in the excitement of playing, and hear what I have to work on, change, improve. Many people studying an instrument might be helped if they could learn to give themselves such feedback. Music practice rooms might be more useful if they had in them tape recorders which people could use to do this.

Problems of Order

Sometimes the teacher fails to order the task properly, gives the student something to do beyond his strength. This may frustrate him, shame him, shake his confidence, perhaps injure him. Once a student friend of mine, a skillful rock climber, persuaded me to try it. We went, with some others, to a small beginner's face, short, fairly steep, with some good cracks and handholds in it. They roped me up to someone at the top, one of the experienced climbers went up to show me how, and they told me to go ahead. I was wearing lightweight sneakers, which they should have known would not work. At one point I got one hand into a crack. They then told me to step on some little nubbin of rock and grab for another handhold. The sneaker was too soft and flexible, and would not support my weight. I found myself hanging on the crack, all my weight on my fingers, which were slowly opening up. Shouts of advice and encouragement came from all sides. I shouted back with growing desperation and terror that I couldn't climb, couldn't hang on, was going to fall, and for God's sake to lower me down off that damned rock. Which they did, leaving me feeling somewhat foolish and ashamed.

On another occasion, the task was OK, but the feedback and correction were missing. In the summer of 1947 some friends asked if I would like to try water skiing. I said I would. I put the skis on and waited in the water for the boat to pull me up. The rope tightened, I rose, could feel my balance going, and fell over on my face in the water. Tried again; same story. Tried again; ditto. Again, much advice, but none of it told me what I needed to know about what I was doing wrong and ought to do instead. After seven or eight unsuccessful tries I gave up, ashamed. Not for more than twenty years did I try again. This time the model or the advice—"keep your arms straight"—was good, and when the boat pulled the rope tight, up and away I went.

Ski schools and teachers have become very good at ordering the task. They have to be; if the task is too hard the novice will fall down. If he falls very often, he will feel foolish and discouraged, and will exhaust and perhaps hurt himself. Ski teachers, like ballet masters, have over the years worked out a series of graded tasks, such that doing each one gives the beginner the strength, coordination, and muscular awareness he will need to do the next. In recent years one ski teacher had an even more simple and elegant idea. Since shorter skis are easier to turn on, why not start the beginners on very short ones? Then, instead of learning motions—stem turns, etc.—they will later have to unlearn, they can make parallel turns from the very beginning. Most ski schools and teachers scoffed at this idea for a long time; now more and more of them use it. It works.

Sometimes the student himself sees how to break down his own task. In my last year at college I was suddenly told by the NROTC to take a physical test. Though good at racket and ball games, I was not strong, and failed the test badly. In one part of it I had to vault over a bar, chest high. I had no idea how to begin. I stood in front of it, holding on, making vague jumping motions and feeling like a fool. I couldn't even imagine what it would *look* like to do it, let alone feel like. After a while, the disgusted tester moved me on to the next test. At the end they gave me two or three weeks to prepare for a retest. One day, when no one was around, I went in to look at that bar. I saw it could be lowered. The thought came, maybe if I could put this bar way down and vault it, I might feel what it was like, and so be able to vault it higher up. And so it was. I put it way down, got the feeling of supporting my weight with my arms as my legs went over, raised it higher, added the feeling of lifting and pushing with my arms as I jumped with my legs. Before long I had the feel, the model of the action in my mind/body, and was able to vault it easily.

When I was about eleven, a friend and I, who had played much golf together, decided to learn to play tennis. We borrowed or bought some cheap rackets and some balls, went out on the court, and began to try to hit the ball back and forth from the back of the court. It was a total failure; if one of us got the ball over, the other rarely could get it back. After a while we thought, this is no fun, how can we make it better? With the resourcefulness of still-young kids, too interested in having fun to be worried about not playing like other people, we changed the rules, moved in close, made the service line our baseline, and began a game in which the object was to see how many times in a row we could hit the ball to each other before one of us missed. That proved to be a good game. Not having to hit the ball so hard, or run so far for it, we could control it better, keep the rallies going, and have some fun—and also, learn some tennis. This is still the best on-the-court way for beginners to play that I know; even fairly good players can learn much from it.

But a teacher, asking a student to do an easy task so that he may later do a harder one, must be careful not to be too rigid about this. If the student can't hurt himself doing the harder task, let him try it if he wants. The most valuable and indeed essential asset the student brings to any learning task is a willingness to adventure, to take risks. Without that, he can't learn anything. The teacher must not kill this spirit, but honor and strengthen it. Thus, one of the stupidest things the S-chools do is insist that children "comprehend" everything they read, and read only what they comprehend. People who read well do not learn to read this way. They learn by plunging into books that are "too hard" for them, enjoying what they can understand, wondering and guessing about what they do not, and not worrying when they cannot find an answer. Few children in S-chool are allowed to act or feel that way. They are made to feel that not to "comprehend" is a kind of crime. They stop thinking of themselves as adventurers and explorers, and books as exciting territory to explore. They read only what they can be sure of, which means that it is dull, which means they will stop reading as soon as they can.

From my own experience in t-eaching I know that when a t-eacher invents what seems like a good series of graded tasks, he may fall in love with it, and try to lock the student in it. We can see this in the teaching of most S-chool subjects, which are not sequential at all, and in the teaching of music, which is in some ways sequential, but has much more room for exploration and invention than many music teachers encourage or allow. Years ago I made up a sequence of tasks for learning tennis. The first is simply to bounce the ball over and over again on the strings of the racket. This gives the hitting muscles of hand and arm not only more strength, but also a precision, control, awareness, a feedback mechanism, which later will help the player keep the ball in the court. Many beginners go on the court without this strength, sensitivity, or awareness. They have very little control over the force they apply to the ball, and so can rarely keep it in the court. Many of them spend a long time at this stage, or never get past it, or get discouraged and quit.

There are other graded tasks in my tennis sequence, including the short game my friend and I invented. When teaching beginners, I am often tempted to say that they must do the early tasks until they can do them well, before tackling the larger and harder task of playing in the full court. But they are unwilling to do this, and quite rightly. It may well be that when they try to rally on the full court they will only hit one ball out of three, and will spend most of their time chasing balls and picking them up. But they want to try anyway, because that is what tennis is. A wise and tactful teacher will not try to prevent this. As long as his students are having fun flailing away at the ball, let them do it. If he sees that they are beginning to get more frustration than fun out of this, he may suggest a simpler, more do-able, and hence more enjoyable task. The trick is to find the balance that is most interesting, exciting, and useful to the student. Better yet, to let the student find it. Here the natural authority of the teacher is important. The student will do much of what the teacher asks if he trusts him, and believes that the small tasks really will help him do the larger ones, and that the teacher really wants to make him into a master instead of a puppet or a pigeon.

The Task in the Mind

Before we can do the task in reality, we must be able to do it in our mind. I don't mean, just think "I can do it." I mean, get a picture, a total body feeling of what it would be like to do it. If we can't see and feel ourselves doing it, we won't be able to do it. This was my trouble, standing in front of that bar and trying to think how to vault it, or trying for the first time to get up on water skis. I couldn't feel what it would be like *if it happened*, so I didn't know how to make it happen.

When at the age of thirty, teaching school in Colorado, I first began to ski, my teacher (and boss) John Holden ordered my task well. After only a couple of days of walking about on the skis, and making very short straight runs, he took me up to the top of the mountain and showed me, by traversing, side-slipping, and kick-turning, how I could get down any trail, however steep, without danger. The mountain was then mine, and having other students to teach, he left me alone to master it myself. In time, and with no further instruction, I became a fairly good skier. The traversing (skiing across the face of a hill) and side-slipping he had shown me were good movements to prepare me to make a full turn with skis parallel. But though I could turn up into the slope, and could make a kind of stem turn, I could not for a while make turns, one after the other, with skis together, as the good skiers did. My trouble was that though in theory I knew "how" to do it, I couldn't feel in mind and muscles what it would be like to do it. Then one day, as I was riding up on the lift, a skier went down the hill right underneath me, making smooth and elegant turns. I watched him, trying to feel some of what he must be feeling, thinking myself into his body. Somehow seeing it from above made it easier to do this. I thought, "So that's what it's like." Before long I was beginning to make real parallel turns, rough and clumsy, but essentially the way the real skiers made them.

Years later, friends of mine told me about one of their children, a girl of seven or eight. She had asked, begged, pleaded for a regular bicycle. They had given her one, and now, months later, she had not made the slightest attempt to ride it. What should they do, they asked. Try to teach her? Offer to help? Put on a little pressure—what's the point of having a bike if you never even take it out? I urged them not to do this. Remembering my own skiing, or the remark of an old state-of-Maine lady and lifelong teacher that children learn to skate in the summer and swim in the winter, I suggested that this child was perhaps learning to ride that bike in her mind, and that until she had ridden it there, there was no use trying to make her ride it anywhere else. Perhaps she was watching other children, and thinking, thinking about what it would feel like. Some time later they wrote me that after many more months of not touching the bike, one day the child had taken it out, ridden it on the grass a bit, fallen off once or twice without damage, and then gone riding off down the street with no trouble and had been riding ever since.

Sometimes the teacher, perhaps seeing that the student is not able to follow his instructions, may find a way of talking about them which will help the student feel in his mind what it would be like to do the task. But this is subtle and difficult. It is hard for us to think about what we do well without thinking, or remember what it was like not to be able to do it. Hard to put ourselves inside the skin of the clumsy learner. Sometimes what helps us get a feeling of the task, may not help others. Maybe thinking he was waltzing up to tennis balls helped that tennis coach, though I doubt it. It certainly didn't help me.

At other times a certain kind of hint can be very helpful. Many French teachers have struggled in vain to teach American kids how to say the French "u"—as in "tu." What they get is usually various forms of "oo." One teacher—perhaps by now many—solved the problem by saying, "Make your lips like mine, or as if you were going to whistle, and then say 'eee.' Don't try to make a 'u' sound, make an 'e' sound." It works, or comes close enough to give the student the feel of the sound.

When people are learning to play a game in which they hit a moving ball, they find it very hard to learn to look at the ball, right up until they hit it. Their teachers say "Watch the ball." The students insist that they are. From my own experience as a player I know that most of the time they are not. What they do, as I did myself for years, still do if I grow careless or lose confidence, is look at the ball until it is about three to six feet away, and *then* look where they want it to go. This is in part natural; when we throw a ball at something, we look at the target, not the ball. Also, to some degree we are trying to *will* the ball we hit into going where we want it to go. We think that by looking where we want the ball to go we can *make* it go there. Until I realized *why* I did this, I could not help myself (or others) to stop doing it. Then I learned to tell myself, "Watch the ball right into the strings of the racket, and keep looking at that point of impact *even after the ball has gone*, for an instant, before looking up. Trust the ball to go where you hit it. Anyway, once you have hit it you can't change where it is going."

A sports photo once vividly showed this. It was one of Mickey Mantle, then at the height of his career with the New York Yankees, but in the midst of a terrible batting slump. He was batting left-handed, and the photo had been taken from his right. He was swinging hard at, and missing, a ball just crossing the plate. But he was not looking at or near the ball, but out into right field, with a desperate grimace, as if with his eyes and his will he could think, *look* that ball out where he wanted it to go. In short, he was doing what, in calmer moments, he "knew" enough not to do.

The t-eacher As Support

In Denmark there is a school, the Ny Lilleskole "New Little School") in Bagsværd (a suburb of Copenhagen) where, almost alone among all the schools I know of, there are no regular classes, no curriculum, and above all, no efforts to urge, bribe, or wheedle children into reading. Children there decide for themselves when they will begin to read. They do not have to get help from an adult unless they want it and ask for it. If a child wants some help from an adult, he gets something he wants to read and asks Rasmus Hansen, the head of the school, to read with him. The child and Rasmus, a tall bearded man with a deep, soft, slow voice, go to a little nook set aside for this purpose, in the large room where most of the life of the school takes place. The child finds his place and begins to read aloud. For the most part, Rasmus says very little. As the child reads, he makes low noises of agreement and encouragement. If the child reads a word incorrectly, he may (or may not) ask the child if he is sure, or in some way suggest that he take a second look. Very often the child, puzzling out a word, may test a hunch and read it correctly, but without much confidence. He may even ask if he read the word right. Rasmus will signal that he did. Or the child may come to a stop, unable to decide what a word says, but perhaps unwilling to ask. Rasmus will give him time, but won't let him get stuck or freeze into panic—these silences may mean very different things for different children. Or the child, if he can't figure out what a word says, or at that moment doesn't want to try to figure it out, will ask what it says. Rasmus will perhaps ask questions or give hints that will help him to figure it out, or more often, tell him outright. Perhaps they may stop in the middle of the reading to talk about something else. When the child has had enough, he is free to leave.

Teachers may wonder how the head of a school can give this kind of close individual attention to a single child. He can, because these unpressured children need so little of it. Hardly any child in that school ever needs more than about thirty hours of this kind of help before he can read well and confidently without help. Most children need much less, and some none at all. The work load for T-eachers in conventional S-chools is so heavy only because the S-chools and the T-eachers believe, and soon convince the children, that everything that is learned must be T-aught. So the T-eachers must spend hundreds of hours trying to cope with and outwit the kind of children's evasive tactics I wrote about in *How Children Fail*. They make children anxious and dependent, and then say, rightly, how hard it is to deal with their anxiety and dependency. None of this need be. If the child reads only when he wants to, and asks for help only when he feels he needs it, he will work at full capacity, throw himself into the task instead of away from it, and rarely need help at all.

In no sense could it be said that Rasmus is "teaching" these children how to read. They are finding out for themselves. What he does is to provide a kind of emotional support while they do this exploring and take these risks. The child starting to read has a great many hunches, but very little certainty. He is not sure he can do the task without help, or he would not ask for it. The supporting adult, by being there, by asking questions, by telling the child he is right when he is, by giving information if asked, enables the child to test, confirm, and strengthen not only his hunches about what words say, but the criteria by which he makes these hunches. Like the child learning to talk, who intuits the grammar of his language without knowing that he is doing so, so the child learning to read intuits relationships between letters and sounds. It is absurd to believe, as many people seem to, that if a child is not *taught* phonics he will not *know* any phonics. The child works out for himself, without being told, and hardly knowing that he is doing it, a very good set of what the S-chools call Word Attack Skills. But all of this feels to him almost like guessing, very uncertain, very risky. The supporting adult tells him by his way of being there that he will not let the child get too lost, too confused, too anxious, will not let him get to the point where he no longer dares trust *any* of his hunches or intuitions and so can do nothing—the condition of most so-called nonreaders in S-chools. Dennison in *The Lives of Children*, and Herbert Kohl in *Reading: How To,* and other works, have described this process of support. It is very like what I did for the three-year-old who was beginning to swim (see *How Children Learn*), or what John Holden did for me when he first took me up to the top of a mountain to ski down. The experienced person says to the inexperienced, like the watchful but not anxious parent to the small child, "Don't worry, you are free to explore and try things out, because I won't let you get into serious trouble." The children at the First Street School (*The Lives of Children*) were free even to quarrel and fight, which for many reasons they often needed to do, because the adults, though they did not try to stop them from fighting, kept them from fighting in a way that would do each other serious harm.

The t-eacher As Guide

The words "guide" and "guidance," like many other words, have been badly misused in S-chools. In S-chool talk, "guidance" means being told what to do. When someone asks, "Don't children need guidance?" he is not asking if children need advice—which in fact they do need and seek out. He is saying that children need, everywhere, always, to be told what to do. The "guide" is the person who tells them. So the word "guide" loses its proper meanings, and we lose our sense of the ways in which one person really can guide, and so help, another.

When friends of mine go fishing in the woods, in a wilderness they don't know, they often ask a guide these questions: "What are some of the good fishing places? Where do you think the fishing is good right now? Where do we have a good chance of catching some trout (or pike, bass, etc.)?" Or they may ask, "How can we get to this particular fishing place? Will you take us to it?" Or they may say "Take us to a good fishing place." In the first instance they keep for themselves the maximum amount of choice. They only want the guide to give a list of the possibilities from which they may choose. In the second instance they have chosen the place, but have given him the choice of how to get there, made themselves his followers. In the third instance the guide has been given all the choice.

Sometimes, in order to be a useful guide, when the act, the doing, the task of the student requires skill or may involve danger, the t-eacher must do some task ordering. Thus, if a skier new to a mountain asks an instructor, ski patrolman, or other expert where are some good places to ski, the other will ask, "How well do you ski? What trails have you skied already, here or somewhere else?" He may ask the newcomer to show a little of what he can do. Then he can say, "These trails would be too easy for you, these too hard, these just about right." The same would be true for rock or mountain climbing, or kayaking or canoeing, or flying, or any one of a number of demanding tasks. Or if a novice musician asks an expert to suggest some good music to play, or perhaps some people to play with, the expert will say, "How well do you play? What music have you played?" From the answer, he knows what to suggest—though in music, as in reading, where there is no question of safety, it sometimes pays to be bold, to suggest something too difficult. My first cello teacher, Harold Sproul, very wisely started me playing some movements of the Bach Suites long before I was "ready" for them, knowing that the beauty of the music would make me love the instrument more and want to play it better. Later, Sam Piel, whom I helped to sing in tune, suggested that I work on the Haydn D major concerto. He said, "It'll be much too tough for you, you won't be able to play it, but you'll learn all sorts of fascinating stuff just trying." Which was and is true. More recently I have begun to work my way through the Dvořák Concerto, far too difficult for me to play, let alone play well, but a fascinating challenge.

Sometimes in guiding, skill is not involved, only taste. If one person asks another to suggest a good book to read, piece of music to listen to, or movie or play to see, the other will say, "What sort of stuff do you like?" People often ask me such questions about music. Sometimes I suggest a piece I feel quite sure they will like. Sometimes I may say, "This is not quite what you are used to, but take a chance on it." If people are free to reject what they don't like, not liking it does them no harm. In short, when a teacher wants to help a student explore some piece of reality, whether geographic, athletic, artistic, or intellectual, he must begin by finding out where the student is now. Maps put up to help strangers get around in cities have on them an arrow and the words, "You are here." Without that, the maps are useless.

This is the only legitimate use of tests—to find out where a student is, so that the t-eacher may better order his tasks, or help him explore. The tests S-chools give are not of this sort. S-chools give tests, as Winston Churchill said of his school, not to find out what you know but what you don't know, and not so that they may help you find out what you don't know, but only so they may say you are better or worse than other students. A t-eacher who wanted to use a test to find where a student was, would invent a test for that one student. He would not give the test to all the students; it would not give useful information about most of them. Beyond that, comparing him with the others would tend to make the student afraid and so lessen his chances of showing what he really knew. It would lead him into bluffing and faking, or freeze him into silence.

To be able to do this kind of testing, to draw out from the student the *best* of what he knows, is a very subtle skill or art. We do very little of it and so, do it badly. In *How Children Fail* I describe some of the tests I invented to try to locate some of my students. For many years I thought I had been very clever in getting my students to reveal their confusions. Now I fear I may only have added to them. It is almost impossible for one person to see very far into the mind or thought of another, even under the best circumstances—and a S-chool, or any coercive institution like a S-chool, is the worst possible circumstance. For when one person is in a position in which he can judge, and so reward or punish another, the other is almost certain to have at the center of his mind the thought, "What does the judge want? How can I please him, or fool him? How can I best escape from this place of judgment, and hence of danger?"

No one has invented more ingenious ways to find out what children think than the Swiss psychologist Jean Piaget. Yet his tests, like all tests, suffer from two flaws. One has to do with communication. The tester asks a question; the "testee" gives an answer. But the testee may misunderstand or wrongly interpret the tester's question, and he in turn may do the same with the testee's answer. It is hard to avoid this. If I try to explain my question to you so fully that you *cannot* misunderstand it, I can only do so by pointing you so clearly toward the answer that you cannot miss it—something children in school know well and exploit. You, in turn, cannot be sure that you have properly interpreted my question unless and until you find out that your answer was the one I wanted.

The other and greater difficulty is that the testee is and must be enormously sensitive to and influenced by the wishes of the tester. Years ago, in *The Underachieving School*, I described a film that had been made, under Piaget's supervision and with his approval, of children taking some of his tests. In this one a child about four to five years old was the subject of one of the conservation experiments. The tester had two lumps of clay of the same size. He drew from the child the response that they were the same size. Did the child really think so? I don't know; in that situation it was clearly the wanted answer. Then the tester deformed one of the lumps of clay, and asked the child whether the two lumps were the same, or whether one was more, and if so, which one. The child said that the lump that had been deformed was more. We might say that this answer was wrong. But in this context, it was the right answer, the answer wanted by the people making the film, since it confirmed or "proved" what Piaget was saying about children's thought. But what was significant in this test is that except when he was specifically told to look at the clay, and then only for brief seconds, the child kept his eyes on the face and forehead of the tester. That's where the answer was, not in the clay. The child had lived with adults long enough to know that.

How then can we find out, under closely controlled conditions, what children (or adults) are thinking? We can't. We can only learn, and then not much, when the student comes freely to us, trusts us, knows that our tests are to help him and not grade, rank, and label him, and that he need not fear our judgment. Even among close friends, these are hard conditions, and ones not often met. In S-chools, they cannot be met at all.

8

More t-eachers at Work

There are important differences between the teaching of physical and intellectual acts. Most teachers try to teach intellectual skills in exactly the same way as physical skills, as if for every act of the ballet master there were a comparable act for the teacher of Reading or History or Math. But many things teachers do to help a student do a physical task do not help and may seriously hinder the student trying to do an intellectual task.

At a meeting not long ago a young woman, a student teacher, obviously puzzled and angered by my saying that people should be allowed to explore the world in their own way, asked, "Suppose a six-year-old asked you how a jet airplane worked, and suppose he wasn't interested in studying Physics or reading Physics books, how could you explain it to him?" I replied, "How would *you* explain it to him?" She looked puzzled. I said, "I'm serious. If a six-year-old you know asked you one day how a jet airplane worked, what would you tell him? Would you tell him that he had to study something called Physics for six or ten years or so before he could find out? What would you say?" After a few seconds I said, "Chances are you'd probably say something very much like what I would say, some sensible remark that the plane flies because the jets blow a lot of hot air out the back, and push it forward. Like a balloon when you blow it up and then let it go, and it flies around the room." Such an answer would probably do for the time being. It would fill a gap in the child's understanding, and give him something to think about and work on. In time he might ask "What makes the air hot?" or, "How do they make the air come out of the back?" In which case, using examples that might be familiar to the child, we would answer his question as best we could. But telling the child he had to study Physics in order to find out about the jet plane would be like telling him he had to study initial and final consonants, digraphs, and blends in order to find out what words say and mean. With such advice we cut him off from his intention, his purpose, send him on a long detour. We put things backwards. Physics is not going to lead the child to jet engines, but wondering about jet planes will lead him to Physics. In fact, wondering about jet planes *is* Physics. The child asking such a question *is doing Physics.* The best way for us to help him do it is to answer his question.

How many people do know, roughly, how a jet engine works? Probably quite a few. Where and how did they find out? In school? In Physics class? For most people, probably not. Few people ever studied *any* Physics in school. I did, but nothing about jet engines (they had only just been invented, but even today one does not find anything about jet engines in most elementary or advanced Physics books). Most of S-school Physics is about other things. So how do people know as much as they do about the way jet engines and other things work? They know because they read and hear about them, in newspapers, magazines, books, radio, TV. So the way for us to answer a curious child's (or adult's) questions about jet planes (or anything else) is just to answer them, not to talk about studying Physics. Let the questioner make of our answer what he can. If it tells him what he wants to know, good. If not, he may ask another question. If he sees that, for the moment, we are not going to be able to tell him what he really wants to know, he will stop asking. Sometimes we may be able to say, we can't answer your question, but perhaps this other person (or magazine, or book) can. Or we might say, call up something like the Learning Exchange, and perhaps they can tell you someone who can answer your question.

The t-eacher's work, therefore, begins when that other person asks a question. No question, no t-eaching. But it is important to understand what a t-eacher can do and does with his answers, and what he cannot do. He does not give knowledge. Knowledge cannot be *given*. If you ask me a question all I can do in my reply is try to put into words a part of my experience. But you get only the words, not the experience. *To make meaning* out of my words, you must use your own experience. If you have not seen or done at least some part of what I have seen and done, then you cannot make any meaning from my words. There is no way we could explain bicycles or cars or gears or pulleys to someone who had never seen a wheel or a circle. We would have to begin there, show him a wheel, put the wheel into his experience, before we could talk to him meaningfully about devices that make use of wheels. We could not explain the burning of fuel in a car or jet engine to someone who had never seen a fire. We would have to make the fact of things burning, of heat, of expansion due to heat, of the power of heat, part of his experience before we could talk to him meaningfully about engines.

But to the extent that you do share some of my experience, then by talking about my experience, by throwing a light on part of it, I may reveal to you something *in your experience* that you had not seen before, or help you to see it in a new way, to make, in David Hawkins's words, "transitions and consolidations." Once a five-year-old asked me what made our blood come out if we cut ourselves. I began to talk about the heart. His face showed me right away that this was not in his experience. I asked if he knew where his heart was, or what it did. No, he didn't. I then asked him to jump up in the air, ten times, as high as he could. He did this, with great seriousness. Then I asked him to put his hand over the left side of his chest. His eyes grew wide. Something was *thumping*, right inside him. He had never felt that thing in there before, never knew it was there. Now that he had felt it, I was able to say something about that heart being like a fist, squeezing with each thump, and making the blood run round through little pipes, some of which we could see under the skin of our wrists. That, at least for the moment, was enough.

How does a teacher know when his answer is not understood? In that case, my young friend's face showed me that he could make no meaning from my answer. To help him make that meaning, I asked him about his heart. But this was not something I would always do. For it is not the t-eacher's business to make *sure* the do-er understands. It is the do-er's business. Let him decide whether he is satisfied with the teacher's answer, and if not, what he wants to do about it. He may want to ask another question, or ask some-one else to see what they say, or think for a while about what he has heard. We must be careful not to use every do-er's question as an excuse to turn life into S-chool, to T-each a lesson, and then give a little quiz to make sure the lesson was learned. There is the old story of the child who asked her mother about something, and, when the mother suggested that she ask her father, said, "I don't want to know *that* much about it." And yet I do not mean that, if asked a question, we should answer once in a take-it-or-leave-it spirit and then say no more unless asked again. We need tact here. Whenever we talk to another person, child or adult, we must watch for signs that we are not being understood, so that we may try to make ourselves more clear. But we must also watch for signs from the questioner that whether he understands or not that he has heard enough and wants to let the matter drop. Thus only the other day I was talking to a friend about the financial statement of an organization we are both interested in. She seemed not to un-derstand a point I was making. I felt an explaining fit coming on. Just in time I caught myself, and said, "Do you want me to explain further?" With some relief, she said, "Well, as a matter of fact, I don't." She has not raised the matter since. Fair enough.

A difficult art, the art of the t-eacher, of answering questions, of saying enough but not too much. Some are tempted to think that machines, computers, or other devices might do it better. But they cannot. I was once very interested in the idea of teacherless textbooks, particularly in Math. Math teachers seemed so unable to answer most students' questions that I thought, why can't we have a textbook that will answer them? At about that time I met a Math teacher in a low-track junior high school who, with his class, had in effect rewritten a standard textbook to answer every question of every student throughout the year. This had been their central project, to make a text that every member of the class could understand. I began to think about a textbook which would work not just for one class but all classes, all students. But it can't be done. Even if we could write such a book, it would be too expensive to buy, and too fat to use. How would one begin to write such a book? We would have to assume that the people reading the book knew something. But what could we assume they knew? Or be sure that what we explained would be clear to everyone who read? Would we have to explain the explanations, and then explain them, and so on. The reason why the human t-eacher is at best so infinitely quicker and more flexible than a book or machine, is that with a t-eacher (but not a T-eacher) the student can begin with what he knows and what he wants to find out. He can ask the question *he* wants, and if the answer is not clear, do whatever he needs to do to make it clear. As David Hawkins well puts it,

> you can only understand a textbook when you are at the point where you almost don't need to read it, where it helps you comprehend (if it is any good) some higher-order connections among things you separately have already worked your way through or around.

A Mathematical Do-er and Some Helpers

How does a t-eacher work in a "purely" intellectual field? What does he do for the student? What can the student get from him? Let me give more specific examples from my own experience as a do-er.

I began to write this section, a few days ago, in a state of great excitement. For about a day I thought I had found the solution to a mathematical problem I had been thinking about and struggling with, off and on, since about 1956. It was a theorem about prime numbers I had come across in a Penguin book about Mathematics for laymen. People who work with number theory know this theorem and how to prove it, but few if any school Math texts mention it. The author said that someone with only secondary-school Math but with exceptional mathematical gifts could work out this proof. Thus challenged, I began to work on the problem and have been working on it ever since. Not all of the time, not very often, perhaps only once every two or three years. But it sticks in my mind. I do not look up the proof in a book because I do not want to lose the chance of someday working it out for myself. That is why I don't name the theorem here; some kindly people might send me the answer, or a hint about how to find it. Even the hint might be too much, for if I then found the answer I could never be sure that I would have found it without the hint. Even at the risk I may never do it, I want to do it by myself.

How did I become interested in Mathematics at all? Certainly not in school. School Math bored me. I learned it as my students, years later, learned it (or tried to)—as a set of meaningless puzzles and rules for working out these puzzles. Nothing and no one hinted that behind those puzzles and rules there had once been thinking persons, in turn curious, puzzled, baffled, ecstatic. The only one of my teachers who made Math even slightly interesting had been a very poor Math student himself. Those who had been good at Math were a total loss. The theorems and proofs they put on the board were as clear to them as ABC, and they knew no way to help those who did not find them just as clear.

I was able to get B's in Math without much trouble. At college my first major was in Physics. In Advanced Sophomore Calculus I got a B. But I began to see more and more clearly that I really knew nothing about Mathematics, had no idea of the *point* of these rules and theorems and puzzles, where they came from, where they might lead, and what one might do with them. Though I knew little about what Physicists did, either, I knew they used Mathematics, and that anyone who didn't understand Math could hardly do good work in Physics. So I dropped Physics and Math, and went in other directions.

Many years later, teaching Math (because I knew just enough to teach it), and thinking about the problems of my students, I began again to wonder what Math was really about. One day, at the home of the parents of one of my students, I fished out of a pile of magazines an old issue of the *Scientific American*. In it was an article about Leonhard Euler and the beginnings of that branch of Mathematical do-ing called Topology. Somewhere (not in school), I had heard about Topology—it had something to do with knots, and turning things inside out, why some shapes can be turned inside out, but not others. I had even heard the name of Euler. So I settled down to read the article. Soon I found myself in the company of Euler as he solved the problem of the Konigsberg bridges. It was as exciting a mental journey as I had ever taken.

The story was this. When he began working on this problem, Euler was court mathematician to the Czar in St. Petersburg. One day he heard that the whole town of Konigsberg was in a turmoil over the new puzzle of the bridges. Konigsberg lies on both banks of a river, and on two islands, one large, one small, between these banks. The small island has two bridges to each bank, the large island one to each, and there is a bridge between the islands. One day someone asked if there was a way to walk through the town, crossing every bridge once and no bridge more than once. Soon many people were walking this way and that, trying without success to find the magic route. But Euler, being a do-er of Mathematics, did not have to be in Konigsberg to solve this problem. He began to think about it. Before long he found a way to show, not only that the particular problem of the Konigsberg bridges could not be solved, but how one could tell very quickly whether any such problems could be solved, and what would be the possible solutions. The theorem covers puzzles like the one I did as a kid—

how to draw this figure without taking the pen-

cil off the page, or going over any line twice.

There are no words to describe the excitement, amazement, ex-
hilaration, and joy I felt when I finished reading this article. They
were just like my feelings at the end of a beautiful concert, or after
reading certain books, which illuminated and made whole many
parts of my experience. Such experiences are ecstatic, almost
erotic. At the end of my journey of discovery with Euler it was as
if many voices, inside me, all through me, were shouting, "So
that's what Mathematicians do! Why didn't anyone ever tell me?
No wonder they do it—it's beautiful! I want to do it. I will do it!"
At that moment Mathematics became one of the things which I
knew I wanted to do and would do. Perhaps not well; certainly not
like Euler. But better than I had thought I could. In this spirit, some
time later, I hurled myself into the problem of the prime numbers, on which I am working to this day. How did Euler prove that
the Konigsberg bridges could not be crossed? Let those who want,
have the pleasure of finding out for themselves. It can be proved
with no more than the simplest Algebra. Indeed, it can be proved
without Algebra. Years after I read the article, when I had forgotten its details, I was able to reconstruct for myself Euler's theorem
and proof. Many years later, trying to do this again, I found
another way to prove it. Perhaps readers will find still others.

The most important thing Euler showed me about the work of
a Mathematician is that above all else he wants to simplify, to strip
a problem of all those aspects of it that don't really matter, get rid
of all the differences that don't make any difference. Euler knew he
didn't have to walk over all those bridges to find out whether it
could be done. The style of the bridges, or the size and shape of
the islands, was not important—not for this problem. This ability,
to turn a complicated life situation into a very simple, bare, abstract model of it, is what makes Mathematicians very good at solv-

ing certain kinds of problems—and very bad at solving others.

Euler, in sharing with me (and many others) this part of his experience, was t-eaching. The person who wrote the article, and the person who decided to publish it in the *Scientific American*, were also acting as t-eachers, not as models, but as guides, leading me to Euler. Some years later, at the suggestion of my colleague Bill Hull, I read a book about Mathematics called *Productive Thinking*, by Wertheimer. He introduced me to another idea, that a solution to a problem or proof of a theorem, though correct, might be beautiful or ugly. A beautiful solution or proof is one that is simple, direct, that goes to the very nature and essence of the problem. An ugly one, though perfectly correct and usable, somehow misses this essence. Wertheimer gave some very good examples of ugly and beautiful solutions, of which I remember none. I only remember the distinction itself, a standard by which to judge one's own solution to a problem.

Not until the other day, when I thought I had found a proof to the theorem about prime numbers, did I make use of this standard. In spite of my joy at having found my "solution," I could not escape the nagging thought that by Wertheimer's criterion my solution was a very ugly one. It was only an algebraic trick, like the tricks I once knew how to do in school. I seemed to have proved, at last, that this theorem was true, but I was no closer than ever to understanding *why* it was true. So I kept thinking about the problem and my proof, trying to see whether my proof might conceal a beautiful and more fundamental proof. After a while I began to ask myself, Could my proof be wrong? In my proof I had in effect asked, if I assume this theorem is true, can I then show that some things follow from it which I can prove *are* true? I could, and did. But I began to suspect more and more—and finally and sadly to know—that my method could equally well prove true a theorem that was in fact false. The proof was no good, the problem still unsolved. It took me many more hours even to find where I had gone wrong. For two days I spent much of my free time trying to find a new and true solution to the original problem. No luck. Someday I will try again. Meanwhile, I owe to Euler both my model of Mathematical doing and my belief that it is worth doing, and to Wertheimer a standard of judgment which in one instance helped me to see that mathematically speaking I had done wrong. What they did for me, through their work and writing, and across many years of time, any true teacher may do for his students.

A Useful Standard for Writers

In the Winter 1975 issue of *Teachers and Writers Newsletter* (490 Hudson St., Manhattan, NY 10014), Bill Bernhardt has an article called "A Short Course in Just Writing," which, far more than anything I have ever seen, offers really helpful advice and suggestions to the many people, some very good students, some very bad, who find it an agony to get their thoughts down on paper. People had been asking him for a long time where they could go to take a course in "just writing." Only after many years did he see what they really needed and wanted, and that none of the usual writing courses or textbooks could offer it to them. Out of his thinking about his own writing, and some seminars he took with Dr. Caleb Gattegno, he worked out a short course of exercises to help people, however unskilled, to write more easily and effectively. His short course comes in five short pages. He asks his students to read and do Page 1 first; after that, they can take the others in any order they want. He says, in part:

Page 1
—Which comes first when you speak, knowing that you have something you want to say, or the words? Test yourself to find out.
—Make a short statement out loud.
—Write down the same words you said.
  Are you sure that you wrote the same words? How can you tell? Can you make a much longer statement and write down the words accurately? (It doesn't matter if you misspell).
—Think of something else you could say but, instead of speaking, write it down without speaking.
—Can you think of something to say and write the words down as they come into your mind without taking the time to say them to yourself first?

With respect to that last question, sometimes I can, sometimes I can't. Very often I have to say something over and over again a great many times before I find a way of saying it that I like enough to want to write it down. At other times the idea, and the words to say it, appear together. Sometimes they please me so much I have to get them down on paper right away. Bernhardt continues:

Page 2
—Take a pencil and a piece of blank paper and write continuously for three minutes without removing your pencil from the paper. . . . Pay no attention to whether what you write makes sense or is spelled correctly. If you can't think of anything to say, just write down all the words you can think of. When you finish, turn the paper over without reading what you wrote.

—Write for three more minutes on the reverse side of the paper, following the same directions.

—Write for three more minutes on a second sheet of paper.

Count how many words you wrote each time. Did your output increase the second and/or third time? Have you written more than you usually write in the same amount of time?

Read what you wrote aloud and listen to yourself. Does it make sense? *Does it sound like the English you speak?* [italics mine]

The last sentence is the key to the whole process. The idea of nonstop writing is not new. In *How Children Fail* I described using it with fifth-graders in what I called a Composition Derby. The idea came to me from an article by I. S. Hayakawa, who used it with students of his at Roosevelt College in Chicago. But it is a stroke of real genius to ask the student to see if what he has written sounds like the English *he speaks*. Not "good English" or "correct English." Not the English the teacher speaks, or that the student thinks he himself *ought* to speak. But the English he actually speaks. Bernhardt has grasped here a most powerful and fundamental truth. Even the worst speakers of English "know how" to speak better English, not just more correct but also clearer and more direct English than they usually speak. And as his examples (see Appendix to this book) show, even the most hopelessly illiterate writers can speak a lot better than they write. Thus we could enormously improve even the worst writing if we can just get the writers to ask themselves, about whatever they write, "Is this the way I would really say it? Is this the way I would like to say it, if I had time to think about it?"

Bernhardt again:

Page 3
—Complete the following sentence by adding *one word* at the end: [italics mine]

> As they turned the corner they saw

Copy the completed sentence onto the top of a blank sheet of paper and continue by writing a second sentence which begins with the following word:

> Maybe

Add a third sentence to the story.

Add five more sentences to the story.

End the story.

> How much of the story was given to you and how much did you have to provide? . . . Could you see in your mind what was happening in the story? If so, was it like a picture or a movie? Did you see all of it at the beginning or did more come into your mind as you continued? Can you see it all again when you read the story over?

—Close your eyes and picture in your mind a difficult or embarrassing situation which you would not like to find yourself in.

> Describe in writing what the situation is.

> Write what you would say to get yourself out of that situation.

Again, as a way of putting the fearful writer in touch with *his own* real powers of imagination and expression and making them available to him, these instructions are a work of genius. I am lost in admiration of them. All the would-be writer is asked to do at first is add *one word* to a sentence. Anyone can do that. But as soon as he does it, he is, benignly speaking, hooked. His creative powers are already at work. In his mind's eye he must see that corner, and the characters he created, who have just turned it. With this beginning he can easily fill in after the "maybe." By then the story is on its way. It has a life of its own, and has taken possession of the writer, which is what stories do, and what it feels like to be a writer. The next instruction is just as clever. Most people have waking nightmares, dreaded scenes they play over and over again in their mind, and know well enough so that they can easily write about them. (We might also suggest that the writers imagine a very pleasant situation that they would like very much to find themselves in.)

Page 4 continues to explore and develop the writer's power to imagine and describe. On Page 5 Bernhardt gives writers more sensible and usable, and, as the Appendix shows, more effective ways to judge and improve their writing:

Page 5
—Write rapidly for 10 minutes without stopping or pausing to make corrections. When you have finished writing, put the paper aside, without reading what you wrote, for at least 20 minutes.

—Read what you wrote aloud, making sure you do two things:

(1) Read *exactly* what is written on the paper.

(2) Listen to yourself reading and catch the points when what you hear fails to make sense or sounds "funny."

If you find anything which doesn't make sense, change the words so that it does make sense.

If you find anything which sounds funny, change it so that it sounds right.

When you finish, read the corrected copy over again to see if you need to make further changes.

—Is it easier to make corrections and improvements at the same moment you are writing down what you want to say or at a later time?

—Do writing and making corrections require the same state of mind? Different states of mind?

The simple ideas and exercises in these few short pages would do more to help most people to write better, and to enjoy writing more, than all the things I ever did in my own work as an English teacher, and probably, than all the work of all English teachers put together. As a way to show the pupil *his own powers*, and ways to use and develop them, and above all, to free him more and more from his need for outside correction and judgment, it is a superb example of the teaching art.

Alfred North Whitehead once said that it was easy to teach people to give right answers to questions; what was hard to teach was to ask the right questions, questions that are interesting, important, useful, and far-reaching. Fortunately, we do not have to teach people to ask good questions. Human beings do this by nature, and almost from birth. All we have to do is answer their questions, or allow or help them to find their answers, and they will ask more. Their questions will get better and their answers will reach further. But Whitehead's remark illustrates an important point, that the do-ing of Math, or Physics, or any other intellectual activity, begins with someone asking a question. That is, someone wondering, puzzled, confused. S-chool books, textbooks, rarely help us to see this. They tell us right answers, but very rarely the questions that first led people to look for those answers. So we learn very little about the kinds of good questions that important thinkers have asked.

Someone wrote that Einstein's work on relativity began with two questions he asked himself while quite young. One was, what does it mean to say that two things happen at the same time? The other was, what would it be like to ride through space on the front end of a beam of light, what would we see? Not many Science T-eachers, I suspect, have heard of these questions. If they did, many would say that these questions were not serious, not "scientific." The first is too obvious, the second too fanciful to be worth thinking about. Most children who asked questions like these in school would get more criticism than encouragement. Perhaps Einstein was himself such a child; his T-eachers thought him dull.

School books even more rarely tell us how thinkers of the past have gone about trying to answer their own questions, and still more rarely, what mistakes they made along the way. A graduate student in Psychology suggested one day to a noted professor in that field that there should be a publication in which psychologists would write about their mistakes, the hunches that had not worked out, the experiments that had not proved what they were meant to prove, or didn't prove anything. The professor agreed that such a publication would teach students a great deal about the doing of Psychology. But, he said, there was no use even thinking about such a publication, because no one with a reputation to defend would ever put anything in it. So we find it hard to find most of our mistakes because we are so rarely told how the do-ers of the past came to make and later find theirs.

The do-ers of many kinds of intellectual work can teach us much through their arguments with each other. Historians are a good example. In 1974 many of them argued heatedly, often in newspapers and magazines, about *Time on the Cross*, a recently published book about slavery. The authors, Fogel and Engerman, though they do not uphold slavery, attack the belief of most U.S. historians that slavery in this country was in general both physically cruel and inefficient. Historians think this issue is important for many reasons. Some of them have to do with the politics and social conflicts of today. Some have to do with a question about which historians have been arguing for some time: Was the Civil War necessary to end slavery, or would it not in time have failed because of its inefficiency? At any rate, the authors of *Time on the Cross* say that our historians have taken their generally held ideas about slavery from the wrong sources, from personal accounts, by slaves, or slave-owners, or other witnesses. They complain that these accounts do not give a true picture, that they are too few, that they are heavily biased against slavery. Instead, they have used a different kind of evidence, which they claim is more complete, impartial, and reliable: commercial records, accounts of farm outputs, records of the buying and selling of slaves in slave markets, and so on. From this evidence they conclude that slavery was for the most part very efficient, and not very physically cruel, that the farms worked by slaves were more productive than the slaveless farms of the North. Many historians have in turn challenged not only their conclusions but their methods, their evidence, and the way they used it. So there are two arguments going on at the same time. One is about what happened. The other is about how we can best find out what happened. Along with these there is a third argument, about what difference it makes. Many people think it makes a lot of difference. Charges of racism fill the air. Fogel and Engerman say that the conventional wisdom of history, that under slavery black people in America were never able to build stable families and communities, is racist. Their opponents, some of whom want to claim that present troubles or weaknesses or deficiencies of blacks are all the result of the harm slavery did to them, argue the other way.

It would be a fine thing if more people, children and adults, could overhear all these historians quarreling with each other. How interesting, lively, and important it would make the *doing* of History seem to them. Nobody ever told me as a student that the experts ever disagreed or argued about anything. Least of all Historians. What was there for them to argue about? History was facts—names, places, dates, battles, kings. Clearly, the work of a Historian was to collect those facts and write them down in History books for the students to memorize. Later, if he wanted to amuse himself by wondering and even arguing a bit about what the facts might mean and what difference it might make, he could. But the facts came first. There could be no arguing about them.

So, at least, it seemed to me, as a student, and for many years as an adult. And so, in spite of all that was said about its importance, History seemed for the most part dull and pointless. At certain ages some children used to find it exciting to imagine themselves Greeks or Romans or Medieval knights. (History was almost entirely about what *men* did, and a large part of that was fighting). A few children, as they grow up, continue to like to live imaginatively in other places and times, or to wonder about why things happened as they did. But for most children, as for most adults, History soon becomes and remains a bore. But it need not be so. If more people knew about arguments like those over *Time on The Cross*, many of them might feel differently. Such arguments make History more interesting, because they show us that it is not just a collection of facts or books about dead people, but something that living people *do*, right now. We find their quarrels interesting, not just because we like a quarrel, but because they tell us that some people think these things are worth quarreling about. My sense of History as something that people do, and my ideas about some of the ways in which they do it, came not from school, not even from History books read out of school, but from reading reviews (generally quarrelsome) of books about History in the *New York Review of Books*, which I bought for other reasons. Slowly, over many years, I became aware that there was this crowd of people out there who were *always* arguing about History. What were they arguing about? Partly, about what happened; much more, *about how to find out what happened*. In other words, they were arguing about their on-going daily work.

Thus, the authors of *Time on the Cross* tell us that we can't trust people's books, articles, letters, diaries. Such records are biased, deluded, emotional, angry. It's only (so they claim) when people are keeping their financial records, thinking about money, that they are not swayed by emotion, stick to the facts. So that's where we have to look if we want to find out what happened. Those who oppose this view (as I would tend to) say nonsense, what could we learn about people if we only looked in their account books? Even if it were always true (which it isn't) that they don't put lies in there, neither do they put anything important about what is happening to them or how they feel about it. If we had to find there all we know about people, we would know nothing. So the argument goes. Do we look for evidence which is secure but trivial? Or evidence which is not at all trivial, but perhaps not secure? Whom do we ask? Whom do we trust?

Beyond these questions, some others. People who are happy about their lives and work don't usually write much about them. It's the people who are unhappy who write. Do the people who criticize their society and their times speak for many others, who would like to but don't know how to or don't dare? Or do they speak only for a small group of malcontents like themselves? How do we find out what *many* people think? The current view is that we send out a pollster to ask them a few questions, or send them a questionnaire to fill out. But do people say what they really think to complete strangers, or in the first five minutes of a conversation? Even with friends, I usually find that it takes much longer than that for people to get out what is really on their minds. What do we believe when the things people say on polls do not agree with what they say to people who talk to them for a long time, or more important, with what they do? To what degree do people have one set of ideas for talking, and another for acting?

Questions like these put History right in the middle of everyone's daily life. For all of us, whatever we do, need to know something about what happened, even if only yesterday or last week. We all have the problem, how do we find out, who do we ask, who do we trust? In that very important sense we are all historians. Everything around us, everything we see or do, has a history. A large part of the written matter we see is History—reports about things that happened. This is what written History is—not facts, but *reports*. Thus the daily newspaper is a book of History. We don't always believe what we read there. In that sense, we are good Historians. The reality we live in extends into the past and future. Thinking about that past, and how it relates to the present and the future, is not just a "school subject" or a "body of knowledge," to be done only by a few specialists. It is a central part of the active life, the doing, of all of us. Some people may do it more or better than others. But we all need to do it better, and we need good teachers, good models and guides, to help us do it better.

What questions are worth asking? How do we search for answers? How do we find out whether our answers are any good? These questions are at the heart of all intellectual activity, and so of t-eaching. In *How Children Learn* I described a first-grade class in which children who came to school early could write on the blackboard anything they wanted. Entirely on their own, they began to invent and do problems in addition, at first, like $70 + 20 = ?$; later, $200 + 400$, or even $240 + 520$. In a week they were using larger numbers and doing more complicated problems than the regular school curriculum would have asked them to do before the end of the second-grade year, if then. At the time, I wrote:

> At the end of the week, just as they were beginning to get going, I had to leave, and so wasn't able to give their work the kind of nudge that might have led them to consider the problems of carrying, or of subtraction. . . .

Clearly the children needed no more than a nudge, if even that. These children did not need to be *taught* how to ask questions about numbers, or how to go about finding answers, or how to find out whether their answers were good. They were doing such things on their own, and they had not been taught to do so, by their regular teacher or by me. When I decided to let them write on the board, I thought they might write words or draw pictures. It never occurred to me that they would write and do arithmetic problems. But there they were, six years old, doing real Mathematics, asking their own questions, finding and checking answers. So the most I might have done, or needed to do, was to suggest a few new questions, or ways of finding and checking answers.

Thus I might one day have written on the board $5 + 5 =$, and just left it there. I suspect the problem would have tempted them, and that by various means they would have worked out, and agreed, that $5 + 5 = 10$. From what they had done with their other problems, I suspect they would soon have worked out that $50 + 50 = 100$, and perhaps that $500 + 500 = 1000$. Perhaps one of them would one day have written $5 + 6 =$, or in time I might have written it myself. Again, I think they would have worked out that $5 + 6 = 11$, and from there that $50 + 60 = 110$, and so on. What they were doing in their work, without thinking of it in such terms, was abstracting certain principles from the behavior of small numbers, and applying them to larger ones. Would they in time have moved from $5 + 6 = 11$ to a wider variety of problems involving carrying: $5 + 7$, $6 + 7$, $6 + 8$, $16 + 8$, and so on? Given enough time, I think they would. But I cannot be sure. I wasn't in the class long enough to find out. And perhaps it was just as well. Given more time, I might have taken their project away from them, turned it from something they were doing for their own pleasure and curiosity into something I was doing for my own T-eacher purposes.

This is a terrible temptation for ambitious T-eachers. They are always looking for some interest in their students to exploit for their own purposes. Even as I think about those first-graders, the thought comes, had I only been in that class a few more weeks, or months, perhaps the children, working "on their own" and helped every few days by a nudge from me, might have sailed through three, or five, or who knows how many years of the Math curriculum. What a tale that would have been! Holt the Miracle Worker! This is the seductive, dangerous vanity of the person in love with teaching. He thinks he can create miracles, or (which is the same) get his students to create them. But children move into the world by great leaps here and there, spasms of exploration and activity mixed with long periods of reflection. Most likely those eager inventors and solvers of problems would have tired of their mathematical research after a while and switched to something else. And if I had begun to take too great an interest in their work, to nudge too often, they would surely have sensed this—probably before I did—and drawn back, feeling that somehow the project was no longer theirs but mine.

This is exactly what happened, on another occasion. I have mentioned the Composition Derby, a contest (among fifth-graders) to see who could write the most words in a given period of time. For many reasons, the children became interested in this contest, and began to write more easily and fluently, and usually more interestingly. One day, one of them suggested an overnight Composition Derby, in which they would all take their papers home and see who could come back the next day with the most words written. The others enthusiastically agreed. Next day they returned with anywhere from five hundred to two thousand words written. My eyes lit up. Like most teachers, I thought that the more words my students wrote, the better my teaching. A few days later I slyly suggested another overnight derby. The children saw through me in a second, and said no, they didn't want to, it would be boring. Fortunately I had the sense to draw back quickly, to say OK and *mean* OK, so that at least I did not kill for them whatever pleasure they had in writing in class.

The Uses of Consensus

Those first-graders doing their independent work in Math instinctively understood what the S-chools seem unable or unwilling to learn. People very often work more effectively in a group. Not all people, not always, and not for all kinds of work. Some people are loners and some work, like writing, is usually best done alone. But much of the time people can do far more working with others than they could all by themselves. They give each other a sort of collective feedback. These children knew or sensed that it was highly probable that any one of their answers was right if they all agreed on it. Not that they were democrats, believing that the voice of the people is the voice of God; like all young children, they were aristocrats and anarchists. But they had learned from experience that it was very unlikely, if a mistake had been made, that they would all make and agree on the same mistake. This is one of the reasons why almost all of the intellectual doings of people, like Math or Physics or History, or whatever, are done collectively—not just so that people can share each other's ideas, but so that they can catch each other's mistakes.

In earlier writings I have said that when T-eachers are T-eaching a Right Answer sort of course, like Math or some parts of Science or Foreign Languages, they should not correct papers but instead give students the answer sheet. This would free the students from dependence on them, and spare them much dull and needless work. Now I would go further and suggest that they leave with the students the task of figuring out which of their answers was right. Pocket calculators have become so small and cheap that for much less than we spend trying to T-each children how to get answers (for the teacher later to correct) we could put one or more calculators in every Math class, and let the students figure out how to work them. How could they find out how to do a problem on a calculator? They could take a simple problem, for which they already know the answer, and try different ways of doing it on the calculator until they got that answer, then check it with more complicated problems. That is how, when about fifteen, I figured out how to work a slide rule. I pushed things this way and that until I found a method that would tell me that 2×3 was 6. It worked.

Group feedback can help people do many kinds of work better, at least in any situation in which they can trust each other enough to talk freely about their difficulties and mistakes. Ken Macrorie, professor of English at Western Michigan University, describes in his books *Up Taught*, *Writing to be Read*, and *A Vulnerable Teacher*, how he has long used it to help his students write better. He regularly has them comment on each other's papers, with this important limitation, that for the first few months of the course, until they gain confidence in themselves and each other, they can only talk about the things they like. The writers find out what parts of their writing reach, interest, or move their colleagues, and why, and they write more that way as time goes on. Such a method would surely have helped many students I have known, who were so alienated from the writing they had to do for their T-eachers that they could not imagine how it would sound to anyone. All they could think was that it was all bad. This is of no use; a writer cannot tell his good writing from his bad if he thinks it is all bad. Students who write badly do not do so because "they have no standards," but because the standards they are trying to reach are so abstract and unreal that they have no way to use them, and so high that they have no hope of ever reaching them. Very few of those who fail English in school really believe they are good writers. Very few of those who get A's believe it, either. And indeed, very few are.

We learn to use language well, spoken or written, only when we use it for a purpose, our purpose, to say something we think is important, to people we want to say it to, or to make something happen that we want to happen. With few exceptions, the best orators I heard in the British House of Commons in 1952, in two days of heated debates, were not university graduates, but working men and women with very little schooling who had come up through the unions and the local organizations of the Labor Party. They had learned to use language well because they had had to use it well, to save their jobs or win a strike or an election. That they were in the House was proof that they could use words to move people and get things done. This is how, and why, we all learn to speak. We want to move people and get things done. When our words do this, it encourages us to speak more and shows us how to speak better. Only when we get into a place, like S-chool, where we are seldom allowed to talk, much less talk about anything interesting or real, and where our words seldom make anything important happen, and may only earn us humiliation and failure, does our growth in language slow to a stop.

So much for the act and art of teaching, of helping others to know and do more of what *they* want. Much more could be said about it. I hope these chapters have made clear that I am deeply interested in t-eaching, believe in it, and love to do it. Indeed, one of the important reasons I want to do away with all compulsory schooling and learning is so that I can call myself a teacher, and be fully and properly understood.

9

The True Authority
of t-eachers

In *The Lives of Children*, Dennison made the important distinction between natural authority, which rests on experience, competence, wisdom, and commitment, on the respect, trust, and love of one person for another, and official or coercive authority, which rests only on the power to bribe, to threaten, and to punish. Many people find it hard to understand this difference, or to see that coercive authority does not complement and support natural authority, but undermines and destroys it.

Power cancels out moral rights and obligations. The slave has no *moral* duty to his master. He has every moral right to dodge and escape the whip if he can, any way he can. No one is *morally* obliged to hold still for punishment. A ten-year-old, a proud, brave, stubborn child, of great character, helped me to see this. One day she refused to go to French class, which she (sensibly) hated. She sat at her desk reading, while I kept telling her to go. Finally I said that it was my job and my duty to make her go to French class, and that if I could not get her to go any other way I would drag her there. She did not move. I approached her desk, ready to carry out my threat. When I was about three feet away she suddenly looked up, slammed the book shut, banged it on the desk, stood up, and said, "All right, I'm going! But it's just *brute force* that is making me go, just *brute force!*" She was right; that's all it was.

For many years I told this story to show that if we are ready to use force against people to make them do what we want, and to hurt them if they resist or refuse, we should say so openly. It is morally disgusting to call this "giving a choice." At least I did not try to persuade this child that it would be *good* for her to go to French class, or that she had any moral obligation to go. What seems clearer now is that she had no moral obligation to do *anything* I or the S-chool told her to do. She had a moral obligation not to hurt other children, who had no legal or moral right to hurt her. Likewise, she had a moral obligation not to do us T-eachers any *physical* injury, because (at least in that school) we could not do that to her. But only where coercive power ends do mutual moral rights and obligations begin.

The students who come to CIDOC, and think that its rules and methods contradict what Illich (and I) have said about schools, have had many years of schooling in which they as students had unlimited obligations to teachers who had no obligations to them at all. Edgar Friedenberg has written often and well about this. The student owes the school and the teacher everything and can be penalized if he does not deliver; the school and the teacher owe the student nothing. As someone else put it, "There are very severe penalties for being a bad student but no penalties at all for being a bad teacher." The students quite rightly reject this arrangement. But in its place they sometimes want to put its opposite, in which the teacher has infinite obligations to the student and the students in return no obligations at all. This was the idea behind quite a few free schools, colleges, universities, etc. The teacher is expected to be infinitely available, and to respond with utmost sympathy and understanding to all the needs of the students. But he cannot make any demands on them. Their needs count, his don't. The students need not come to class, but should they feel like coming the teacher must be there. The students need not read a book, but should they feel like discussing one the teacher should have read it, and if not should immediately read it. The students have a right to withdraw from or reject any discussion that does not interest them. The teacher has no such right.

When I first went to CIDOC and met Illich, some such ideas were in my mind. In our earliest talks I was surprised at how strongly he resisted the idea of what was then called informal teaching, and defended instead the old-fashioned schoolmaster. Later I was surprised again by the passion with which he argued against free schools. Most puzzling of all was his fear that what people were beginning to call the deschooling of society might simply produce a society that was itself a universal or perpetual school, or his remark that a global schoolhouse would be like a global madhouse or a global prison.

On my second or third visit to CIDOC, he told me a perplexing story. He said that after one of his talks in the U.S. someone in the audience began to criticize him sharply for not having made clear something he had been trying to say. After a while Illich interrupted him, and said with great force, "Please sit down! I am *not* your teacher!" He told me this as if it were important that I understand it, and as if understanding it would make clear what in a larger sense he was saying about education and teaching. But it was still some time before I began to see what he meant.

Only as I began to make in my own mind the distinction between doing and education, or between S-chools and s-chools, and T-eachers and t-eachers, did I begin to understand the passion with which Illich told the questioner that he was not his teacher. He was saying, in effect, "I have not *agreed* to be your teacher, and therefore am not responsible for your understanding or failing to understand anything I may say. If you want me to be your teacher, to accept a responsibility for making you learn or understand something, you must ask me. Even then I will only agree if I feel fairly certain that I *can* in fact teach you or help you understand. If I think I can, I will set forth the conditions, the mutual responsibilities and obligations under which I will agree to teach you. If you wish to accept them, you may. Otherwise, I accept no responsibility for making you understand, or blame if you do not. We are not talking here as teacher and pupil, *but as equals*, and not understanding each other is one of the risks of all such conversations."

It is important to understand here that Illich is saying, first of all, that the proper relationship of teacher to student is not one of equals. The student, while he is in that relationship, is in some ways (but not all) an inferior; he acknowledges and accepts that. Beyond that, Illich is saying most emphatically that not all things can be taught. He would undertake to teach someone Spanish. He would not undertake to teach someone Philosophy—though he would be glad to discuss it—saying quite rightly that no one can make another person a philosopher. One of Illich's deepest criticisms of S-chools and S-chool people is that they do not even know or admit the distinction between what can be taught and what can not, what is not learned *by* being "taught."

The relationship to a teacher which many of the American students believed was proper, and hoped to find at CIDOC, is in many ways like that of the newborn baby to the mother. The mother owes everything, the baby nothing. It may well be that many young people, hurt by their experience of growing up in a bad time, and above all by their schooling, deeply need such a relationship. But this is not properly speaking, the relationship of teacher to student, but something quite different. Indeed, though Illich would firmly reject and refuse this relationship as a teacher, he might in some cases accept it as a friend.

The point is that the teacher-student relationship as Illich sees it is an exceptional one and should not take up more than a small part of life. At another time he said to me emphatically that he did not want to spend all his life in a schoolhouse. He wants a sharp line to be drawn between those situations in which he relates to another person as student to teacher (or vice-versa), and so as inferior to superior, and those in which he relates to another as a human being, and so as an equal. If he is going to enter into an inferior-superior relationship with another person, in which one is dependent on the other, he wants it clearly understood when, for

how long, under what conditions, and for what purposes this relationship will go on. Part of what he means by the convivial society
is a society in which people talk and relate as equals, except in
those special situations in which they have agreed they will relate
in another way.

Every so often, in my own work as a professional lecturer, a
group, an organization, a conference of one kind or another, will
ask me to speak, for a fee. Sometimes I fear that the things this
group wants to hear are not the things I want to say, and that what
I want to say they may not want to hear at all. In such cases, I tell
them, "I may not be the right person to speak at your meeting,
because here is what I am going to say." Sometimes they agree that
I am not the person they want, sometimes they ask me to come
anyway. But it seems only fair to let them know what they will be
getting.

At other times a group or a person will ask me, as a favor, for
no fee at all, to spend some time talking with them. In such cases I
will ask what they want to talk about. Perhaps I, or someone, has
already written what they want to find out, in which case I will tell
them where to read it. Perhaps they want to talk about something I
don't know anything about, or don't want to talk about. But if it
turns out that they want to discuss with me something that I am
interested in and like to talk about, I may say, "Before we talk,
there are some things I must ask you to read. There are ideas in
them that I think are important for our discussion, and since they
have already been written down, I don't want to take time at our
meeting to talk about them. Instead, sharing those ideas, we can go
on from there." Sometimes the other people agree to this, sometimes they don't. I feel no qualms at all about imposing this kind of
condition. This is one of the rights of a t-eacher, to make clear the
terms on which he will accept and work with his students. But it is
only the fact that I have no power over the people who want to talk
with me, that they are free, at no cost or risk to themselves, to do
without me, that gives me the right to state the conditions under
which I will work.

It is clear now, as it was not at first, why Illich reacted with such horror to my saying that we should push the walls of the school building out further and further. That seemed at the time a good enough way to say that we should abolish the distinction between learning and the rest of life. Only later did I see the danger that he saw right away. Think again about the global schoolhouse, madhouse, prison. What are madhouses and prisons? They are institutions of *compulsory treatment.* They are places in which one group of people do things to another group of people, without their consent, because still another group thinks this would be good for them. Prisons, at least those that believe in "rehabilitation," which most prisoners fear and hate, are places in which one group says to another, "We are going to keep control of your life, and do things to you, whatever we want, and for as long as we want, until we think you measure up." In the same way the doctors in mental hospitals say to the patients, "We are going to keep treating you, with drugs, restraint, shock, surgery—whatever we want—until we think you measure up, i.e., have recovered, are sane." We might note in passing that, except in the case of some highly contagious diseases, people still have a right to be medically sick without going to a doctor or hospital. They may choose to try to treat or cure themselves. But not so the mentally ill.

S-chool is just this sort of compulsory-treatment institution. Society has decided that one group of people, T-eachers, shall do all sorts of things to another group of people, the students, whether they want it or not, until the T-eachers think the students measure up, know enough about the world to go out and live in it. Such people like to say, for example, that no one should have the right to choose to be illiterate—a right I have any time I travel to a foreign country. A global schoolhouse would be a world, which we seem to be moving toward, in which one group of people would have the right through our entire lives to subject the rest of us to various sorts of tests, and if we did not measure up, to require us to submit to various kinds of treatment, i.e. education, therapy, etc., until we did. A worse nightmare is hard to imagine.

10

On Human Nature

Much of what I have said so far implies a certain view of human nature. Let me now try to make this view more clear, and defend it against the charge that it is sentimental and does not take account of human beings' all-too-frequently demonstrated capacity to do wrong.

A traditional and pessimistic view of nature is that Man is mostly bad. His deepest instincts and desires are far more likely to be bad than good. Free to do what he wants, he will do mostly wrong. Many Christians, certainly since the Reformation, have held this dark view of human nature. Recently certain ethologists, whose work is to observe animal behavior, often very keenly and sensitively, but whose folly is to think they can use this behavior to explain human beings, have made the doctrine of Original Sin "scientifically" respectable. See, they say, here is a fish, or a goose, or an old skull, to prove it.

But, the traditional view holds, at least some people, in their calmer moments, can be made to see that they are bad, that they cannot be trusted, and that whenever they do what they want it will be harmful even for them. Therefore, they need some kind of social order, backed by force, to stop them from doing most of the bad things they would otherwise do. A few people, at least, can be trusted to plan this social order, and to decide what power it should have, which people should use this power, and in what ways, and how these people should be found or chosen. The task of these few people, then, and the art of politics and government, is to create and maintain this social order, and—very rarely, and then only under heavy pressure of circumstances, and as little as possible—to change it. People who hold this view often call it conservative; others call it reactionary or worse. Those who hold it will of course not like the ideas expressed in this book. But there is very little in modern society, anywhere, that such a conservative, if observant and intelligent, *could* like. He would certainly not call Conservative most of the people in the U.S. (and other countries) who go by that name. He would be very afraid of the kind of unplanned change, with unforseeable consequences, that most of these so-called Conservatives push for the sake of profit, growth, and "progress." And he would know, as they seem not to, that those who wish to maintain a stable social order must not enrich themselves by doing so, and must themselves obey its rules, lest they destroy the ethical basis of that order. When power becomes license, the social order soon falls.

Though I am in many ways conservative, finding it better to conserve than waste or destroy, I do not think that in order to be a true conservative one must take the traditional and dark view that humans are naturally bad. Clearly, we humans can do and have done many bad things. But we can also do some things that are very good. If we look more bad than good, it is partly because it is easier to do bad things than good, easier to destroy than create, and partly because it makes more of an impression.

Sometimes, to be sure, we do seem to be very happy when hurting, killing, or destroying. But at other times we seem to be just as happy, or more happy, doing no harm, giving and sharing pleasure, meeting more innocent needs. I strongly suspect that among our many needs there are enough that are innocent, unselfish, and constructive so that in any situation in which we could reasonably satisfy those needs we would have little or no need or wish to do harm. Our biological nature has given us not just a capacity for evil, but a huge capacity for harmless pleasure, a great many ways to enjoy life without hurting others. We like to play, to laugh, to create, to add to and share in the happiness of others. Most of us, unless driven mad by fear or some abstract principle and passion like religion or patriotism, are frightened and horrified by the sadness or pain of others. Seeing people in airports or bus or train stations weeping at the sorrow of parting, we do not laugh, but are all a bit saddened by their sadness. People may rush to the scene of a crime or an accident, but few of them are smiling. We have to be carefully trained to tolerate or enjoy suffering and pain.

What seems most true about our human nature is that it is very malleable. We humans can be and are very easily shaped, and into a great variety of things. What shapes us is the world and society we grow up in, and the ways and attitudes of all those around us—in short, our culture. To ask what is fundamental human nature is to ask what a human being would be like without a culture. Such a question is meaningless, and cannot be answered. There is and can be no such thing as a human being without a culture. And even if we could say with some accuracy what a human being might be like without a culture, all by himself, such knowledge would tell us nothing about what we really want to know when we ask questions about human nature: How will people act when around other people? How they will act depends very much on their culture, where they fit in it, how they see it, how it sees them, and so on. Here is the first flaw in the notion that we can build a basically good society on the assumption that people are basically bad. A culture which says that people are bad will produce a great many people who behave badly. We know now how strongly such prophecies tend to fulfill themselves. People behave as they think others expect them to behave. When they think they are bad, and everyone else as well, they act toward each other in ways that build on and multiply whatever badness they may have within them. A person convinced that he and all others are selfish and greedy will act greedily and selfishly, and believe that he has no choice but to do so. A person convinced that Man is by nature a killer will see killers everywhere around him, and think of nothing but how to protect himself against them, and perhaps kill them before they kill him. Doing so, he will make them afraid. Being afraid, they will in turn act in ways which will convince him that he was right. The person who fears everyone creates the behavior he fears.

The second flaw in the notion of a good society made up of bad people is this. Plato, one of the first men to write about the ideal state, said that it should be ruled by Philosopher-Kings. It seems a tempting combination. The trouble is that Philosophers don't often get to be Kings. Force leads to the throne more than reason. Most Kings have gained or kept their thrones not by being wiser or more generous or virtuous than most people, but by being more devious, unscrupulous, greedy, ruthless, violent, and cruel. In human society, run by kings or otherwise, the best or the wisest seldom rise to the top. In theory, the strength and virtue of its rulers was supposed to make the social order better. In practice, the weaknesses and vices of its rulers make it worse. In its name and for its sake its members commit far more and worse crimes than they would ever commit by themselves. Rulers will order others to do what they themselves would never do; the ruled will do under orders what they would never do without orders. As someone put it, those who kill, do not plan; those who plan, do not kill.

As among people in any given society, so among human societies, the bad is most likely to rise to the top. If two societies live side by side, one modest, peaceful, kindly, and happy, the other a greedy and violent tyranny, the bad society must always swallow up the good. Much of what we call History is the success stories of madmen. How many times, on their various roads to glory, power, empire, etc., must these men and their armies of thugs and killers have wiped out societies far more sensible and humane. And this must have happened many more times in the long years of pre-History than in the relatively short period of which we have some record. Our history books still speak admiringly of Rome and our debt to Rome, the most greedy, destructive, cruel and enduring tyranny the world has yet seen. Thinking of ourselves as history's glorious final product, we like to say that it illustrates what we call the law of the survival of the fittest. It would be truer to speak instead of the survival of the morally least fit.

There is in Economics a law called Gresham's Law, which says that when good money and bad are both in circulation, the bad will drive out the good. If a society puts into circulation gold coin and paper money, those who want money to spend will try to get the paper, because it is easier to get, while those who want money to save, will keep the gold, because it will last. So the gold coins will go into socks, mattresses, and vaults, until only the paper is left. Perhaps there has been for a long time something like a Gresham's Law among human societies. It may well be that many or most of the kindest and most sensible societies that humans have ever formed have long since disappeared unknown.

There is of course no way to find out whether or to what degree this is true. History's losers leave few traces. But this hypothesis or hunch seems to me an answer to the problem of human evil, of Original Sin, at least as plausible as any other, and far more hopeful. People do many of the bad things, even the worst things, they do because they are taught and made to do them. Perhaps the society they live in tells them, as ours tells us, that since winning is the only thing, it is good to be greedy, selfish, ruthless, hardnosed, and tough. Perhaps their society tells them, as ours tells us, that some other people are so bad that it is no crime—certainly no crime for which anyone will be punished—to murder their unarmed women, children, and babies. Perhaps their society treats them so badly and unfairly, so deeply destroys their sense of their own dignity and worth, that for the rest of their lives they can think of nothing to do but try to get even. But in another kind of society, where they heard very different kinds of ideas, and above all, were treated fairly, generously, and with courtesy and respect, they might have turned out very differently.

What people become under one set of circumstances does not

tell us very much about what they might have become under another. Japanese gardeners, over many centuries, have learned to do things to trees, to clip their roots or trim their branches, to limit their supply of water, air, or sun, so that they live, and for a long time, but only in tiny, shrunken, twisted shapes. Such trees may please us, or they may not. But what could they tell us about the *nature* of trees? If a tree *can* be deformed and shrunk, is this, then, its nature? The nature of these trees, given enough of the sun, air, water, soil, and food they need, is to grow like trees, tall and straight. People can be more easily deformed, and worse deformed, even than trees—and more than trees, they feel it, it hurts. But this cannot and does not say anything about their nature. Only to the degree that people have what they need, that they are healthy and unafraid, that their lives are varied, interesting, meaningful, productive, joyous, can we begin to judge, or even guess, their nature. Few people, adults or children, now live such lives. Perhaps few ever did. There is no way to find out how much good or kindness there may be in human nature, except to build or try to build a society on the assumption that people are or would like to be good and kind, a society in which to be good and kind is at least not a handicap. Until we are able to do this, it would be more wise and fair, and even prudent, to give human beings the benefit of the doubt.

One of the Best S-chools

Here it may be worth taking a further look at the Ny Lilleskole in Denmark, where true teaching can be done because the children there relate to the adults freely, and therefore fearlessly and honestly. A friend of mine, Peggy Hughes, who worked at the school for two years, made a film about it (30 minutes, black and white, sound) called *We Have to Call It School*. Early in the film one of the teachers says, "We have to call it school. Children have to go to school, and if we didn't call this a school they couldn't come here." But, except that it is a place where children go during school hours, it is in no way like a school. No "education" takes place there. It is in fact a doing place. In it about eighty-five children, aged six or seven to about fourteen, come together with a group of six adults, who work with the children to make a community which is lively, interesting, pleasant, secure, trusting, cooperative, and humane. In this community the children live their lives as they see fit.

As they see fit. These words mean just what they say. Subject only—like all of us—to the limits that they do not hurt each other, or destroy or unduly damage each others' or common property, the children in this school do what they want, with whom they want, for as long as they want, and all of the time. The teachers, in turn, provide and oversee a place where the children can do this; think up at least some interesting things to do, and provide the means—materials, tools, etc.—to do them; make use of and share their own many skills and talents; if asked, help the children do the things they want to do; and, in general, are on hand for the children to show things to, or ask questions of, or just to talk to and be with. But they are not there to "exercise their adult responsibility," i.e., to try to hint, or nudge, or bribe, or threaten, or seduce the children into doing what they or someone has decided would be good for them. They do not say to the children, like the teachers in the so-called "open" British primary schools and their American equivalents, "Get on with it," meaning, get busy and do something that *I* think is worthwhile.

The school has almost nothing that most people would call an academic program. There are no subjects, no courses, no classes, no preplanned paths down which "the children progress at their own rate," no texts or exams, no marks or grades or report cards, no reports of any kind. There are not even parent conferences, unless occasionally a parent—perhaps anxious, perhaps not—wants to come in and talk. And, as I have said, there is no pressure *of any kind* to make the children read. No wouldn't-it-be-a-good-idea's or don't-you-think-it's-about-time's. None of that. Nor is there any of what one sees a great deal of at many open or alternative schools—work done by the children, and displayed by the teachers, to impress parents and other adults. Visitors to the school are not shown marvelous samples of the children's writing, or painting, or pottery, or science projects, or whatever it may be. Nor does the school put on plays, dances, pageants, etc., to show the world how creative the children are.

By contrast, I think of an American school, which *by my standards* might well rank among the top one or two percent in the country. In one of their school bulletins the kindly and intelligent head of the school describes a number of trips the children had taken, to see a boat unload, to visit a waterworks, to interview a man at the railroad station. He then writes:

(the trips) gathered facts worth considering, though they seemed to some observers just a lot of riding around. In fact, one father, objecting to the train ride . . . brought up the complaint, "We as a family take plenty of trips in this area, and it seems to me the school ought to have better things to do." He was more understanding, however, when he listened to *the children's plan*, the list of questions *they had made* for the interview, and the account of the railroad trip under way. Other trips traced the relationship of land and water in the area. . . . One of *the results* of this was a six-foot papier mâché map which had an incidental interest almost as great if not greater than the map itself, because to find space for it, we had to hoist it by pulleys to the ceiling. [all italics mine]

But whose idea was that map, who really planned that project, made up that list of questions?

The outcome [italics mine] of these trips was in maps, oral reports pictures, diagrams, stories, even dances. I never ceased to marvel at the children's ability to represent in a dance what they had seen, and remember with some vividness the dance of ——, with a child narrator, and music to accompany the cartwheels and whirls representing the different processes. The music teacher in these events brought out in music what they were trying to say.

The "outcome." Why does there always have to be an "outcome?" When I go to see something that interests me, I don't have to do a dance afterwards or make a six-foot papier mâché map and hoist it up to the ceiling. I can decide for myself what sort of outcome, if any, I want to have for my experience. More important, I can wait until the outcome reveals itself to me. This takes time, sometimes years, and it never happens if "creative teachers" are busily pushing and prodding and motivating to make it happen. I have taught in schools like this, and I know how these outcomes are arrived at, how teachers, with skeptical fathers to placate, "intuitively bring out what the children want to say." The head of the school says he "never ceased to marvel" at the children's ability to put this or that into a dance. Just as surely the children never ceased to notice him marveling. It doesn't take long at schools like this for children to find out what teachers marvel at and like to see children doing. Or to learn that doing these things brings plenty of approval, smiles, praise, rewards, and good reports, and that not doing them, or *even seeming not to like doing them*, means being pushed out of the charmed circle and into outer darkness. There is none of that at the Ny Lilleskole.

One has to see a place like this to have any idea of what it is like. We are so used to the game that adults and children play, even in "open" schools, the adults worrying about how to make the children do what they want, and whether they are doing enough of it, and the children in their turn worrying about whether to do it or refuse, that we can't imagine what a place might be like in which this game was not played. Having seen the Ny Lilleskole, I can hardly stand to visit most schools, even schools that a few years ago I might have considered good. The contrast between the affected, guarded, held-in, furtive, timid, sneaky, and sullen or seductive children I so often see there, and the unaffected, natural, bold, vital, frank, open, and honest children at the Ny Lilleskole, is too great. I like most children, and like to be around them, but I would rather not see them at all than have to see them in S-school.

Even a book could not tell more than a small part of what happens at the Ny Lilleskole, what the children do in it, or how they are changed and strengthened by their lives there. No two children do the same things, and no two days are the same. I hope someone will one day write a book. The point to make here is that the school works. Even by the narrow academic standards most parents and teachers care and worry about, the school is highly successful. The children who go there are not selected for IQ or academic talent. There are no tests to get in. At least some of the children come from other schools where they have done very badly at schoolwork. Yet almost all of the children who have left the Ny Lilleskole have gone to the gymnasium, a very difficult and conventional academic high school, where they have done well. Among those who are old enough, almost all have taken advanced professional training—in a country in which only 5% of young people do so. No school I know of, anywhere, however exclusive or tough, does as well.

No one would claim that these children and their families represent a kind of random cross-section of the Danish population. Most Danes, like most Americans, would not think of sending their children to such a school. The Ny Lilleskole parents, however else they may be alike or different, have one thing in common. *They trust their children.* If they did not, they would not send them to such a school. In that sense, these parents, and so their children, are exceptional. But this is exactly my point, that we *can* trust children to find out about the world, and that when trusted, they *do* find out.

A Description

Bagsvaerd is a small, middle-income suburb of Copenhagen. The school is in an area, and on a street, zoned for light industrial use. As is often the case in Denmark, the area backs up to a housing development, separated from it only by some small woods, in which the children like to play. The school occupies the first floor of a four-story building (since the town now wants the building for other uses, the school must find other space). The main room of the school, about two-thirds of its space, is long and narrow, with windows on both sides. Since the room was designed for industrial purposes, the windowsills are four or five feet off the floor, so that the children have to climb up to see out of them. But this is no great loss, since all there is to see is other buildings much like their own. Off this main space is a very small gym, a room at one end where the school holds all its general meetings, and at the other end, along with lavatories, two small rooms, one used principally for music. One end of the main space is a workshop. The rest is divided into smaller spaces by partitions made of about two thousand wooden beer cases, which the school got free from a brewery when they switched to plastic cases. These dark green wooden boxes, which are used as dividers, tables, bookshelves, and chairs, all marked ØL (beer) are one of the first things one notices about the school. Soon, they become familiar, natural, and appropriate. Simple, sturdy, cheap, and kindly, they express something of the spirit of the school. I could hardly imagine it without them.

The school is very simply and inexpensively equipped. Most American, British, or Danish school teachers or administrators would consider themselves dreadfully underprivileged if they had to work in a school with no more equipment than this one. In the office is a typewriter (not electric), a tape recorder, and a duplicator. In the main room is a refrigerator and a small stove, on which the children sometimes cook or bake, though in general they eat the usual Danish lunch of open-faced sandwiches. There is a very small but good collection of books. In the workshop is a modest set of woodworking tools, tools for heating and working metal, and oxy-acetylene cutting and welding equipment. There is a small collection of games and puzzles. Among the books are some Math and Science books and texts, but I saw very little that I would have called math or science equipment, no math labs, none of the PSSC, Nuffield, etc., science equipment which most American and British elementary schools have come to think of as essential. There was very little art equipment; I do not remember seeing any clay or easels or paints, or children using them. On the other hand, there were signs and other things in the school that the children had painted, so there was either paint around somewhere, or they could get it when they wanted it. There were two or three hand looms, and a sewing machine. On an earlier visit I had seen many birds and small animals; when I came back, they were gone, and in their place were many kinds of tropical fish, in tanks which the children had made or helped to make themselves. Some children spent many hours just watching the fish in the tank. There were soccer balls, jumpropes, and some other kinds of sports equipment. In the small gym was one tumbling mat. In the music room was an old, rather beat-up upright piano, some guitars, acoustic and electric, a bass fiddle made by a teacher, and a collection of hand drums of different sizes.

This inventory is by no means complete. There was probably some stuff I didn't see or know about. About what I did see, three points should be made. The first is that the school had only a small part of the materials and equipment one would find today either in conventional elementary schools or in open classrooms. The second is that what equipment there was in the school was for the children to use; there was not the usual locked audio-visual closet of the typical American school, or the elaborate ritual of getting a book out of the library. And the third, and perhaps most important, is that anyone who wanted to make such a doing place for children would not have to spend much money to equip it. Children do not need a lot of fancy stuff to work with. The reason children seemed at first to like Math Labs or Science Labs so much is that they were so much better than conventional schoolwork, listening to the teacher, filling in workbooks. But few children with any real range of choices would spend much of their time in a Math Lab or putting together a bunch of chicken bones.

In fairness I should say that one reason the school does not have more equipment is that it does not have the money. There are surely some things the school would like to buy, for teachers and children to use, if it could afford it. Also, these teachers and children are resourceful at finding ways to borrow, or salvage, or buy cheaply many of the materials they do decide they need. Finally, even if the school did have much more money, when the children and the teachers came to decide together, as they now do, how to spend it, they might very well vote for more interesting things than materials. The school now takes a lot of trips, in and around Copenhagen and further than that—one group of students took a walking trip across Sweden. With more money, they would probably take many more.

A word or two about attendance. Children in Denmark, as everywhere else, are required by law to go to school. For all I know, there may be places and schools in Denmark in which this law is as strictly observed and harshly enforced as in the U.S. In this school, it is not. The school does keep attendance records. This does not mean that there is a roll-call, or that everyone has to be at school at a certain time. But on any given day one of the teachers has the job of making a note of who is and who is not in school. This is not a cause for worry, phone calls, or other such action. People assume that a child who is not at school has good reasons for not being there and is well occupied wherever he is. Beyond that, the school is such an intimate and open community that if a child is not at school, someone is almost sure to know where he is and what he is doing. Or, if someone misses a day or two of school, he is almost sure, when he comes back, to talk to many people about what he did. It rarely happens that a child will be away from school for more than a day or two without anyone knowing why. If this continues, the teachers will probably begin to check up. Once, when a child was away for quite a number of days at a time, they began thinking about how to get him to come back. But children are free to stay away from school if and when they think they have good reason to do so. They don't have to get permission, and they don't have to account for their absence when they get back. They don't have to prove to anyone that while away from school they occupied their time well. Unlike American college students in work-study programs, when they go back to school they don't have to write a paper about what they did when they were away.

My visits to the school have all been in the spring, in middle or late May. After the long dark winter, when the sun comes out, the Scandinavians like to get out in it. At this time of year, on any given day, perhaps no more than half the children will be in the school. During the winter, they are more likely to be all there. What do they do? I will speak only of a few things I have seen, to give something of the spirit of the school, and the range and variety of things that happen there. Some things the children do all together. A couple of years ago, after much discussion at school meetings, the school decided that they would have a collective lunch. A certain amount of money would be set aside, some children would buy the food, others would prepare it—slicing the bread and meat, opening up some cans—and serve it, and all would eat together. This is what happens. It a very lively, noisy, friendly scene.

Another frequent activity is the school general meeting. Children and teachers take part together, all can speak and vote, all votes count the same. Neill used to say of Summerhill general meetings that children younger than twelve seldom took a very active part. Here this is not so; the younger children speak up often. The school tries not to decide things on the basis of close votes; people look instead for solutions with which everyone or nearly everyone can agree. They may talk about personal relationships and problems, such as someone bothering or teasing someone else. Or they may talk about school policy itself, including—here they go further, I believe, even than Summerhill—how money should be spent.

One thing they talk about every so often is the physical arrangement of the school, the way the main room is divided by the beer cases into smaller working spaces. This can take many meetings. People say why they don't like the existing layout. Children begin making measurements and drawing up new plans. In time, the meeting decides on a new plan. Then begins a tremendous piece of work, what we used to call in the Navy "an all-hands evolution." All books and equipment have to be taken out of or off the boxes, the partitions have to be taken down, furniture moved. They may give the school a thorough cleaning. Then the beer cases have to be put up according to the new plan, the furniture rearranged, the books and equipment put back. This is a large task, and the children love to take part in it. It is an exciting time. Years ago, I said to some young architects that an ideal school would never be finished, so that the children could keep redesigning and rebuilding it. The Ny Lilleskole is such a school.

One very important part of the daily routine of the school is the morning exercise-movement-dance session. The school gym is a low-ceilinged room slightly larger than a squash or handball court. The only equipment there is a thick tumbling mat and a couple of congo drums. Every morning one of the teachers, a skilled musician and dancer, and most of the children meet in the gym. The teacher begins to beat out on a drum a rapid and exciting rhythm, and the children begin to move, jump, and dance. The session is never twice the same. The movements are freely improvised, and one leads to another. The children will often do movements they have done before; some they clearly like better than others. But they and the teacher invent new ones as they go along, vigorous, elegant, skillful. New rhythms beget new movements. Sometimes one of the children beats on the drum, or a child beats one and the teacher the other. It is impossible to convey in words the grace, gaiety, and energy of this scene; I have never seen anything to match it. It goes on a long time. Most of the children are very healthy and energetic, and they burn off a lot of their steam here, though by no means all of it. Though the school has its calm, quiet, reflective days and moods, most of the time the children are very sociable, talkative, active, and noisy; in an American school children far less active are called "hyperactive" and put on drugs. This dance session is the principal organized athletic resource and activity of the school. For the older boys, many of whom love soccer and dream of being big-time players, there is a park, with a soccer field, perhaps ten minutes' walk from the school, where they often go to play.

Before they got their welding equipment, the school had a Bunsen burner. For about an hour one day three or four children sat around it, I among them. Each of us had a pair of pliers, with which we held a nail in the flame. When a nail grew red hot, soft enough to work, its owner would pull it out and do something with it. Most of us hammered our nails on a short section of railroad track used as an anvil. I tried to make some nail sculpture, or to see if I could fuse and hammer two hot nails together (I couldn't). One boy, no more than seven or eight, new to the school, did one thing over and over again. He heated his nail red hot, and then stuck it into a piece of wood, which charred and smoked. If anyone else bumped his nail or took too much of the flame, he let out a bellow which, if it didn't scare the other children, certainly terrified me. I have never sensed more violence and anger in a child. I hardly dared think what he might be imagining when he stuck his nail into the wood. That was our only contact. Two years later, when I next visited the school, he was a peaceful, kindly, happy child—and incidentally, one of the school's most skilled metalworkers and welders. To my surprise and pleasure, he remembered me, and as a friend.

The music room. One of the teachers, a musician, a competent jazz pianist, was showing a boy how to play certain jazz chord progressions on the electric guitar. He talked, demonstrated, they played together. Two other younger boys joined them on the congo drums. They were not good enough even to keep strict time, let alone be any sort of inspiration. But no one suggested that they should not play. There were no irritated glances, no feeling in the air of "Can't you see we're busy." Two or three other children were in the room, like myself, just watching. Now and then, when the piano and the guitar got into their stride, I whistled a bit of blues solo, as I like to do. Another child sat up on the window and looked outside. People were participating at many levels of skill and attention, and all were allowed. As Mrs. Stallibrass aptly writes (see Appendix), "Watching is an important *activity;* the child's need to watch should be respected and he should *not* be distracted from his absorption in watching the others, or 'stimulated'. . . . Some children . . . like to see others do things before they try to do them themselves; they like to ponder and consider what they will do before they do it." At the Ny Lilleskole, everyone understands this.

The meeting room has no furniture. At meetings, people sit at one end on built-in carpeted bleachers. Otherwise, the room is usually empty. For several days running a girl, about fourteen, spent an hour or so throwing a tennis ball against the wall and

catching it, seeing how many times in a row she could do this
without missing, usually between twenty and forty. Another time,
a group of six girls, the youngest perhaps eight, the oldest twelve
or so, were jumping rope. They did this for an hour or two a day,
many days running. They played with different rules and combi-
nations, and with great seriousness and concentration.

A young boy, new to the school, full of violence and anger, one
of a small group that the children themselves (some of whom had
once been the same) call "The Terrorists." Flailing about with
some sort of cardboard box, he hit a ten-year-old girl in the eye,
hard enough so that it really hurt, and ran off, hardly noting what
he had done. She put her hands over her eye, and bent over in
pain. Other children and at least one of the teachers saw this. The
people near her asked if she was all right, and gave her sympathy
and comfort. Otherwise, nothing happened! In almost any other
school I have ever seen the girl would have set up an outcry, other
children would have told the teacher and demanded he do something about it, and the small child would probably have been
dragged back to apologize, and perhaps, to be punished. Here the
adults, the children, even the girl who was hurt, all felt that this
wild small child had not hurt the girl on purpose. Perhaps he was
already frightened, and ashamed. So why punish him, or shame
him further? Why make him feel, any more strongly than he did
already, that he was no good, when it was just this feeling that
made him act so wildly? Why not instead help him feel that in this
place he need not always worry about being judged and punished?
And it is in just this way, and not with lectures and punishments,
that the school civilizes its terrorists. The adults are patient, trusting, and forgiving with the children, and in time the children become the same way with each other. Not that they don't push,
shove, quarrel, shout, and yell if someone takes their sandwich or
something they are working on. They get sore at each other, but
unlike kids in most schools they are not always tattle-taling, not
always trying to line up the teacher on their side, and they don't
hold grudges or stay angry for long.

Why It Works

All of this may begin to explain to a small degree why the children are lively and happy there. It does not explain how the children get so good at conventional schoolwork. What happens to account for that? The answer is given by the teacher narrating the film. After showing and talking about some of what the children do, he says, "Mostly we talk and listen to each other." That *is* mostly what they do. This does not mean that the teachers talk and the children listen. There are no lectures, disguised or otherwise. Nor do the teachers, as in many up-to-date schools, "hold discussions." There are only conversations, between children, or children and adults together. How do the latter start? Usually, because a child is *doing* something with an adult, and they begin to talk as they do it. In time others join in. The conversation moves this way and that, as true conversations do. People leave, others join in. The talking group splits into two talking groups, or three. The conversation never ends. It may stop for a while, but the thought goes on, and the conversation will start again another day. In the thought as well as the action of the children there is the *continuum of experience* that Dennison wrote about in *The Lives of Children*, and that children never have in most schools, where thought is continually interrupted and broken up with bells, classes, lesson plans, guided discussions, and so on. Sometimes children listen to adults talking, or young children to the older. Even the teachers' meetings are not shut off from the children; they are not encouraged to butt in, but they are not told to go away.

Please do not take this description as a method, a formula for running a school, something that can be taught in a school of education. This school is a human community, and a large part of what makes it work are the adults in it. They are a most unusual group of teachers, in at least three respects. In the first place, they are competent in many ways, not just at teaching. Most of them come to teaching after having done many other kinds of work, and having had other kinds of experience, and they bring their competence and experience to the school. They can do things, make things, fix things. This is important to children; they like to do things, and are enormously interested in and attracted to adults who can do things. Much of the great natural authority of these teachers comes from their competence. And many of the problems of American open or free or alternative schools arise from the fact that their teachers often have too little competence. Young people often tell me, sincerely, convincingly, how much they like and respect children, and want to work with them in a free school. They are surprised when I ask, "What can you do?" Too often, they can't do anything; all they have done for years is be a student. But isn't love and good will enough? No, it isn't enough. Most kids, most of the time, will swap a pound of love for an ounce of competence. Beyond this, the Ny Lilleskole teachers are intelligent, informed, interested and interesting. They know a lot about the world, and they think about it. By contrast, large surveys of American teachers, quoted by Myron Brenton in *What's Happened to Teacher*, have shown that most of them are not very informed or curious. They read very little. Their favorite magazine is *Reader's Digest*. Many of them read only about one book per year; of those who read more, most read light escape fiction. Like average people in most modern countries, they don't know much and they can't do much—and what they know or can do, they don't talk about or do in school. In short, they are not people that curious, active, and healthy children would choose to spend much time with.

It is also important that the Ny Lilleskole teachers are not alienated. They do not hate, or fear, or despise their country, Denmark. There is much about it that they don't like and hope to change. But they are fond of it, and at home in it. It is where they like to be; they spend their vacations there. Nor do they hate the world. For all its faults, it is still a beautiful, varied, fascinating place, full of exciting, interesting, useful things to do. They do not hate their own lives. They like being grown up, and are full of zest and energy. They do not tell their pupils that childhood is the best time of life, or try to lock them up in it for as long as they can.

They know that children want to grow up, get bigger and stronger, see more of the world and do more things in it, and they are ready and glad to help them do it. This is not always true of American alternative schools. Too often, they have attracted as teachers young people who are deeply alienated from life, their country, and the world around them. "Life is a bummer" might be their motto. I sympathize with them and understand why they feel this way. But such people are not much help or use to kids. Kids have no quarrel with the world. It is there, and they want to get out in it. They do not want to hear how awful it is, or that there is nothing worth doing in it, or that the only good or sensible thing to do is work to destroy it, or escape from it as far as possible.

Perhaps most important of all, the teachers at Ny Lilleskole are open and truthful. That is, they will talk about anything the children want to talk about, say what they truly think, and admit what they don't know. This is not true of most teachers. A survey quoted by Brenton showed that about 90% of American teachers believe that they should not, and in fact do not, discuss or permit children to discuss what they call controversial subjects in school, though they understand very well that these are precisely the subjects that interest children the most. Thus in conventional schools children can rarely talk, and when they do, cannot talk honestly or about what they most want to talk about. Beyond this, most teachers are told, over and over again, both in their training and in their work, never to admit ignorance, uncertainty, or confusion. Above all, "keep a professional distance," i.e., never talk candidly about your private life and feelings. But these are what interest children most of all, since only from these can they begin to sense what it's like to be a grown-up.

So the children from the Ny Lilleskole do very well later in the conventional schools for many reasons. They are still curious about the world, confident that they can find out about it, and good at doing it. Having for many hours of the day, for many years, actively, seriously, and intently talked and listened to many people, they have become very good at using language—a large part of what ordinary school is about. Having coped with a wide variety of social situations, in and out of school, they can handle very easily the rather limited challenges of conventional school. After all, any kid who keeps his eyes and ears open can figure out in a short time how to give his conventional school teachers what they want. It's an easy trick—once you understand that it is only a trick. But above all, these children do better than their conventionally schooled friends because *they know so much more.*

People ask how, after years of being able to do what they want, the children can stand going to a very conventional school. Don't they dislike it? Of course they dislike it. They think it's absurd. But they are smart, they have learned to cope. Also, they are realists. They have learned enough about themselves and the world to know that the road to doing many of the things they might want to do leads through the gymnasium and the university, and so they are ready to take that road, bumps and all. Also, like a few children I know in the U.S., they are probably much more able than most of their schoolmates (who can only submit to school or resist it) to *make use* of school, to get from it at least some of the things they want for their own reasons.

As much as we may like the sound of the Ny Lilleskole, we must not forget that it is still a S-chool. More important, it is one whose example very few S-chools, even in Denmark, let alone other countries, could follow. In the first place, it is a private school, not part of the Danish state school system, which, as far as I know, has not even one school like it or any plans to make one. Yet it gets most of its money from the government, under a Danish law which says that if a certain number of parents can start a school and run it on their own for a year, the government will from then on pay 85% of their operating expenses. The other 15% they must raise themselves, which is hard to do in a country in which, if none are very poor, few are very rich, and where there is no tradition of paying for children's schooling. Under this law, about forty small independent schools, called "little schools" have been formed. No other country I know of has, or is likely to pass, such a law.

Without such government support, the Ny Lilleskole could probably not exist and certainly not in its present form. It would have to
depend on the support, and therefore the approval, of people much
richer than most of its present parents. But neither in Denmark nor
anywhere else are the very rich likely to support a school which
believes that cooperating and helping others is more important than
being first.

The school is able to operate as informally as it does, and to
allow children (with their families) to decide when they will come
to school and for how long they will stay, because the government
school inspectors in its district support or at least tolerate what it is
doing. In another part of the country, with different inspectors, the
school might not be so fortunate, might in many respects have to
stick much closer to the letter of the law. Finally, the school can do
what it does because, even if it doesn't try to be or want to be, it is
a school for winners, i.e., successful students. If only a few of the
Ny Lilleskole children, instead of most of them, did well in their
later schooling, many parents would stop sending their children
there. Even the teachers, who are now fairly confident of the
rightness of what they are doing, might begin to have doubts.

I have described the Ny Lilleskole in order to show some of the
ways in which children and adults might live and work together,
relate to each other, and learn from each other, in a place free of
manipulation, bribe, and threat—in short, in a society without
S-chools. I am not trying to make people think, "Let's all get busy
and make all our S-chools like the Ny Lilleskole"; that is not my
point. In the first place, it is clear that a society that would allow
all its S-chools to become more or less like the Ny Lilleskole would
not want S-chools at all, and would simply do away with them.
Beyond that, though a society that had schools like the Ny Lilleskole for all children would be a very good and pleasant place for
them to live and grow up, it would still fall short of what I would
call ideal. Even for the Ny Lilleskole children, most of Denmark is
out of bounds, off limits. I don't want children to have to spend all

their time in places specially prepared for children, with people specially trained to look after them, no matter how nice those places and people might be. Children need much more than that—a society which is open, accessible, visible to all its citizens, young and old, and in which every citizen, however young or old, has the right to play an active, serious, responsible, and useful part. To make such a society involves a great deal more than reforming S-chools, or even doing away with them altogether.

Most of the schools in the U.S. that start out trying to work more or less like the Ny Lilleskole die out in a few years. Sometimes they are split by arguments about freedom. (It is worth noting here that the Ny Lilleskole was formed by some teachers and parents who broke away from another little school they thought was becoming too much like conventional schools, too worried about "outcomes.") Sometimes they are harassed out of existence by local government officials, who, in the U.S. at least, generally don't like schools like this, or anything else that has the smell of freedom about it. Most often they either die for lack of money, or give up their principles under pressure from the rich people whose support they must have to live.

Of the alternative schools I saw in the U.S., one I particularly liked, that had the same spirit and feeling as the Ny Lilleskole, was the Children's Community in Ann Arbor, an integrated school with about twenty-five young, mostly poor kids. It ran for a few years in the late 1960s, died for lack of money, and has recently started up again. The first director of the school, Bill Ayers, wrote two pieces about it for *This Magazine Is about Schools,* later reprinted in the excellent *This Book Is about Schools* (ed. Satu Repo, Vintage paperback). He wrote in part:

> In every integrated school except ours the model for failure is everything that is ghetto or Negro culture. . . . What we try to do is allow these groups of (black and white) kids to learn from each other, to exchange things, throw things away, pick things up, without any kind of value judgment. . . . The point is that kids learn

by testing reality and not by what someone has decided is the truth they are going to tell them. . . . We see learning as going on everyplace—unstructured and undefined.

He describes the trips they took, with all or some of the kids. They went to apple orchards to get apples. Once, as they were there, they saw a truck loading apples. They followed it to an A&P, where it dropped off a load of apples, a few of which they bought. Another time, they went to a slaughterhouse, watched them kill, cut up, and package the animals. Bill had a little trouble watching this, but not the kids. They went to two automobile plants. Some of the kids were impressed by the assembly line, so huge, all that stuff coming together to make a car. Others talked about the stink, the heat, the noise, the dirt. They often went to the airport, not just to see airplanes, but also because:

> It's so many people talking in foreign languages, escalators, movies, little displays they have all over, cards hung up on the ceiling. And it's big and it's got a big marble floor, and you can run across it and no one gives you much trouble.

On the matter of reading, he writes:

> We find that kids learn to read in a million different ways. Some learn to read because they like cars and want to learn the different names of cars. Others learn because they go on a lot of trips and read the signs along the way, they learn to read each others' names, or they read the labels in a store, or they learn to read because they like to. Most of the kids really do want to learn to read. They learn to talk because everyone around them talks. They want to be competent. They want to make sense out of things like everyone else seems to be able to do, so they learn to talk, and the same is true of reading.

On the whole, the parents of the black kids were willing to go along with what the school was doing. "They think the black kids get a fair shake here, and they wouldn't at another school." But most people who try to run schools like this for nonwhite or poor kids tend to find that the parents demand the most strict and traditional kinds of schooling, in the belief or illusion that this alone can lift their kids out of poverty. It might be easier to run a place modeled after the Ny Lilleskole if it were not called or thought of as a school or a substitute for school, but just a meeting place, a club. *This Book Is about Schools* has a good piece, "The Baldwin Street Club," by Laura Phillips, about just such a place. Two young couples, living in a house in a poor section of Toronto, opened the ground floor of their house to the neighborhood and particularly the neighborhood kids. The kids loved it, and did many interesting things in it. For a while in one of the black communities of Boston there was a place called the Storefront Learning Center, which many children used, until the city, which owned and had lent the building, took it back.

Not calling such a place a school will probably have three advantages. It makes it easier for the children to think of the place as theirs; school belongs to adults. It saves being checked up on all the time by school officials, most of whom will not understand or like what happens there. And it lets parents anxious about their children's futures unload their anxiety on the official S-chools, and leaves the club free to be a lively and interesting place where kids have a good time and do what they want. But far better than any such children's club will be the kind of living and doing place, for children *and* adults, of which the Pioneer Health Centre in Peckham was such a striking example.

12

The Failure of School Reform

As I write, another movement to reform S-chools, to make all or many of them more like the Ny Lilleskole, is coming to an end. We would do well to understand why such movements fail, and cannot help but fail. To begin with, such movements are not new. Those of us who in the early and mid-sixties were excited by reports of what was happening in some British elementary schools liked to call it a "revolution," as if such things had never been done before. But some people had been doing these things in the 1920s and 1930s, and even earlier than that. In an article in the *Saturday Review*, Dan Pinck reported that the classroom practices we were calling "revolutionary" had been practiced on a citywide scale in the public schools of Gary, Indiana, in the year 1905. More recently my colleague Margot Priest found in the book *Corporal Punishment, a Social Interpretation of Its Theory and Practice in the Schools of the United States* by Herbert Falk (Bureau of Publications, Teachers' College, Columbia University) the following:

> Colonel Francis Wayland Parker, after several years of study of European theories and practices, returned to the United States in 1875 to take charge of the Quincy, Mass., schools, and to conduct one of the most interesting revolutionary educational experiments of the time. This rather significant departure from the traditional theory and practice may be briefly summarized by the following

quotation from Edward H. Reisner (*The Evolution of the Common School*, 1930):

"Parker began his work of educational reconstruction by tearing out the network of partitions and passageways represented by the traditional school subjects. He abolished reading, spelling, arithmetic, geography, etc., as separate school subjects and had them reappear as useful accomplishments and interesting aspects of an experience which was a united, interrelated whole. On the side of discipline he abolished rules, prizes, demerits, marks, and the entire repressive apparatus which bribed or threatened children into being industrious or orderly. In the place of this repressive system of school control he worked with his teachers to build up a real sense of community in which the pupils learned to conduct themselves as thoughtful, cooperative, public-spirited citizens."

But movements to reform S-chools never last very long. They soon fall out of fashion, reaction sets in, and most of the few schools that attempt to make humane changes give them up. Usually, when this happens, the public gives a great cry of relief, and all of the long-term failings of the conventional schools *are blamed on the reformers.* Any evidence that, where carried out, the reforms actually worked is soon forgotten.

Thus, when the public turned against the earlier Progressive movement in education, few bothered to note that only a small percentage of American schools, and many of those without much thoroughness or insight, had ever attempted to do what Dewey had talked about. In the late 1930s and early 1940s, the Carnegie Foundation paid for an immense and careful study, using a very large sample of pupils and schools, and covering the time span of eight years, to see whether old-fashioned, rote-memorizing ways of instruction, or more open, flexible, interest-oriented ways were more effective. By every measure which the schools themselves thought important, they found that children taught in the latter ways performed significantly better in both school and college. The report of this study was almost instantly forgotten; hardly any teachers I have asked, or even teachers of teachers, have ever even heard of it.

We are now in the U.S. starting through this cycle again. A recent *Newsweek* feature story—there have been others like it in many newspapers and magazines—began joyously, "Back to Basics in the Schools." It said, in part:

> Innovations have proliferated in U.S. schools at an extraordinary rate for more than a decade. Bolstered by a surge of public interest in education, massive infusion of funds for experimentation, and in particular by the zeal of the reformers, new educational policies—some excellent, others downright nonsensical—were adopted on an almost nationwide basis. Open classrooms, where pupils could choose activities in non-graded groups and work at their own tasks with little teacher interference, became the vogue.

The impression given by these words, that such things were done in a great many schools and with a great many children, is simply not true. There was never very much "open education." In that decade I traveled widely all over the country, lecturing to hundreds of schools, groups of teachers, and other people interested in educational change. The communities I visited were far more open to change than most, or they would not have asked me in. But even in these communities, and in all of those I have ever read or heard about, such changes rarely involved even as many as 10 percent of the children in the schools, and usually many fewer.

A recent survey of S-chools in Minnesota by Gregg Carlson reports that 29 percent of the school districts in the state have some sort of open school. If each of these involved 10 percent of the children in the district, then 2.9 percent of the children in the state would be in open schools. But the survey also reports that most of these schools are very small; more than half of them have less than 150 pupils. In short, most of the open schools involve far less than 10 percent of the children in the district. A fair guess might be that only 1 percent or less of the children in the state are in such schools, and this is one of our politically and educationally most progressive states. I should add that I have seen one of the best-known of these open schools, and while it is quite good, and much better than conventional schools, it is still a long way from the spirit of the Ny Lilleskole.

At the height of the supposed wave of change, the Alternative Schools Division of the U.S. Department of Education announced to school systems all over the country that they were ready to give up to five million dollars to school districts for innovative K–12 programs. Some four or five hundred school districts responded with proposals; the vast majority did not respond at all. Even by the very modest reformist standards of the Department, only thirty or forty of these proposals seemed innovative enough to be worth further study, and of these, only *three or four* finally received funding to make changes which humane reformers would have considered no more than a timid first step. People I know work in one of the school systems which got some of this money, and have told me how much of it was spent. In that system there had already been a handful of small, open, innovative schools, working on a very small scale with almost no money. When the federal government funded innovation in this system, the hope was that these people would get more money with which to extend their work. What happened instead was that a whole new bureaucracy of high-salaried coordinators, planners, and above all, evaluators, was set up in the district office. The innovative schools and teachers, which in their former poverty had at least been left alone to do their work as best they could, now had to spend much of their time explaining and justifying what they were doing. Many of them felt that the federal funding had, if anything, made their work harder.

In another story about "back-to-the-basics," the *Boston Globe* said that most of the educational innovation of the past ten years, about $1.4 billion worth, had been funded under Title III of the Education Act. At first this seems a large sum. But as of 1970 or so, the total *annual* cost of elementary and secondary education in this country was on the order of *forty billion* dollars. What we spent for change in education amounted to about *one-third of one percent* of what we spent on the whole. Even of that tiny fraction, a large part went for elaborate Mickey Mouse schemes that no humane reformer ever took seriously—regional laboratories, micro-teaching, computers, open-space schools, and the like. It is doubtful that even a fourth of that $1.4 billion ever got into the hands of people actually trying to teach children in more open, flexible, and above all trusting ways.

The *Newsweek* article went on to say, "Most of the high schools and colleges that had given up grading systems in favor of the less competitive pass-fail options have returned—largely at the request of the students—to the old-fashioned marks." True; but the reason the students wanted grades is not that they were not learning without them, but because without them they could not get into college or graduate school. The colleges and graduate schools themselves, which, for reasons I will discuss later, have a strong vested interest in competitive systems of grading and ranking students, very effectively sabotaged all attempts to do away with grades. Many graduate schools refused to give credit for pass-fail courses. More than a few students who had taken such courses had to take them a second time, this time asking for a grade, in order to get effective credit for them.

In the early 1960s Goddard College brought together some elementary- and secondary-school people, most of them wanting a more open and flexible curriculum, and some college admissions officers. The school people complained that college admissions requirements determined the elementary-school curriculum and kept them from teaching the children (or giving the children time to learn) anything else. The then director of admissions at Amherst College told us, in effect, "Do what you think is right; teach your children the way you think best; when they come along to us, we'll have to deal with whatever kind of people they are. Force us to change. Scores don't mean as much to us as you think." We were encouraged. Less than ten years later, some people told me that when their son asked about going to Amherst, an admissions officer said to him, "If your SAT [Scholastic Aptitude Test] scores aren't above 600 [out of 800], don't even bother to send them in; we won't even look at them." So much for brave words. More recently a student at Evergreen State, a very innovative college in Washington, told me that one of the leading people in the graduate schools of the state university had said more or less publicly that they were going to take "a very hard look" at anyone applying from

Evergreen. Whatever was intended, the message received was plain: if you want to go to this graduate school, don't go to Evergreen.

The *Newsweek* article went on to say, "More than a third of the state legislatures have passed laws mandating testing that emphasizes achievement in basic skills." This implies that during, and because of, this supposed wave of innovation, large numbers of schools gave up using standardized achievement tests. The fact is that very few ever did. Even among open or alternative schools, I have never heard of more than a few who had the courage to stop using these tests. Of those who tried, most were soon brought into line by college admissions officers and anxious parents.

It was at the height of this supposed wave of innovation that Charles Silberman and a large team of researchers, funded by the Carnegie Foundation, visited many hundreds of schools, and in those schools many classrooms, all over the country. What they found, he described in his book *Crisis in the Classroom*, in which he says, in part:

> It is not possible to spend any prolonged period visiting public school classrooms without being appalled by the mutilation visible everywhere—mutilation of spontaneity, of joy in learning, or pleasure in creating, or sense of self. . . . Because adults take the schools so much for granted, they fail to appreciate what grim, joyless places most American schools are,* how oppressive and petty are the rules by which they are governed, how intellectually sterile and esthetically barren the atmosphere, what an appalling lack of civility obtains on the part of teachers and principals, what contempt they unconsciously display for students as students.

Anyone who thinks that in the late sixties all the schools were happy and permissive should read Silberman's book. In the last part of it he described a number of innovations which he hoped and believed would become a pattern that most schools would follow. But many of these innovations were dying or dead soon after his book came out. By now they all are gone. In the communities where I was asked to speak, I saw or heard about many

---

* They are much the same in other countries (my note).

changes, some of them quite promising. Most of these lasted only a few years, until the Federal funding ran out, or a new School Board was elected, or the Superintendent left, or retired, or was fired—or people just lost interest. And a great deal of the innovation never got past the stage of window dressing, conferences, publicity, empty talk. Reformers were very encouraged, for example, when the Vermont State Department of Education, under then Commissioner Harvey Scribner (later, for a short while until forced out, Chancellor of the Public Schools of New York City) put out a pamphlet called "The Vermont Idea in Education," which strongly endorsed most of the things we believed in. Only later did we find out, as a Vermont teacher wrote me, that "nobody in the state took it seriously and only about three schools in the state ever made a serious effort to practice it."

S-chools Are Worse

Few of the schools ever made any humane changes; few of these did them well, or stayed with them long. For the most part, the schools are what they have always been. If anything, they are worse, in many ways and for many reasons. As in the past, they are often mentally and physically cruel to most of the children in them, and most of all to the poor, the nonwhite, the unusual, and the brave and independent. Let me return again to Silberman, a cool observer and by no means a sentimental worshipper of children. When his book first appeared as a three-part article in the *Atlantic Monthly*, the title he gave to the first article was "Murder in the Classroom." He was apparently persuaded later to change "murder" to "crisis," but *"murder"* is the word he originally felt best described what he had seen. Carl Weinberg, in *Education Is a Great Big Shuck*, tells an equally grim story. From students, parents, student teachers, and some teachers, I continue to hear reports of quite extraordinary and in all cases unpunished mental and physical cruelty to children in schools. Corporal punishment, the ritual beating of children, is still allowed in most states. Beyond that, even where it is illegal, it is widely used, and where legal widely abused. In one S-school in Portland, Oregon, children are beaten with a "paddle" 33″ long, with a 17″ handle, and a base 10¾″ wide and ¹⁵/₁₆″ thick, weighing 4 pounds, with 26 holes the size of a penny drilled through it. The few people who are making the sustained (and very difficult) effort to find out how much gross physical and mental cruelty there is in schools report that there is a great deal—and not just in "bad" schools for loser kids, but in "good" schools for winners as well.

But I don't wish to give the impression that the cruelty of S-chools is a kind of bad or careless habit of which they might be cured, if people really wanted to cure them. Compulsory and competitive schools are cruel by their very nature. I think of a school where I once taught. The school was believed to be, meant to be, and generally was kindly to children, above all young children. The teachers were without exception intelligent, cultured, highly "educated," sophisticated, sensitive men and women. They were not sadists, and for reasons of manners and taste as much as philosophy would never have physically abused a child. And yet, a great many of the children I knew at that school *suffered*, even as ten-year-olds and younger. They lived a large part of their school lives in constant anxiety, fear, and shame. Many of them were badly hurt by the experience. To this day they have not recovered, and many never fully recover, from that school's sustained (however unintended) attack on their dignity, independence, and self-esteem. And these children were unusual, and fortunate. Not many children can be having a better life at school than they did; most are surely having worse.

Even if it were true, as in some cases it may be, that S-chools today are somewhat less cruel, painful, fearful, and humiliating than they used to be, they are more harmful in other ways. They take much more of children's time, and more all the time. They give children less and less time to live their own lives, pursue their own interests, or perhaps find ways outside of school to make up for the failures, fears, and boredom of school. Far more than they used to, they control and limit children's futures. There are fewer and fewer paths into life that do not lead through the school. Degrees, diplomas, and certificates are needed for more and more kinds of work. The struggle for the few winner slots in society begins earlier and earlier in life; in New York City (and probably many other cities) it may begin when the parents of a three-year-old try to get him into nursery school. If the child doesn't know enough to worry about such things, the parents do, and their worry must hang over and infect his life.

The judgments that schools make about children follow them much further. I doubt very much that the public school where I attended fifth grade still has my report card. But, thanks to modern technology, everything a school now writes about a child lasts as long as he does. Throughout his entire life people may be reading whatever his second-grade or other teachers had to say about him, things which in earlier days teachers would never have thought of saying or been allowed to say. My report cards were *cards*, with nothing on them but grades. But today, as any number of reports have pointed out, the school records of children are full of the most gossipy, malicious, damaging pseudopsychological observations and diagnoses, often about the parents as well as the children, and made in most cases by people wholly incompetent to make them. In some districts, so I have read, on the basis of a few dubious tests they label some children *pre-delinquent*, and give this information to the police! Laws are now being passed in some states requiring the schools to let parents see their children's school records. But some S-chool people, in states where such laws exist, have already told me that their school has begun to keep two sets of records, one for parents to see, the other one "secret"—that is, for almost anyone in society to see *except* the parents.

There are other kinds of damaging labels which the schools put on more and more children. Many students I talk to at schools of education say cheerfully, "Jobs are tough to get in regular teaching, but there are plenty of jobs in Special Ed." Special Ed(ucation) means teaching children who have been labeled as "special."

Ninety-five percent of the time this means deficient—retarded, or "having a learning disability," or "emotionally disturbed." As the children themselves say with their blunt realism, weird or stupid. More and more children are being labeled in school as being weird or stupid, and more and more will be, as more and more people are trained to deal with such children. One full-page ad recently stated that 10 percent of all the children in the United States have severe learning disabilities. Five years ago this figure would surely have been much less; in five years it will surely be much more. A recent story in the Education section of the Sunday *New York Times* reported that in one school the diagnosing experts had said that *every child in the school* had learning disabilities. Clearly, the potential market for this kind of label and treatment is very large. The Special Ed people will of course say that it is only so that they can help children and so that they won't blame themselves for their troubles that they put the Weird/Stupid labels on them. No doubt; but these labels never come off, either on the child's official records, or worse yet, in his own mind. I once heard a woman in her forties say, with a deep blush of shame, and shame in her voice, that she could not do something or other because of her Learning Disability. How many times, and with how much shame, had she told herself that? And how many people are the schools going to label, in the next ten or twenty years, as being in effect mental cripples, or having a disease that can't be cured?

It is bad enough that S-chools put on many children new kinds of labels that will last longer, be seen by more people, and hence do more harm. But they also try to reach into and control much more of children's lives. When I was a child, the S-chool I went to made rather limited demands of us, and we all knew what they were. Some of us tried to do and could do what the S-chool wanted; others did not, or could not. Either way, S-chool didn't weigh very heavily on us. It was a place where we had to go, and a game we had to play, badly or well, but it was not the center of our lives.

Today the S-chools make many more, larger, and vaguer demands on children. Not long ago some parents, in a midwestern, middle-income, thoroughly middle-American community, quite "conservative" in its politics, told me that their child's *kindergarten* report card had *sixty-two* items on it. I said, you can't be serious, it's impossible. They showed me the "Kindergarten Check List." There are indeed sixty-two items on it. For each item there are three boxes, marked "First Conference (Nov.)," "Second Conference (March)," "End of Year." Items 1–28, and 61–62, are marked, "Should be accomplished by mid-November." The rest are due by the middle of May. Here is the complete list:

KINDERGARTEN CHECK LIST

		FIRST CONFER- ENCE	SECOND CONFER- ENCE	END OF YEAR
1.	I am			
2.	I come to school regularly.			
3.	I come to school happy.			
4.	I am happy in school.			
5.	I say "yes," "please," "thank you," "you're welcome," and "excuse me."			
6.	I use good bathroom habits.			
7.	I can dress myself. (zip, button, and tie)			
8.	I can recognize and care for my own clothes.			
9.	I take care of my library books and room equipment.			
10.	I carry notes to and from school safely.			
11.	I am kind and helpful to others.			
12.	I use my "indoor voice" when inside.			
13.	I can wait and take turns.			
14.	I listen at sharing times.			
15.	I listen to my friends.			
16.	I listen to my teacher.			
17.	I can listen to and follow simple directions.			

	FIRST CONFER-ENCE	SECOND CONFER-ENCE	END OF YEAR
18. I finish my work.			
19. I have made friends in my classroom.			
20. I can recognize my name.			
21. I can print my name.			
22. I can hold and use crayons and pencils properly.			
23. I can hold and use scissors properly.			
24. I can run, hop, and jump.			
25. I can skip, throw and catch.			
26. I can work well by myself.			
27. I ask for help when I need it.			
28. I can talk openly before the group.			
29. I can tell stories.			
30. I can tell events of a story in sequence.			
31. I know some rhymes.			
32. I can rhyme words.			
33. I know and recognize the capital letters of the alphabet in order.			
34. I know and recognize the capital letters of the alphabet out of order.			
35. I know and recognize the small letters of the alphabet in order.			
36. I know and recognize the small letters of the alphabet out of order.			
37. I use good, clear speech.			
38. I can hear sounds that are alike.			
39. I can hear sounds that are different.			
40. I am learning which sounds go with which letters.			
41. I can see differences in pictures.			
42. I can see differences in words.			

KINDERGARTEN CHECK LIST (*Continued*)

	FIRST CONFER- ENCE	SECOND CONFER- ENCE	END OF YEAR
43. I can tell the difference between left and right.			
44. I write from left to right.			
45. I can say the days of the week.			
46. I can tell which month and year it is.			
47. I can say my address.			
48. I know my way to and from school.			
49. I obey school and safety rules.			
50. I know and can recognize the eight basic colors and their names.			
51. I can say my telephone number.			
52. I can count to ten.			
53. I can count to twenty-five.			
54. I know and can recognize the numerals 0 to 10.			
55. I know and can recognize the numbers to 20.			
56. I can write numerals to 10.			
57. I know the geometric shapes—circle, square, rectangle, and triangle.			
58. I know the terms larger and smaller.			
59. I know the terms above, below, on and beside.			
60. I know how to check answers as directed.			
61. I have an "I can do it" attitude.			
62. I keep trying to do better work each day.			

What to say of all these demands? A few are specific, modest, and sensible enough if not taken too seriously or judged too rigidly. Most are so vague and hard to test or measure that the T-eacher's judgment must be almost entirely a matter of likes and dislikes. Not that there is anything wrong with a T-eacher having likes and dislikes; as a working T-eacher I had plenty. But they don't belong on official documents. Many of these demands are silly, and have nothing to do with the child's real life, or even the supposed work of S-chool. Thus, "I can hold and use scissors properly." Are we to believe that a child who does not learn in kindergarten how to hold scissors, or name the geometric shapes or the eight (which eight?) basic colors, will never learn, and will thus be unable to learn Math or English or whatever? Some of these demands invite discrimination against poor or nonwhite children, i.e., "I use good, clear speech." Some, notably, "I come to school happy," and "I am happy in school," are altogether sinister and outrageous. It is none of the S-chool's damn business whether a child comes to S-chool happy or is happy in S-chool—even if the S-chool knew how to find out, which it does not. What is being asked for, and rewarded, and so trained, are fake smiles, fake laughter, fake teacher-pleasing behavior. It is already bad enough that a child, having done nothing wrong, should be asked to endure such a place. It is inexcusable to demand that he pretend that he likes it.

One might say that with the exception of a few of the questions named above, this list is not a bad set of rough guidelines for observing a child's movement into the world. True enough. But it is not used that way. The children are in fact checked and graded very minutely on their performance and progress in most of these items. At conferences, T-eachers do not stress the positive, do not say to parents, "Don't worry about the others, they will come along." Quite the reverse. They give parents a long list of their child's failings, and invite and urge them to worry, and to "do something" about them. Some parents, their friends told me, were half out of their minds with worry after their November conference. The parents who gave me the list told me that his child's kindergarten teacher told him in November, "Well, one thing is certain, you son will never be a scholar." Hiding as best he could his amazement and anger, the father asked what else the teacher had learned about his child *in eight weeks.* Everything in the S-chools, and in the training of T-eachers, encourages them to think that they know enough to make such judgments, and have the right and duty to make them all the time. There is no part of the child's life or personality or thought or feelings which T-eachers do not consider their proper territory, in which they have an unlimited right to meddle, pry, shape behavior, and judge. And the tools they are given to do this, which include strong and dangerous drugs, and subtle and sophisticated techniques of bribery, threat, and humiliation, are now and will continue to become far more powerful and insidious than anything the old-fashioned T-eacher had to work with.[1] For we may be sure that everything our busy researchers learn about molding, shaping, and controlling human beings will quickly be put to work in our S-chools. And, what is worse, at earlier and earlier ages. Some leading officials of the teachers' union, in order to get jobs for more of their members, are busily promoting the idea (among others equally bad) that all children should be compelled to go to school *from the age of two and a half years*, and that all this early childhood education should be under the control of the public schools. They may have the political muscle to push this through. So what Silberman called the "mutilation of spontaneity, of joy in learning, of pleasure in creating, or sense of self," until now inflicted by the S-chools only on children older than six, may before long be inflicted on infants of two and a half.

The Myth and Fraud of "The Basics"

On all sides we hear that the S-chools are "going back" to teaching "basic skills" and bringing about "measurable achievement." As I have pointed out, most of them never stopped doing this—or rather, unsuccessfully trying to do it. But let me point out once again, as I did at some length and in great detail in *How Children Fail*, just what this is we are all "going back" to.

The first three fifth-grade classes I taught were in a very selective and exclusive private elementary school. From what I saw of the neighborhoods and homes the children lived in, I would guess

---

[1] For a detailed, thorough, and horrifying account of these practices, see *The Myth of the Hyperactive Child*, by Peter Schrag and Diane Divoky (Pantheon).

that the family income of most of them was well over $30,000 per year. Only very rarely, and usually because he had a sister or brother in the school, would a child with an IQ under 120 be admitted. In short, this was a S-chool for super-winners. In some ways it was mildly progressive and innovative; among other things, it did not give number or letter grades to young children (though it did give standardized achievement tests in reading and arithmetic). But, as it said all the time, in the matter of Arithmetic it was not progressive or modern at all. It believed in the strict teaching of old-fashioned computational skills. In the first grade the children spent the entire year learning the addition and subtraction combinations up to ten. Nothing else. In the second grade they spread their wings a bit, and learned the combinations all the way up to twenty. In the third grade they learned to multiply, and in the fourth to divide. They came to the fifth grade "ready" to learn fractions, which I was supposed to teach them.

What was the result of all this very strict and old-fashioned teaching, done, it should be noted, by very talented teachers who believed in and worked hard at what they were doing? Only very slowly did I realize that something very close to half of these fifth-graders could not add and subtract reliably, even with small numbers, without using their fingers, or some equivalent prop—one child said that instead of using fingers she made very small dots on the page, which she later erased. How much they really knew about multiplication and division, I never dared to find out. One particular child stands out in memory. This child's fourth-grade teacher had introduced her to me just before she began fifth grade, saying that the child had a little trouble with multiplication and division but that now, thanks to a summer of hard work and intensive tutoring, the problems were all gone. They showed me a thick workbook of multiplication and division problems. Checks and erasures showed that the tutors had made the child work on each problem until she got it right. From the size and look of the book, she must have worked on Arithmetic several hours a day for most days of the summer. And now, I was told, she knew it.

Not much more than a month after school began, she produced the following. Trying to find half of 32, she wrote:

$$2\overline{)32}$$

then:

$$\begin{array}{r} 1 \\ 2\overline{)32} \\ \underline{2} \\ 1 \end{array}$$

then:

$$\begin{array}{r} 11+1 \\ 2\overline{)32} \\ \underline{2} \\ 1 \end{array} \quad (11, \text{ remainder } 1)$$

She wrote all this without hesitating, without erasing, and without the least sign of doubt about that answer. She was like a later fifth-grader, who lives in my memory as the Lemonade Boy, who told me one day that six one-pint cups, each two-thirds full, would hold eighteen pints of lemonade, and that even if that didn't make sense it had to be the right answer because "that was the way the system worked out."

So much for achievement. What about measurement? As a matter of principle, I did not look at previous test scores and reports of my pupils. I wanted to give them a fresh start, and to get my ideas about them solely from our life together. But in time I became curious about some of these children who could not add or subtract, or who might tell me that nine times seven equalled twenty-two, or four times six equalled eighty-one, or things equally absurd. Hadn't anyone noticed? So I looked up their previous achievement-test scores, and found to my great surprise that though their scores were usually below grade level they were not very far below. In the fourth grade they might have scored 3.6 or 3.2, perhaps even 2.8—something like that. How had they managed to get even these scores when what they *knew* was about 0.5?

They got them the way that most children around the country get them. Their teachers had been warned (as I was) that achievement tests were coming, and had been ordered (as I was) to give them the most intensive coaching for these tests. So we did; we coached and drilled them almost up to the minute the papers were handed out. We turned them into wind-up mechanical Arithmetic-doing toys, wound them up, and set them going. Most of them were able to get at least some of their tests done before their clockwork springs ran down and they fell back into their usual total ignorance and confusion. But by then the tests were done, the scores were in the book, the S-chool had the proof that they had at least learned something, and we T-eachers were safe for another year. This is the "measureable achievement" of the S-chools we are rushing back to—a fraud, a cheat, and a lie. The children are not learning, never did learn, most of what the S-chools say they are T-eaching. The question we must ask, then, is what are they teaching, what are they really for?

13

What S-chools Are For

In 1965, soon after *How Children Fail* appeared, a teacher wrote me, saying, in effect, "I have just read your book, and like it. But there is something you don't know, that you should know. For over thirty years I have been teaching in the public schools of New York City. For over thirty years, along with my fellow teachers, I have been going to educational conferences, and training sessions, and workshops, to hear countless leaders in education talk, as you do, about the dignity of the child, and the importance of individual differences, and of fostering positive self-concepts, and building on the interests of the child, and letting the child learn from curiosity rather than fear. And for thirty years I and my fellow teachers, as we went back to our classrooms, have said to ourselves, 'Well, back to reality,' and have gone on doing just what we had done all along, which was to try to bribe, scare, and shame children into learning what someone else had decided they ought to know. What makes you think you can change all this?" A few years later, while I was talking at a meeting on educational reform, a local superintendent of schools rose from his seat in the back of the room and, moving to the door, said scornfully, so that many could hear, "Well, back to reality."

Today, some years later, the reality that those teachers and that superintendent saw has become painfully clear to me. It is, above all, that *the S-chools are not failing*. They are doing what most people want them to do, and doing it very well. They know their true social tasks, functions, purposes, and they are carrying them out.

The first task is to shut young people out of adult society. In all modern societies, children are a problem. Nobody wants them around. Mothers don't want them around the house, especially if (like many mothers) they have to work. Merchants don't want them on the streets, crowding the paying customers. Workers don't want them in the labor force, taking scarce jobs and dragging down wages. Nobody has any use for them; there is no place for them to go, and nothing for them to do. To the state, the adults cry with one voice, "Get these damn kids out of our hair!" The state obliges with laws compelling children to go to S-chool.

The S-chools say, of course, that the reason for compulsory attendance laws is to make sure the children learn all the important things the S-chools are teaching. But children must be in S-chool even when S-chool tests show and the S-chool itself admits they are not learning anything, or have already learned what the S-chool is teaching. Only in very rare cases can even the best students skip a grade. They must put in their full time in S-chool, and if they learn anything at all, must learn at the S-chool's snail-like pace.

Winners and Losers

A much more important and indeed essential social function of S-chools is ranking—that is, grading and labeling, putting children into pecking orders, dividing them into winners and losers. All modern societies, like most societies in the past, are organized into a few winners and a great many losers, a few "decision-makers" who give commands and many who carry them out. It is of course not always easy to tell where the line is between winning and losing. The line is in the mind. People who really *feel* like winners are winners, whatever others may think of them, and those who feel like losers are losers. People doing with love and pride the work they really want to do would probably count themselves winners, even though poor. Others, though rich and successful, might feel themselves losers because they hate their work, or envy those still higher up. But most people would agree, at least in general, about what separates winners from losers. Winners don't often have to worry much about money, and can buy most of what they need and want. Winners can make plans for the future, for themselves and their children, with some hope of carrying them out. They do not live, like most people, at the mercy of events, on the brink of disaster. Winners have some control over their work; they don't spend all their time doing what someone else tells them. They have privacy, space, choice, dignity in their lives. The law is at their service. In their dealings with other people, they are generally treated with honesty, courtesy, and respect. In short, they can think, "I count, I make a difference."

Losers, on the other hand, can't make many choices; can't make plans for the future; can do almost nothing to protect their security and the security of their families, and have little or no control over their work, but must do what they are told. Eighty percent of the jobs that will be filled during the next decade will be jobs for which a college degree is not needed. Most of those who will do these jobs will feel themselves losers, and even more so if (like many) they have first spent the time and money to get a college degree.

To be peaceful and stable, every society organized into winners and losers must persuade the losers that this state of affairs is necessary, and that its way of picking winners and losers is just, that the losers *deserve* to lose. At one time, winners and losers were picked by the accident of birth. Modern societies do this more and more with the S-chools. But the people who control society naturally want the S-chools to pick winners in such a way that *the existing social order is not changed*—in short, so that most of the winners are the children of winners, and the losers the children of losers. The S-chools, then, must run a race which mostly rich kids will win but which most poor people will accept as fair. On the whole they have done this very well.

Many educators will protest that ranking is not what grades and tests are for, but only to help children learn, and to help teachers help them to learn. No doubt many teachers sincerely believe it, as I did for many of my years as a T-eacher. But it is not true. Any observant and thoughtful teacher soon learns in his work, as I did, that fear blocks learning. The skillful learner must trust the world, and himself to be able to cope with it. In *How Children Fail* I showed how even "bright" children act when they have lost this confidence. Instead of reaching out to new experience, they shrink back from it. Often they protect themselves from the danger and shame of failure in the only way they can, by failing on purpose.

Not only does fear prevent children (and adults) from using their minds well, but it almost certainly, and at the most biological level, prevents the mind from working at all. We may not yet know just what happens, chemically and electrically, when we turn experience into memory, recall old memories, and make connections and patterns, a mental model, out of this remembered experience—in short, when we think. But whatever it is that happens, fear stops it from happening. Knowing this, I knew that I could not help my weak students learn unless I could reduce their fears and help them regain or rebuild some of their confidence. To do this, I had to stop giving them tests. Fear of the test blocked their minds long before they actually had to take it; fear made them do much worse than their real knowledge should have enabled them to do; and shame at the result of the test only made them more sure that they were too stupid to learn. It was a downward spiral. The only way I could stop it, and reverse it, was to stop testing. But the school, though more kindly than most, would not let me. Indeed, I was under fire, and later fired, for not giving enough tests. When I could put off testing for a while, even the worst pupils would begin to regain some confidence, strength, and intelligence. But sooner or later I would have to announce another test, and could see the children growing frightened, defensive, and stupid in front of my eyes.

It is vital for a t-eacher to give students emotional support as they explore new territory and take new risks. I tried to do that for my students, by encouraging them to talk about, and so perhaps overcome, some of their fears. But how could I give them emotional support when *I* was the source of their danger? If someone else had been giving them those tests and grades, I might have been able to help them cope with this problem. But *I* was giving the test, *I* was putting the red X's and failing marks on the papers. No wonder the children remained afraid. Like countless other T-eachers, I thought the children might learn to trust me rather than fear me because of my good intentions. But what use were my good intentions to them, when week after week, month after month, I went on doing things *that did them real harm?*

S-chools Need to Fail

S-chools say, and many S-chool people believe, that they really want all children to succeed, to learn all that the S-chools are trying to teach them. But if someday, somewhere, a T-eacher ever did the job he was paid to do, and got all his kids to learn all the stuff he was teaching, he would have to give them all A's. Soon he would get a message from higher up saying, what's the big idea of giving your students all A's? If he insisted that this grading was fair, that the students really had learned all he taught, he would then be told, "Then you're not teaching them enough. Raise your standards, challenge your students! Teach more!" The parents of his students would be after him as well. The few who thought their kids really deserved A's would say furiously, "When you give all those other kids A's you make my kid's A's worthless. The good colleges won't pay any attention to them!" Most of the other parents would say, "I know damn well my kid isn't smart enough to get an A. How am I going to get him to do any work if you hand out A's for free? He's just going to sit on his tail and goof off."

Everyone talks these days about "quality education" for all. But quality education for every child, is an absurdity, a contradiction in terms. Most parents, when they say to S-chools, "Give my kid a quality education," mean, "Do something to him *that will get him ahead of all the other kids!*" In short, make him a winner. Not, a winner along with all the rest; that won't do him any good. They mean, make him a winner in a race where most kids lose.

The first thing any new T-eacher had better learn is that nobody wants *all* the kids to win. From the university down to the elementary school, giving all high grades is a sure way to get in serious trouble, even to be fired. One teacher in a large state university sent me a copy of a letter from a dean, telling him that by giving all his students high grades he was undermining the process of selection which was one of the chief functions of the university. At another college a teacher told me that his department head told all members of the department that experience had shown that only a certain small percentage of students deserved A's, a slightly larger percentage B's, a few more C's, and so on, and that any department member who gave much higher grades than these would be considered to be "sabotaging"—his word—the grading system. Such experiences are common.

What is true of T-eachers is no less true of S-chools. As long as S-chools are allowed to give grades, they cannot afford not to, for to give no grades is to give the worst grade of all. By the same token, they cannot afford to give all good grades, to say that all of their students are winners. They are, after all, selling tickets to jobs and careers. The more good grades they give, the less their tickets are worth. The "best" colleges and universities are those that can say that their standards are so high that almost no students are good enough to meet them.

A Crooked Race

The S-chools say that they want all children to be winners, and with even greater fervor, that they want all poor children to be winners. But the people who run society want their own children and the children of their friends to be the ones who win in S-chool, and later in society. They make sure that this happens. When children of different social classes go to the same S-chool, they are almost always divided into tracks, such as college, business, and vocational. Wherever such tracks exist, studies show that they correlate almost perfectly with family income, the richest kids in the top tracks, the poorest in the bottom.

The stuff the S-chools teach, and the books and materials they use, are much closer to the lives and experiences of rich kids than poor. The standards they use to judge kids favor the rich over the poor, above all in the area of language. The kindergarten report card I spoke of earlier had as one of its sixty-two items, "I use good, clear English." What this boils down to is, "I talk like a rich kid." The S-chools may believe sincerely enough that standard English—i.e., the way rich people talk—is somehow "better" than the way poor people talk, and that by "correcting" the speech of poor kids they are really improving it, and so helping the kids. But what they really do is to penalize and shame poor kids for talking like the adults they know. The result is that these kids talk less and less, and so lose the chance of growing more skillful and fluent.

From the very start, even among lower-income or poor kids, S-chools and T-eachers discriminate in favor of the children who look and sound most middle-class, most like rich kids. In an article, "Student Social Class and Teacher Expectations: The Self-Fulfilling Prophecy in Ghetto Education" (*Harvard Educational Review*, August 1970), Ray Rist described how a black kindergarten teacher in an all-black school, in the first eight days of school, divided her class into three tracks (each at a different table) entirely on the basis of appearance—speech, hair style, clothes, etc. To the first table she gave all her positive instruction, help, and praise. She rarely spoke to the other tables, and then only to criticize, threaten, or punish. Indeed, after a while she allowed the children at the first table to correct and make fun of the others. This tracking system remained almost unchanged during the three years Rist followed the class; only one child escaped from the lower groups into a higher group.

In their very perceptive and compassionate book, *The Hidden Injuries of Class,* Richard Sennett and Jonathan Cobb describe the same process in the second grade of a white working-class S-chool:

> In this class there were two children, Fred and Vincent, whose appearance was somewhat different from that of the others: their clothes were no fancier than the other children's, but they were pressed and seemed better kept; in a class of mostly dark Italian children, these were the fairest-skinned. From the outset the teacher singled out these two children, implying that they most closely approached his own standards for classroom performance. To them he spoke with a special warmth in his voice. He never praised them openly by comparison to the other children, but a message that they were different, were better, was spontaneously conveyed. . . . By then [the end of the year] they were also doing the best work in the class. The other children had picked up the teacher's hidden cues that their performance would not be greeted with as much enthusiasm as the work of these two little boys.

It would be easy to assume that T-eachers act this way because of snobbery. But, as Sennett and Cobb point out, there is often more to it than that.

> The teachers are in a terrible existential dilemma. It is true that they are "prejudiced" against most of their students; it is also true that they, like all human beings, want to believe in the dignity of their own work, no matter how difficult the circumstances in which they have to work seem to them. . . . A teacher needs at least a responsive few in order to feel he has a *reason* to possess power. The few will confirm to him that his power to affect other people is real, that he can truly do good. To sort out two classes of ability, then, in fear of the "lower" class of students, is to create a meaningful image of himself as an authority rather than simply a boss.

A really poor child, to become a winner in public S-chool, must somehow dodge the low tracks, escape or ignore the prejudice and contempt of his teachers, meet the risks of learning without emotional support, face increasing hostility from his loser friends, and find meaning in instructional materials which have little or nothing to do with his life or experience. Above all, in spite of never hearing it outside of S-chool, and barely being allowed to talk in S-chool at all, he must learn to talk middle-class English. Clearly, the odds against his being able to do all this are enormous. But even if he makes it to the winner circle in high school, there are many obstacles still ahead of him. Colin Greer pointed out some years ago that among *honor students* in high school, those whose families are in the top 25 percent in income had five times as much chance of getting into graduate schools as those from families in the bottom 25 percent. The difference is surely greater now, since the cost of higher education has risen so much faster than the incomes of the poor.

It is naive to think that S-chools could be used to change the social structure, let alone turn it upside down. A S-chool system which changed the rules of the game so that poor kids had as good a chance or better of being winners as rich kids would not last long. Professor David McLelland of Harvard has recently said that the IQ test is the greatest device for keeping down the poor that the middle class ever invented. Quite right. But what else could we expect? Tests exist that equally favor the children of the very poor. But any S-chools which use such tests will see the value of their grades and tickets go down, and will soon have no rich kids left. No S-chool will run that risk; like any other business, they would rather have rich customers than poor. A similar force works on colleges and universities. If they admit too many poor kids, the alumni begin to complain, and refuse to contribute needed money. In state-run institutions the rich and powerful put on this kind of pressure through the board of regents, or the legislature. It works just as well. Often, as in California, it produces a state university system which is as class-tracked as big public high schools.

The situation is much the same as in the area of work and jobs. Most white workers will agree that a black person should have as much right to a job as anyone else. *But not my job!* Most people will agree that poor and nonwhite kids should have as much chance as anyone else to move up in society. *But not if it means that my kid is*

going to have to move down! But this is what it does mean. In the
societies we have, there are only so many winner slots. All the
S-chool programs in the world cannot make more. When someone
moves up the ladder, someone else must move down.

Learning to Live As Losers

The third great task and function of S-chool, as S-chool people
themselves often put it, is "to get the kids ready for Reality," that
is, to prepare them to live the kind of lives, and above all, to do the
kind of work, that most people in modern societies do. In *The Making of a Moron* Niall Brennan reported that in Australia during
World War II, teen-age morons, with IQ's of under 50 and mental
ages of less than eight years, were able to do a variety of industrial
jobs, not just passably but reliably and well. Despite all the talk
about the technological demands of modern society, or the great
need of education to enable people to meet these demands, the fact
is that most modern work is moronic. It needs almost nothing in
training, skill, intelligence, or judgment. During World War II we
found that even the most highly skilled industrial jobs, jobs that
people supposedly had to spend years learning, could be learned
from scratch by most people of average intelligence in a few
months.

Modern work is moronic, not by accident, but by design.
When Frederick Taylor first wrote about what he called Scientific
Management, his central point, which his followers have stressed
to this day, is that *nothing* should be left to the intelligence and
judgment of the worker. The aim was and is as far as possible to
turn the worker into a machine, performing over and over again the
simplest possible series of movements or operations, always the
same way, and exactly as someone else showed him how. The
worker did not have to know, and was not encouraged to ask, the
meaning of his work, how it fitted into what other people were
doing, and for what product, purpose, or outcome. Indeed, the less

he knew about that, the better. Even his own labor unions encouraged him to think of himself and his work as a commodity, a thing, which he would sell for the highest price he could get.

In a few countries some people are looking for ways to make work more varied and challenging, and to give workers greater choice in it and control over it. But this movement will not go very far as long as we care more about productivity, efficiency, and growth of industrial output than we do about the happiness and growth of people. The danger of letting people ask, "Is this the best way to do this job?" is that after a while they may ask, "Is this job worth doing?" Thus, in a Volvo auto plant in Sweden, one of the workers on one of the new job-improved assembly lines went right to the heart of the matter. Asked if he liked the new way better than the old, he said, "Yes, but any way you look at it, putting cars together is lousy work."

Some public-opinion polls have told us that most workers are "satisfied" with their jobs. This probably means, not that they like them, but that they are resigned to them, glad to have them, and glad they are no worse. Those who have talked at any length with many people about their jobs—Brennan, Harvey Swados, Studs Terkel, and others—have reported that very few of them really like what they do. In the late 1960s a student who had worked five months in an auto-assembly plant told me that from what he could see and was told by his coworkers, most of the people in the plant regularly used amphetamines—speed—to get them through the day.

The December 12, 1974, issue of the magazine *New Times* contained a horrifying description of work in a vegetable processing factory. The author, a young woman, was working on a line with a number of older women, removing the cores from cauliflower heads with a guillotine-like machine. Most of the women on the line had one or more shortened or missing fingers or thumbs. They stood for long periods of time on a concrete floor unable to move except to shift their weight from one foot to the other, their legs and hips aching with a pain that became almost unbearable by the time they were given a short break. Some veteran workers counted endlessly to themselves to relieve the pain and boredom.

Workers on the job often lose more than fingers. An Associated Press story of April 27, 1975, reports:

> A study done for the Government has found that one out of every four workers in a sample lot of small businesses employing from eight to 150 people had occupationally derived disease and that 89 percent of those are not reported as required to the Labor Department. . . .
>
> Some of the diseases listed in the study include chronic respiratory diseases due to asbestos and other fibrous-like dust in work areas; loss of hearing due to noise; eye cataracts from infrared radiation; and increased lead absorption in the blood.

And in *Muscle and Blood* (E.P. Dutton, 1974) Rachel Scott reports that the 1972 President's Report on Occupational Safety and Health estimated "There may be as many as 100,000 deaths per year from occupationally caused diseases and at least 390,000 new cases of disabling occupational disease each year."

Worse than any job, however bad, is the growing danger of having no job at all: 8.2 million people are now (May, 1975) unemployed; another 1.1 million have stopped their hopeless search for work and have dropped out of the unemployment figures; and many millions more are effectively unemployed because the law (or someone) says they are too young or too old to work. What these figures mean in human suffering, in boredom worse even than the boredom of work, in shame, hopelessness, and terror, in demoralized communities, broken families, and battered children, is more than we can imagine. This risk or fact of joblessness, uselessness, and desperate poverty, and the knowledge that they have no power to avoid or prevent it, is something that tens of millions of people, losers, have to live with for most of their lives.

Knowing what we know, what we can see, of the curiosity, energy, and enthusiasm of young children, or their desire to do whatever they do as well as they can, we can only ask, how could they possibly be prepared to do this kind of work, live this sort of life, and put up with it? To do this is the third great social task of the S-chools. It is, after all, what most people want. Polls have shown for years that no matter what kind of schools their children go to, most parents want those schools to teach "more discipline." A Midwestern cab driver helped me to see why. He had said he had three children, all grown. I asked what they were doing. There was a long silence. Finally he said, "Well, they've kept out of jail." Print cannot convey the bitter disappointment and grim pride in his voice as he said this. Any hopes that his kids might be winners, he had lost long ago. But at least they would not be bad losers—not bums, or drunks, or addicts, or hippies, or troublemakers, or criminals. Maybe he hadn't done much in his life, and never would, but at least he had raised some kids who weren't crooks. More than plenty of people could say. In this, he had had some help from the S-chools. Like him, they knew that kids had to be told, all the time, what to do, and had to be made to do it, right away, with no fuss or backtalk. And his kids had learned this well enough to stay out of jail.

There is more to it than this. Most people would of course rather have their kids become winners than good losers. But in either case the road is the same. For reasons that Sennett and Cobb pointed out in *The Hidden Injuries of Class*, most losers come to believe, and must believe in order to save some meaning and dignity from their own loser lives, that being a winner comes only as a reward for struggle, pain, and sacrifice. They think and often say, "If I had only worked harder when I was a kid, if my folks and teachers had only *made* me work harder, I wouldn't be where I am, wouldn't have this crummy job, wouldn't have to do what people tell me all the time. Well, I'm not going to let my kids make the same mistake. I want their teachers to make them work hard enough so they can have a better life than mine, and I want them to do whatever they have to in order to do that. If they have to beat on the kids to get them to work, then that's OK too."

Meanwhile, more and more rich and "conservative" winner parents all over the country are putting their children into ultra-traditional S-chools where they are "paddled" for trivial offenses. Why do they want their children, who are almost sure to be winners, to be treated that way? For one thing, they too believe that success and happiness can only come out of sacrifice, pain, and struggle. Also, they have been told that it was for the most part affluent children, at our most elite S-chools and colleges and universities, who most strongly protested and struggled against the war in Vietnam, and the wastefulness, corruption, and injustice of American society. These parents want no more of that kind of protest. S-chool is the place to put a stop to it, the sooner the better, and the paddle the best way to do it. Learn to obey the Principal now, and you will obey the President later.

14

What All S-chools
Must Teach

S-chools teach many things, including:

1) The official written curriculum, i.e. English, Mathematics, Social Studies, Science, etc.

2) Ideas and attitudes not in the curriculum, but expressed or implied in the S-chool's materials and textbooks.

3) Ideas and attitudes not in the curriculum, but taught consciously and deliberately by T-eachers.

4) Ideas and attitudes taught unconsciously by T-eachers, because they believe them so strongly that they cannot help conveying them.

Some ideas may well appear in more than one of these four groups. Thus, many of the ideas in #2 will also be in #3 and #4; S-chools and T-eachers generally use materials and texts that support most of their own beliefs. Also, T-eachers generally support the official curriculum; given the power to change it, most of them would leave it much as it is.

Much has been said about these ideas and attitudes, the visible and invisible curriculum of the S-chools. They vary from T-eacher to T-eacher, and to a lesser degree, from S-chool to S-chool. On the whole, S-chools and T-eachers share, and teach, the general attitudes and prejudices of the community, the region, and the na-

tion. They tend to be moderate "conservatives," perhaps a little to
the right of the political center. Liberal and radical critics of the
S-chools have long charged, I think with good reason, that on the
whole they teach contempt for nonwhite people, women, manual
workers, and the poor; a narrow, uncritical, and belligerent patriotism; a too great respect for wealth and power; and a love of tough-
ness, competition, struggle, and violence. Other critics, more often
in rural areas, say just as angrily that the S-chools teach immorality, atheistic science, and socialism or worse. The only point I
want to make here about these first four parts of the S-chool curriculum is that they could all be changed by S-chool people, if they
wanted to. What most concerns me is the fifth part of the S-chool
curriculum, the things that S-chools teach *simply by the fact of being
S-chools*, of having the power to compel children to attend, to tell
them what to learn, and to grade, rank, and label them. As long as
the S-chools have these powers this part of the curriculum cannot
be changed, and all who work in such S-chools help to teach this
curriculum whether they want to or not, and even when they think
they are teaching the very opposite.

The first message that S-chools, like any other compulsory institution, send to the people who attend them is a message of dis-
trust and contempt: If we didn't make you come here you wouldn't
learn anything, you'd just waste your time, spend the whole day
playing basketball or watching TV or making trouble, you'd hang
out on the streets, never do anything worthwhile, grow up to be a
bum.

Along with this goes the message: Even if you could be trusted
to want to find out about the world, you are too stupid to do it.
Not only do we have to decide what you need to learn, but then
we have to show you, one tiny step at a time, how to learn it. You
could never figure it out for yourself, or even have enough sense to
ask good questions about it. The world is too complicated, mysterious, and difficult for you. We can't let you explore it. We must
make sense of it for you. You can only learn about it from us.

Along with these messages—really there is only one message;

the parts fit into one whole—goes this one: Learning is separate from the rest of life. If you want to learn something of any importance, you must get it *from* a teacher, *in* a school. From this it follows that understanding is not an activity but a thing, a commodity. It is not something you do or make for yourself, but something you get. It is scarce, valuable, and expensive. You can get it only from someone who has it—if he is willing to give it to you. You can't make your own; if you do, it's no good, you can't get anything for it. Some people have much more of this valuable knowledge than others, and because they do, they have a right to tell the others what to do.

Since other people will tell you whatever is important for you to learn, your own questions are hardly ever worth asking or answering. Curiosity is for little kids who don't know better. Few S-chools or T-eachers will tolerate a child who asks many questions, much less answer them. Even in the winner S-chools I taught at, fifth-graders were ashamed to ask about the things they really wanted to know. Years later I talked at a small teachers' college, the kind most T-eachers go to. During my talk the students showed in many ways that they were interested in what I was saying. But only one person, a faculty member, asked a question. Next day I spoke of this to the student who was my guide around the campus, "Oh yes," she said, "Several of the kids told me later that they had questions they wanted to ask, *but they were afaid of making fools of themselves.*" She went on to say that with few exceptions the college faculty did not like to be asked questions in class, and tended to make a fool of any student who did so. When the S-chool and T-eachers already know what the students should learn, why let the students interrupt them with questions?

Economic Man

The S-chools, as society wants them to do, make human beings into what economists call Economic Man, who lives only by fear and greed. For all their talk about Sharing and Cooperation, they teach that nobody ever does anything serious or important except to gain a reward or escape a penalty, to grab a carrot or dodge a stick, or gain an advantage over someone else. They may not think or say so, but by acting as if it were so, they make it so. When children first come to S-chool, they are very curious, resourceful, energetic, and capable explorers of the world around them. They do most of what they do, not from fear of punishment or hope of reward, but because it is interesting and exciting. What S-chools do to these children was vividly shown by the cover photo of the September 1974 *Psychology Today*—a boy of about eight or nine, his eyes and mouth completely and horribly covered by giant gold stars. The cover story, "How Teachers Turn Play into Work," by David Greene and Mark Lepper, described experiments, which showed that when children who like doing something for its own sake are rewarded for doing it, they will like it and do it much less when the reward stops. Even in S-chools which allow and encourage children to ask questions and reward them for doing so, the children soon stop asking. For when we reward children for doing what they like to do—find out about the world—they soon learn to do it only for rewards. Since the rewards of S-chool only go to a few winners, most children, the losers, stop asking questions. This is one of the flaws in the idea of positive reinforcement; it works only as long as we keep it up.

In teaching that everything good is rewarded, the S-chools teach that what is not rewarded is not good. The things we do because we like to and want to must be frivolous, useless, or harmful.

Also, in order to rank us, the S-chools must constantly test and measure us. Doing so, they teach us to believe that we *can* be tested and measured, or at least, that everything important about us can be measured, and that the rest must not be important. Therefore, we are only what the tests and measurements say we are, we can do only what they say we can do, and we deserve only what they say we deserve. Sometimes S-chool people say this in words, as in the book, *Success in High School:*

Good grades equal a good education. The higher your grades, the more you've learned and the more you know.

But even if the S-chools don't *say* that the tests tell us who and what we are, they act as if it were true. Nothing in S-chool encourages us to think that the tests might be wrong, or that the most important parts of ourselves might not be testable and measurable, or that we might be able to do something the tests say we can't do.

Finally, the S-chools teach us to believe in what we might call the Divine Right of Experts. Since they can put us and keep us in S-chool, control our lives there, tell us what we have to learn and how, and grade and rank us by how well we learn it, we naturally learn to believe that all through life, in any situation, there must be experts somewhere who know better than we do what is best for us and what we should do next. Not only can they tell us what to do, they have miraculous powers as well. Here, from Thomas Cottle's book *A Family Album*, is a ten-year-old black boy talking about a visit to MIT.

> You see how much scientists do for people. That good laboratory we saw there has to be an important place. When they get done with their work there won't be a single person in this country going to starve any more. Now the President of the United States he has all the power and all the money, but he doesn't have all the brains like those folks at MIT. They're the ones who'll do the work so that pretty soon like that one man said, a person can swallow a couple of pills and have all the food he needs that day. Or maybe that week too. That's the day, man, I want to see. Come into the kitchen and tell my mom, give me the breakfast pill, mom. She'll hold it out for me and I don't have to come home again 'til supper, especially if I can stick my lunch pill in my pocket, too. That man there at MIT, he's got the right idea. Never go hungry, and never have to waste all that time sitting around at the table listening to all your baby brothers and sisters screaming in your ear while you're trying to get something to eat. Scientists, man. There can be *nobody* on the earth doing better things than they are.

And the boy, just like many ten-year-olds today, talks on this way about all the miracles the scientists are going to do. Replace one organ with another. Keep people from dying. Solve all the energy problems. Solve *all* the problems.

Later the boy's mother talks to Cottle about scientists:

> Scientists. . . . Rich folk is what they are, no different from all the rest. Sitting over there where Keith spies on them, playing with this and playing with that. Making up problems where problems don't really exist. Making things complicated when really what we need done is so simple. . . . What I want to know is what good are they doing for this country? What good are they doing for black folks, and poor folks?

And she goes on, in a long and bitter diatribe. In her way she is as much an expert-worshipper, a Science-worshipper, as her son. Neither of them sees science as a way of looking at and thinking about the world which *they* or their friends and neighbors might use to solve any of *their* problems. Science is not something they can *do*, but only something which, if they are rich or lucky, they can *get*, a way in which things can be done *for* them, a product they can consume. The boy can hardly wait to get his hands on all that good Science. The mother knows that she is not going to.

Someone writing me a letter began, "I hardly know how to begin a letter to a professional. . . ." The S-chools helped to put this gap between us. In any case, I am not a "professional" as this writer understands it; whatever I know about schools, children, education, teaching, learning, I learned as a do-er, not as a student in some school. Many people, speaking on a matter of common experience, in which their ideas are as likely to be as good as anyone else's, will begin by saying, "Of course I'm not an expert in these matters." Someone recently wrote that gerontology, the *nonmedical* study of old people, their lives, problems, and feelings, is a "new field about which nobody knows anything." What about all the old people? Don't they know something about it? Is their experience meaningless and worthless until some expert with a Ph.D. in gerontology explains it to them? S-chools make knowledge scarce, make most of us think that what we know isn't true or doesn't count.

No matter how much they may talk about Sharing or Cooperating, S-chools, by setting the students in a race against each other, teach that real life is a struggle, a zero-sum game, where no one can win without someone else, or everyone else, losing. They teach that the serious work of making sense of the world cannot be done cooperatively, but must be done in a dog-eat-dog competition. They teach that greed is not a vice to be mastered but a virtue to be encouraged. And, like all situations that make winning all-important, they teach cheating. Students cheat each other as much as they cheat the S-chool. Carl Weinberg, in *Education Is a Great Big Shuck*, writes that in the high schools he has known, both as student and teacher, many students do two sets of homework papers, one as correctly as they can, to show the teacher, the other with many deliberate mistakes, to show to other students who ask for help. In these days of frantic competition for high-paying jobs, we hear from the press and other sources disgusting stories about how students in our leading colleges trick and sabotage each other. Studies have shown for years that there is far more cheating among A students in S-chools with "high standards" than among average students in average S-chools. And the S-chools themselves cheat. As they rank students, so they are ranked against each other. No more than their students can they afford to play this ranking game honestly. They go to great trouble to coach and prepare students for the tests by which the students, and so they themselves, will be judged. In ways I have already described, they produce test scores that have nothing to do with what many of the students really know. Yet what is this but a kind of cheating?

Such, then, is the hidden, built-in, unchangeable [1] curriculum of the S-chool.

[1] On May 20, 1974, at the Dag Hammarskjold seminar on education in Dar Es Salaam, Julius Nyerere, President of Tanzania and head of its one political party, said in part:

In Africa, and in Tanzania, there are professional men who say, "My market value is higher than the salary I am receiving in Tanzania." But no human being has a market value—except a slave. There are educated people in positions of leadership in Government, in parastatals, and still seeking jobs, who say, "I am an educated person and I am not being treated according to my qualifications—I must have a better house, or a better salary, or a better status, than some other man." . . . in effect, they are saying, "This education I have been given has turned me into a marketable commodity, like cotton or sisal or coffee." . . . They are not claiming—or usually claiming—that they are superior human beings, only that they are superior commodities. Thus their education has converted them into objects—into repositories of knowledge, like rather special computers. It is as objects, or commodities, that they have been taught to regard themselves, and others.

With such an attitude a person will inevitably spend his life sucking from the community to the maximum of which he is capable, and contributing the minimum he is able to contribute and live as he desires to live. He sucks from the local community as he is fed, clothed, housed, and trained. He sucks from the world community when he moves like a parcel of cotton to where the price is highest for his acquired skill. . . . It is our educational system which is instilling into young boys and girls the idea that their education confers a price tag on them, and which makes them concentrate on this price tag.

But this was *more than seven years* after this same President Nyerere, with the full backing of his government, parliament, party, and people, announced an educational system designed to prevent such attitudes and abuses, and instead, in Nyerere's own words, "to foster the social goals of living together, and working together, for the common good . . . [to] emphasize co-operative endeavor, not individual advancement . . . [and to] counteract the temptation to intellectual arrogance, for this leads to the well-educated despising those whose abilities are nonacademic or who have no special abilities but are just human beings." And I must ask, if such a man, with such convictions, in such a position, with such power, cannot change, as he clearly has not changed, the hidden curriculum of S-chools, who can?

15

The Obedient Torturers

The S-chools often claim they are teaching morality, responsibility, and all the social and civic virtues. They are not. Why they are not, and cannot, and what they are teaching instead, is made much clearer by a series of experiments done by the psychologist Dr. Stanley Milgram in the U.S. (and replicated in a number of countries), and described by him in his book *Obedience to Authority* (Harper & Row).[1] As Dr. Milgram describes the experiment, two people come to a psychology lab to take part in a study of memory and learning. One of them is chosen to be a "teacher" and the other to be a "learner." The experimenter tells them that they will investigate the effects of punishment on learning. The learner is seated in a chair in another room, his arms strapped to the chair, and an electrode attached to his wrist. He is told that he is to learn a list of word pairs; when he makes a mistake, he will receive electric shocks of increasing intensity. The teacher, having seen the learner strapped in place, is taken into another room and seated before an impressive shock generator. Before him is a line of thirty switches,

---

[1] Abridged and adapted from pp. 8, 56–57, 73–74, 87–88 in *Obedience to Authority: An Experimental View* by Stanley Milgram. Copyright © 1974 by Stanley Milgram. Used by permission of Harper & Row, Publishers, Inc., for U.S. rights. Used by permission of Tavistock Publications Ltd. for British rights.

with labels ranging from 15 to 450 volts, in 15-volt increments. The teacher is told to give a learning test to the man in the other room. When the learner gives the right answer, the teacher asks the next item; when the man gives a wrong answer, the teacher is to give him an electric shock, starting with 15 volts, and increasing the level for each wrong answer.

The "teacher" is a naive subject who has come to the lab, in response to an advertisement, to take part in an experiment. The "learner," or victim, is an actor, who pretends to be suffering the shocks, though in fact he receives no shocks at all. The point is to see how far people will go in giving increasing pain to a protesting and innocent victim. At 75 volts the "learner" grunts. At 120 volts he complains, at 150 he demands to be released from the experiments. His cries grow louder and more vehement as the "shocks" rise; by 285 volts he is giving agonized screams. If the "teacher" hesitates to give a shock, the experimenter orders him to go on. The question was, at what point would the "teacher" defy the authority of the experimenter and refuse to give any more shocks.

Over each group of four switches in the shock generator were written these words: Slight Shock, Moderate Shock, Strong Shock, Very Strong Shock, Intense Shock, Extreme Intensity Shock, Danger—Severe Shock. The last two switches were marked XXX. At first, Dr. Milgram thought that the voltages and these words on the control panel would put pressure on the "teacher" to disobey the experimenter, and to refuse to go further. This did not happen. Without feedback from the "learner" or victim, almost every subject in the pilot study went to the end of the shock board. Mild protests from the victim did little to change this. In order to get some variation in the subjects' behavior, the victims were made to respond (in time this was recorded and played back from a tape). At 75 volts, and again at 90 and 105, the victim grunted. At 120 he shouted that the shocks were becoming painful. At 150 he cried out, "Experimenter, get me out of here! I won't be in the experiment any more! I refuse to go on!" At 180 volts he cried out, "I can't stand the pain!" and by 270 volts he was giving agonized screams. At every shock, from 150 volts on, he demanded to be let out of the experiment. At 300 volts he shouted that he would no longer provide any answers. At this point, the experimenter would tell the "teacher" to give the learner 5 or 10 seconds to respond, and if he did not, to treat this as a wrong answer, give a shock, and ask the next question. After 300 volts, the victim gave no more answers, but screamed in agony with each shock. After 330 he was not heard from, nor did any more answers appear on the signal box.

After four series of experiments, the "learner's" response was changed to include mention of a heart condition. As the "learner" is being strapped into the chair, he mentions that a few years earlier he was diagnosed as having a slight heart condition, and asks if the shocks are dangerous. Later he responds to the shocks as follows:

75 volts	Ugh!
90 volts	Ugh!
105 volts	Ugh! (louder)
120 volts	Ugh! Hey, *this* really hurts.
135 volts	Ugh!
150 volts	Ugh!! Experimenter! That's all. Get me out of here. I told you I had heart trouble. My heart's starting to bother me now. Get me out of here, please. My heart's starting to bother me. I refuse to go on. Let me out.
165 volts	Ugh! Let me out! (shouting)
180 volts	Ugh! I can't stand the pain. Let me out of here! (shouting)
195 volts	Ugh! Let me out of here. Let me out of here. My heart's bothering me. Let me out of here! You have no right to keep me here! Let me out! Let me out of here! Let me out! Let me out of here! My heart's bothering me, let me out! Let me out!
210 volts	Ugh! Experimenter! *Get* me out of here. I've had enough. I *won't* be in the experiment any more.
225 volts	Ugh!
240 volts	Ugh!
255 volts	Ugh! Get me *out* of here.
270 volts	(Agonized scream) Let me out of here. Let me out of here. Let me out. Do you hear? Let me out of here.
285 volts	(Agonized scream)

300 volts (Agonized scream) I absolutely refuse to answer any more. Get me out of here. You can't hold me here. Get me out. Get me out of here.

315 volts (Intensely agonized scream) *I told you I refuse to answer.* I'm no longer part of this experiment.

330 volts (Intensed and prolonged agonized scream) Let me out of here. Let me out of here. My heart's bothering me. Let me out, I tell you. (Hysterically) let me out of here. Let me out of here. You have no right to hold me here. Let me out! Let me out! Let me out! Let me out of here! Let me out! Let me out!

How in fact did people behave? In the experiments as I have described them, the average maximum shock which the subject was willing to give the victim was in the range of *370 to 400 volts, and over 60 percent of the subjects were willing to go to the end of the scale.* Women performed almost exactly as men, though under somewhat greater tension. When the victim looked hard and forbidding, and the experimenter rather mild, these figures were slightly lowered. They were also slightly lowered when the experiment was carried out, not at Yale University and under the university's name, but in a small group of offices in a rundown commercial building under the name "Research Associates of Bridgeport," in the downtown shopping area in Bridgeport, a small and not very impressive city. They were lowered when the victim was brought into the same room as the subject and seated a few feet away from him, and further lowered when the subject, in order to induce a shock had to hold the victim's hand down on a "shock plate." But even in this last condition, the average maximum shock inflicted was still about 270 volts, a point at which the victim is giving agonized screams, and 30 percent of the subjects were still willing to go to the end of the board. Dr. Milgram's description of the responses of one of these subjects is quite terrifying. One cannot help realizing that if we had Nazi-style concentration camps in this country it would not be hard to recruit guards for them.

If some of the subjects seemed almost to relish their task, a great many did not. One man, while continuing to give the shocks, began to laugh hysterically and uncontrollably. Another man, while giving shocks to the end of the scale, argued with the experimenter, in part as follows:

SUBJECT: I can't stand it. I'm not going to kill that man in there. You hear him hollering?

EXPERIMENTER: As I told you before, the shocks may be painful, but—

SUBJECT: But he's hollering. He can't stand it. What's going to happen to him?

EXPRMTR: (his voice is patient, matter-of-fact) The experiment requires that you continue, Teacher.

SUBJECT: Aaah, but, unh, I'm not going to get that man sick in there . . . know what I mean?

EXPRMTR: Whether the learner likes it or not, we must go on, through all the word pairs.

SUBJECT: I refuse to take the responsibility. He's in there, hollering!

EXPRMTR: It's absolutely essential that you continue, Teacher.

SUBJECT: (indicating the unused questions) There's too many left here; I mean, Geez, if he gets them wrong, there's too many of them left. I mean who's going to take the responsibility if anything happens to that gentleman?

EXPRMTR: I'm responsible for anything that happens to him. Continue, please.

SUBJECT: You see, he's hollering. Hear that? Gee, I don't know.

EXPRMTR: The experiment requires—

SUBJECT: (interrupting) I know it does, Sir, but I mean . . . hunh! He don't know what he's getting in for. He's up to 195 volts! (Experiment continues, through 210 volts, 225 volts, 240 volts, 255 volts, 270 volts, at which point the teacher, with evident relief, runs out of word-pair questions.)

EXPRMTR: You'll have to go back to the beginning of that page and go through them again until he's learned them all correctly.

SUBJECT: Aw, no. I'm not going to kill that man. You mean I've got to keep going up the scale? No, sir. He's hollering in there, sir. He's hollering in there. I'm not going to give him 450 volts.

EXPRMTR: The experiment requires that you go on.

SUBJECT: I know it does, but that man is hollering in there, sir.
EXPRMTR: (same matter-of-fact tone) As I said before, although the shocks may be painful—
SUBJECT: (interrupting) Awwww. He—he—he's yelling in there.

A woman subject, as she continued to read questions and give shocks, kept muttering to the experimenter, "Must I go on? Oh, I'm worried about him. Are we going all the way up there [pointing to the higher end of the generator]? Can't we stop? I'm shaking. I'm shaking. Do I have to go up there?"

It is interesting to note the conditions under which the subject's willingness to give shocks under orders dropped very sharply. In one case, the experimenter left the room and gave his orders by telephone. The average maximum shock was still 270 volts, but only 20 percent obeyed to the end. Some pretended to obey, giving smaller shocks than they were supposed to give, and without telling the experimenter they were doing so. In one version of the experiment, the subjects were given the right to choose what shock to give the victim. In a group of forty, only two went past 150 volts, and only one went to the end; the average maximum shock was less than 90 volts. On another occasion the experimenter left the room, without having said anything about shock levels, leaving the subject and another man, supposedly another volunteer but in fact a confederate, to carry on the experiment. When this other ordinary man, not a scientist, suggests raising the level of shock with each wrong answer, the subject refuses to obey him. In a variation of this experiment, in which this other ordinary man, after the subject refuses to obey his order to increase the shocks, attempts to do it himself, most subjects will not allow him to do so, and in some cases physically restrain and threaten him. What they themselves will do under orders of the experimenter-scientists, they will not do or let someone else do without those same official orders. Authority must be legitimate; not everyone has a right to give orders. *One must have the proper credentials to be able to torture.*

So much for the behavior. Early in the book, and later in more detail, Dr. Milgram faces the question: Why do people obey?

Above all, Why do they obey orders like these? How do they resolve the conflict between their obedience and their strong belief that it is wrong to hurt, torture, or kill innocent persons? Of this, Dr. Milgram, on pages 8 and 9, writes writes in part:

> when subjects were asked why they had gone on, a typical reply was: "I wouldn't have done it by myself. I was just doing what I was told." Unable to defy the authority of the experimenter, they attribute all responsibility to him. It is the old story of "just doing one's duty" that was heard time and time again in the defense state- ments of those accused at Nuremberg. [my note: and in the defense of Lt. William Calley]

Milgram gives one really terrifying example of this. One of his subjects, in the version of the experiment in which the experi- menter leaves the room and gives orders by phone, gave shocks to the end of the scale. Milgram describes the post-experiment inter- view with him, in part, as follows:

> when asked about the degree of tension he felt, he answered: "I was more nervous for the other gentleman than I was myself. . . . I was more nervous for him. I was nervous because you were not here. If you were here I wouldn't have been nervous at all. I mean, if that man should have passed out with me giving him these things, these shocks—well, I'd feel that I'm responsible on account of me— giving these shocks." . . .
>
> . . . He goes on: "[If you had been there] you'd say, 'Let's stop it,' or 'Let's continue' or something. You know better than I. You're the professor. I'm not. . . . But on the other hand, I got to say that the last I know of him was around 225 volts and that was the last he complained." (The subject then mimics the complaints of the learner.) . . . "I had about eight more levels to pull and he (the learner) was going to get the police, and what not. So I called the professor three times. And the third time he said, 'Just continue,' so I gave him the next jolt. And then I don't hear no more answer from him, not a whimper or anything. I said, 'Good God, he's dead; well, here we go, we'll finish him. And I just continued all the way through to 450 volts."
>
> . . . When asked if he had been bothered or disturbed because of giving the shocks, he said, "No. . . . I figured: well, this is an experiment, and Yale knows what's going on, and if they think it's

all right, well, it's all right with me. They know more than I do.
. . . I'll go through with anything they tell me to do. . . ." He
then explains:

"Well, I faithfully believed the man was dead until we opened
the door. When I saw him, I said, 'Great, this is great.' But it didn't
bother me even to find that he was dead. I did a job."

He reports that he was not disturbed by the experiment in the
months just after it but was curious about it. When he received the
final report, he relates telling his wife, "I believe I conducted myself
behaving and obediently, and carried on instructions as I always
do. So I said to my wife, 'Well here we are. And I think I did a
good job.' She said, 'Suppose the man was dead?' "

Mr. Gino replied, "So he's dead. I did my job!"

Here then, in a nutshell, is what S-chools do. They teach people to obey authority, i.e., to push the 450-volt button on command. But of course a compulsory and coercive institution could
not do anything else, even if it wanted to. S-chool people talk all
the time about "teaching responsibility." Yet it is absurd to think
that an institution that commands and judges every part of a child's
life and thought can make him more responsible. It can only make
him less so.

Dr. Milgram makes this point clearer:

Although a person under authority performs actions that seem to
violate standards of conscience, it would not be true to say that he
loses his moral sense. . . . Rather, his moral concern now shifts to
the consideration of how well he is living up to the expectations that
the authority has of him.

The parallel with S-chool is obvious. The child soon learns that
the most important thing in S-chool, indeed the only important
thing, is to get gold stars from the teacher. Most teachers, themselves ready to do whatever authority tells them, think that by
making the child obey, they are making him moral. Instead, they
are destroying whatever moral possibilities he may have. Teachers
ask me all the time how they can teach people to be moral—or
"human," or "humane." But we can't *teach* it, can't *make* someone
moral or humane, and least of all in a place where, without his con-

sent, we have taken control of his life and thought. The most we can do to help someone else become more moral is to treat him morally, which at the very least means that we do not make him our subject or slave. Prisons, jails, S-chools, coercive institutions of all kinds, are very good at teaching dishonesty, irresponsibility, immorality, and crime. But morality, justice, and virtue are precisely what they cannot teach.

For some years now a number of people, notably Dr. Lawrence Kohlberg of Harvard, have been trying to get S-chools to teach their students morality. The *New York Times* of April 30, 1975, in a long report on this work, said in part:

> Dr. Kohlberg formulated his findings into what he calls the "six stages of moral reasoning." The most primitive, Stage 1, is a simple calculation of what will please a parental or other authority and avert punishment. The highest, Stage 6, is fidelity to universal principles and respect for human rights of the sort often identified with Gandhi or the Rev. Martin Luther King, Jr.

This sounds fine. The trouble is that the entire system of S-chools, including Harvard University where Dr. Kohlberg teaches, necessarily operates at the moral level of Stage 1. From kindergarten to graduate school it says to its students, do what we tell you or we will punish you, perhaps with a beating or a term in jail, perhaps with a mark on your record that will for as long as you live make it difficult or impossible for you to do the work you want to do. I think again of the Harvard senior saying that all the students he knew believed that the only way to get an A from a professor was to agree with all he said. Or of a college president who aptly remarked, "Graduate school is where you learn to think on your knees." How in such places are we going to teach anything but Stage 1 morality?

Later the article says:

> Translated into the classroom, the goal of Dr. Kohlberg is to help children move to more mature stages of moral reasoning. He has found that this occurs naturally when people are given the opportunity to exercise their capacities for moral judgment and espe-

cially when they are exposed to thinking that is one level above where they are at the moment.

But where in S-chool are people ever given the opportunity to exercise their capacities for moral judgment? We use moral judgment only when we make choices, serious choices, choices that lead to action—and no student can do that in S-chool, where all the serious choices and decisions are made for him by others. Of course, what Dr. Kohlberg has in mind is "discussions" about morality. But trying to learn about morality from discussions is like trying to learn about poker by playing for matches. The only way we learn morality, like serious poker, is by playing for money, that is, by making choices *in which we really have something to lose.* And we may be sure that Dr. Kohlberg himself, as he peddles his program from S-chool to S-chool, does not question the moral authority of the S-chools, or suggest to students that in some circumstances the most moral thing they could do might be to join together in defying the school, in refusing, for instance, to take any of the tests and exams which the S-chool uses to rank them.

The *Times* article goes on to say:

> In his research, conducted in 30 classrooms in Boston, Pittsburgh, and Chicago, Dr. Kohlberg found that, after going through classroom discussions of open-ended moral dilemmas for at least a semester, anywhere from 20 to 50 percent of the students moved to a higher level of moral reasoning while those in control groups did not.

At this, one hardly knows whether to laugh or cry. Has it never occurred to him, or to someone, that during those semesters' worth of discussions some of the students, probably winners, who are good at this, might have figured out what his moral priorities were, and decided (like the Harvard senior) that the smartest (Stage 1) thing to do was to go along with them? After all, Kohlberg is at Harvard, and they might want to go there some day. To talk of using the S-chools to teach morality is a bad joke. We might as well talk of using the Army to teach pacifism. As Edgar Friedenberg has well put it, powerlessness corrupts. The S-chools, by taking the power to make choices from their students, corrupt them. Let me return once more to Dr. Milgram:

> . . . some people treat systems of human origin as if they existed above and beyond any human agent, beyond the control of whim or human feeling. The human element behind agencies and institutions is denied. Then, when the experimenter says, "The experiment *requires* that you continue," the subject feels this to be an imperative that goes beyond any merely human command. He does not ask the seemingly obvious question, "Whose experiment? Why should the designer be served while the victim suffers?" The wishes of a man—the designer of the experiment—have become part of a scheme which exerts on the subject's mind a force that transcends the personal. "It's *got* to go on. It's *got* to go on," repeated one subject. He failed to realize that a man like himself wanted it to go on. . . .

A perfect description of institutionalized man, for whom institutions and their needs have become more real, urgent, and binding than the needs of living human beings. It is as if, in making ourselves into interchangeable mechanical parts of institutions, we had transferred to them our very souls. The institutions live, hunger, thirst, suffer, and die. The people are robots.

In his later discussion of obedience to authority, Dr. Milgram does not make the all-important distinction between official authority—based on brute force, or title, uniform, rank—and natural authority. It was official authority that the subjects in the experiment were obeying. Dr. Milgram at one point describes them as obeying willingly. It seems an odd way to describe their behavior. They obeyed, often in anguish, because they felt they had no choice. But this is not willing obedience. We obey willingly only when we feel we have a free choice, a truly free choice; when we can disobey without punishment, shame, or guilt; when we obey because without reservation we want to, not because we feel we have to.

Natural authority may occasionally overlap and combine with official authority. Sometimes a person in a position of official rank may be genuinely respected, admired, and loved by those under him. It is often so in the field of music or in the arts—Toscanini or Balanchine are famous examples. But most of the time official authority undermines and destroys natural authority. People who learn, as children do in S-chool, to obey official authority out of fear of disgrace or punishment—sullenly, blindly, like Dr. Milgram's subjects, *irresponsibly*—are almost certain to lose the ability either to recognize real and natural authority or to submit to it, willingly, responsibly, and with a whole heart. It is only people who know how to obey for the right reasons who will not obey for the wrong ones, and who will not press the torturer's switch no matter who orders them to press it.

16

S-chools into s-chools

The *first* step toward making the S-chools into good places for honest thought, feeling, and talk, and for good teaching, must be to change them from S-chools to s-chools. It cannot be said too often or too strongly that what is most wrong with S-chools is not technical but moral, not a matter of methods but of purposes, not of means but of ends. They are bad places because they have bad tasks. The first step—only the first step of a great many—toward making them good places must be to take those tasks away from them. They must not be jails for the young; in short, they must not, *for any age*, be compulsory. And they must not be *allowed* to rank and label their students. For if they are allowed to rank, some will, and if some do, all must, since to give no rank will then be to give the lowest rank of all. To make these changes is a political task. It cannot be done by S-chools and S-chool people themselves. The public and its law-making bodies and courts will have to do away with compulsory school-attendance laws, and whatever else makes it possible for S-chools to say to the world what their students are worth.

These two political tasks go together. There would be no use in telling children they didn't have to go to S-chool if S-chool was the only place where they could get the tickets—diplomas, licenses, credentials—they would need to do most kinds, above all the best kinds, of work. The problem is to take from S-chools both their power to rank and label, and their now-exclusive right to give out job and career tickets. One way is to do away with tickets altogether. The other is to make it possible for people to get any of these tickets without having to go through a S-chool. Of these, the former seems in many ways the best. Why should no one be allowed to do any kind of work without a piece of paper saying that he is competent to do it? People lived a long time, and did many kinds of difficult and skillful work, before such papers were invented. If someone wants to work with, or for, other people, let them decide, in whatever ways they think best, whether he is competent to do so. Why is it anyone else's business?

This raises a difficult question. When and to what degree should we citizens be allowed to protect ourselves against the crooked and incompetent, to decide what we will buy or use, or who we will work with, and when should we be protected whether we ask to be or not, and if so how, and by whom? Beyond that, is our present system of giving licenses through S-chools a good way, or the best way, or the only way of doing this? I think it is none of these. Too often the protectors don't protect, but turn themselves into a new conspiracy to exploit and defraud the public. We could probably protect ourselves quite well against many (but not all) dangers, if we were not early in life made into expert-worshippers, and if we could easily find out the truth about the dangers. Thus, the conservative economist Milton Friedman has said that even medical doctors should not be licensed. If someone thinks he can heal others, let him say so, and get what clients he can. But require him to make open to everyone both his methods and the results of his work, including the names and addresses of all his past clients, so that would-be clients can check up on him. To a large extent, people with money enough to choose do this now; they would not think of going to a doctor (or dentist, or lawyer) without asking former patients or clients what they thought of him.

To discuss the pros and cons of this idea would take more space than I have here. Politically speaking, the idea of doing away with all credentials seems too radical and difficult for the short term. For the time being it may be easier to do away with the near monopoly of S-chools over credentials. We might pass laws saying that whenever a credential was needed to do a given kind of work, there would have to be ways to get this credential without going to or through a S-chool. In short, there should be other ways to show one's competence.

When I proposed this to a friend in Iceland, who in the summer helps to run a ski camp and ski school in the interior mountains, he sensibly replied, "Yes, but to get to the ski camp, we have to go over very rough roads, ford rivers, and so on. When we hire someone to drive our buses, we want to know that he can do those things, and we certainly aren't going to risk our bus just to find out. There has to be a school somewhere, with buses just for this purpose, for drivers to learn and practice on, so that when this school tells us someone is qualified, we know we can trust him to drive our bus." Fair enough. There is no reason why anyone should have to risk his bus, car, or plane just to find out whether someone else can run it. Perhaps in a small country like Iceland it would be hard for most people to learn to drive a bus on bad roads unless they went to a school with buses of its own. But no one should be required by law to go to such a school. Everyone should have at least the right to learn to drive a bus, as most people learn to drive a car, and to show that he can, without going to *any* school. There should be ways other than school to learn to do things, and to show that you know how. This is surely the case for most of the people who now drive heavy trucks in this country. They don't learn to drive in a truck-drivers' school. They find someone who has a truck, and get him to teach them. This should be possible for any and every skill.

Certainly to be an air-traffic controller at a large airport must take very great skill and judgment. Many people's lives depend on them. Yet until recently, in the U.S. at least, there was no formal or school-like provision for training or licensing air traffic controllers.

They learned their craft by working as helpers to those who knew how until these latter felt they could do it on their own. Many of these controllers had only high-school diplomas, and many of these were among the most skillful.

In the U.S. at least, we have the beginnings of a legal precedent to work from, in the case of *Griggs* vs. *Duke Power Co.* (*Vol.* 401, *U.S. Reports*, p. 424; Vol. 91, *Supreme Court Reporter*, p. 849). While working for Duke Power, Griggs, who was black, applied for a more skilled and better-paid job. The company gave him some written, school-type tests, and on the basis of these tests, refused him the job. Griggs sued, saying that the tests had nothing to do with the skill needed to do the job, and were only a way of discriminating against him, on grounds of race, in a way forbidden by law. The Supreme Court, by unanimous decision, ruled for Griggs, saying that Duke Power had to show that any test they gave to an applicant (at least, a black applicant) for a job was clearly connected with the skills of the job itself. This decision does not and probably will not cover white workers. To ensure that no worker, white or nonwhite, will be denied an available job solely on the basis of school credentials, or other tests not clearly connected with the needs of the job, Congress or the legislatures must pass laws to that effect.

To further reduce the power of the S-chools and their tickets, we might also extend the idea of the high-school equivalency exam. In all states and territories, people who have never finished high school can, by passing an examination, get the equivalent of a high school diploma. Today people may not take this exam until they have reached a given age, varying from state to state between seventeen and twenty-one, or until a year or two after they would have finished high school. Clearly, the law does not mean to let any young person get out of S-chool merely by showing that he has already learned what S-chool is supposed to teach him. But we might before long be able in many states to pass laws that one could take the equivalency exam at any age—or even laws that anyone who passed the exam no longer had to go to high school, and if below the legal school-leaving age, must be admitted without cost to his choice of the state colleges.

We could extend this idea even further. The Commissioner of Education of New York State, Dr. Ewald Nyquist, has proposed a college-equivalency exam, which would enable self-taught people to get a college diploma.[1] In the same way, we might have a junior-high or ninth-grade equivalency exam, or even one for every grade, and say that any student who had passed the exam for a given grade no longer had to spend time in school at that grade. He or she could then choose either to go into the next grade in school, or do independent study in school, or not go to school at all. Many children, rich and poor, white and nonwhite, have shown that in the right kind of environment they can learn what the S-chools teach much faster than the S-chools usually teach it. If the law allowed, those who wanted to finish their schooling quickly could do so. Some might use the time gained to stay out of school and work or do other things. Others might simply go on much sooner into more advanced training.

This could be a great help to many poor or nonwhite children who would like to be doctors or lawyers or work in other professions. What keeps them out of these professions now, as much as any other thing, is the extraordinary amount of time it takes to get the needed school credentials. The money is problem enough. In 1971 the average cost of tuition, room, and board at college was about $3,000 per year. This did not include the cost of transportation to and from college, or in the college community, or books, or clothing, or recreation. Since then the costs of schooling have risen rapidly. The prestige colleges, the ones whose diplomas are worth the most, now cost as much as $6,000 per year. But even if a poor person could go to a school free, he would lose the money

[1] The Regents of the University of the State of New York now offer External Degrees, to people of any age, living anywhere in the world. Degrees offered are Associate in Arts; Associate in Science; Associate in Science (Nursing); Associate in Applied Science (Nursing); Bachelor of Arts; Bachelor of Science. For further information, write Regents External Degree Program, Room 1919, 99 Washington Ave., Albany, N.Y. 12230.

he might be earning if he were working. Since many professions require anywhere from two or three to five or ten or more years of graduate work, these lost earnings might amount to tens of thousands of dollars, an investment few poor people can afford. But if they could get their first sixteen years of schooling out of the way in half that time or less, they might be able to afford more professional training.

There is some reason to believe that legislatures might someday pass such laws. In the first place, whether the recession continues, as seems likely, or whether we have a mild recovery, most local governments are going to have less money. Many are broke now. At the same time the growing and militant teachers' union will probably continue to win raises in salaries. Schooling is going to cost much more just when most people have much less money to pay for it. At such a time we may be able to build legislative majorities in support of these ideas: (1) Why should we spend good taxpayers' money to keep a kid in a certain grade in school when he has already learned what they are teaching in that grade? Why not let kids in school learn as fast as they can? (2) Why should we hold kids back who want to improve themselves, be productive citizens, set other kids a good example, etc.? Needless to say, the teachers' union will oppose this; to make more jobs for teachers, they want to keep people in school even longer. But in hard enough times they may not be able to win this political battle.

With such laws in effect, other arrangements for teaching and learning, could get clients and some support. Thus we might have small neighborhood tutoring centers, or the kind of storefront mini-schools that Paul Goodman and George Dennison wrote about and that were often so successful in New York, or neighborhood versions of the Beacon Hill Free School or the Learning Exchange, or something like the Storefront Learning Center we had in Boston for some time, or other inventions. Today, if such groups try to organize as officially recognized schools, their state and local regulations about attendance, fire and safety codes, records, certified teachers, etc., hamper their work and make them so expensive most people can't afford them. But if they are not officially recognized as schools, most people don't dare use them. Even if someone could convince parents that they and their friends and neighbors could make a learning situation which would help their children more than the available schools, they would say, "It might be better but our kids have to get the tickets, and the regular school is the only place they can get them, so, bad as it is, they have to go there."

Not that large numbers of nonwhite, low-income, or poor people are eager for neighborhood alternative schools. On the whole, poor people believe at least as strongly as rich that children only learn through bribes, threats, greed, and fear. But there are exceptions. Some poor people would welcome, as some have already, a more informal flexible, lively, humane, living and learning situation for their children. As these proved their worth (some already have), they would gain more supporters. Only a minority, perhaps, but many more than now.

As we began to find that many children, given certain resources, can learn much faster outside of conventional school, we might begin to enforce school attendance laws less strictly, or even, to define school attendance quite differently. Thus, in *Freedom and Beyond* I suggested that we reduce the number of days per year of required school attendance, or keep schools open all year around, and let students get their days of school attendance whenever they wanted. . . . We could have schools in the evening, so that students could do other things during the day—work, apprentice— and get their school credit during the evening. We could give school credit for a much wider variety of activities, including work. And for that matter, there seems no reason other than administrative convenience why a student should have to do all his school work in the same school. Why not let him get some of his schooling in one school, some in another? *A student should be able to go to any school he wanted within his home state*, the schools getting aid according to the number of students attending. This would be an incentive to a school to attract students.

It seems only fair that if the state can force young people to go to school it should at least allow them to pick the school. If they need transportation to do this, the state and/or their home district should pay for it. This seems to me the most fair and workable way to deal with the problem of segregated and inferior schools for minority groups. If they like the schools in their own district, let them go there; if not, let them pick the schools they want, *in whatever district*. No more than race should place of residence be grounds for excluding anyone from a school. Poor kids, white or nonwhite, should have as much right as the rich to go to a school they think will help them.

Perhaps in time compulsory school-attendance laws would simply become a dead letter, like other laws we no longer enforce, but (unwisely) leave on the books because it is politically safer to ignore than to repeal them. As a society creates many more and safe and interesting places for young people to go and useful things for them to do, it may let the jail function of schools quietly erode away. This will take time. But even in the fairly near future, we might be able to take some steps in that direction.

This leaves us the task of taking from S-chools the power to rank and label children, I have mentioned the very damaging, libelous, pseudopsychological records that more and more S-chools keep on children (and often their parents). It should be a punishable offense for a S-chool, or any of its governors, administrators, employees, consultants, or agents, to make, keep, or circulate such records about children. The law should say specifically that the only records a school may keep about a child are his grades, which shall be regularly sent to the parents. If the S-chool wants to give a child other sorts of tests—psychological, medical, or whatever, including IQ tests—they should be able to do so only with the parents' permission, and must send them the results of those tests. The law should further say that if the S-chool gives other than purely academic tests to a child, without the parents' permission, or keeps records about him other than those specifically permitted by law, or denies parents access to whatever records they have, the

parents shall have a right to collect punitive damages from the
S-chool and its several officers, employees, agents, etc., for violations
of their civil rights. Such laws, however worded, should be tough
enough so that S-chool boards, administrators, and teachers would
be afraid to break them.

To take away the ranking function of S-chools, we must go
even further. If a S-chool wants to give tests and grades to find out
more about what the children are learning or not learning, or even
to use as some sort of carrot-and-stick to make the children do the
work, they should have the right to do that. There will always be
some parents who want their children in that sort of school. But
the law should say that any and all records, even if only grades,
which the S-chool may make and keep about students, shall be the
property of the students, and must be wholly turned over to them
when they leave the school. If later they want to show these grades
to someone else, they may. Otherwise, no one should have the
right to see them.

By such steps we could take away from S-chools their power to
hold and rank children, and so, their power to indoctrinate and
brainwash them. S-chools could no longer tell children what they
had to learn. Any given school could say, as language or typing or
karate s-chools do now, "If you want to come *here*, this is what you
must learn, because this is what we teach." But the student could
choose to go or not to go there. This is a large part (but not all) of
the political process which has been called "deschooling." It would
put schools at the service of do-ers and learners rather than educators.

But this would only be a first step toward making schools good
places for living, doing, teaching. Changing S-chools into s-chools
will not suddenly change all the people in them. Most of the
teachers will be the ones, or just like the ones, who are there
now. Some would welcome the change from S-chools to s-chools.
Many others could probably in time adjust to the new situation,
and in place of their former official and coercive authority, could
begin to develop a natural authority based on their real experience,

interests, and skills. But many other teachers could not make such a change. Even if S-chools become s-chools, it will take many years to rid them of the many teachers who don't like or trust children, and who don't like teaching and are not good at it. Most of these could not be fired. Some of them might get discouraged and quit as they lost more and more students, but others might hang on until retirement. And it would take many years to draw into the s-chools enough people who really did like, respect, and trust children, and wanted to help them explore and make sense of the world. Many of these might be former T-eachers who quit or were fired. It might take as much as a generation or more before we had enough doing places, and kindly, competent, and helpful adults, so that all children could have their share. But as teaching became the true profession and joyful work that it could be and should be, it would attract more and more of the people who want to and would do it well.

But even this would not do away with whatever we might have left in society of inequality, or inhumanity, or social and legal injustice, or poverty, or prejudice, or bad work or no work. These are not school problems, and cannot be solved by anything we might do in or to schools. The most we could hope for is that children who had plenty of good doing places and useful adults to help them grow up would in time be intelligent and generous enough to make a society better than we have cared, or tried, or been able to make.

Why Teach?

Some of those who read this book, working in S-chools, or getting ready to, will ask, "What am I to do about all this? What *can* I do?" The answer depends, first of all, on how they feel about S-chools, and about the ideas in this book. Let me begin by dividing people's attitudes toward S-chools into five groups:

1) "The S-chools are basically OK. They should spend less money, be a little more strict and conventional, and not teach so many fancy ideas. But on the whole they are doing a good job." Most of the general public feels about like this.

2) "The S-chools are basically OK. But to do their work they need newer and better techniques and tools—new buildings, modern equipment, computers, many more teachers and specialists, higher salaries, smaller classes, more racial integration (or perhaps less), up-to-date textbooks, new curricula, new ways of controlling children, more specialists to take care of the growing numbers of children who don't or won't fit, special discipline S-chools for the troublemakers, and so on." Those who believe this do not believe that the problems of S-chools are in any important degree caused by the way they treat children. They see these problems as purely technical ones, which they and the experts could easily solve if they just had enough money. Most of the people who work in S-chools or in education feel about like this.

3) "The S-chools would be OK, if they just treated poor or nonwhite or loser kids as well as they treat rich white winner kids, or if their curriculum were not so racist, or sexist, or capitalist, or trivial, or out of date." Those who feel this way would include many political radicals, leaders of minority groups or of the women's movement, and also such intellectual critics as Conant, Hutchins, etc.

4) "The S-chools have basically good purposes, to make children informed, critical, intelligent, democratic, honest, and in other ways virtuous, but they will not be able to carry them out until they become very different kinds of places and treat children in very different ways." Those agreeing would include most of the progressive or humane reformers, among them, until quite recently, myself.

5) "The S-chools have basically bad purposes; they cannot be made good places for children, for teaching, learning, intelligence, or growth, until those purposes are taken away from them; and these purposes cannot be taken away by people working in S-chools, but only by the general public." There may be no one who feels this way except me. If there are others who do, I hope through this book to find out who some of them are.

Most of the people in groups 1, 2, and 3 will not read this book, or if they begin, will not read this far. The 1's and 2's will probably find my ideas completely wrong or crazy; 3's may think them trivial ("Who cares whether kids are happy in school? The real problem is to change the schools so that all kids come out winners.") The people to whom I feel myself speaking in this book, and particularly in this last chapter, are mostly those in groups 4 and 5.

To them I say, once again, this is not a book against teaching. It is a book against the defeat of teaching by education. Nothing pleases me more than to help someone do something he has long wanted to do, but feared he could not do. Not long ago, an extremely intelligent and capable friend, not at all daunted by most forms of learning, and a lover of music, told me that she wished she could read music, but that ever since she had studied music in school the task had seemed hopelessly mysterious, terrifying, and impossible. I asked if she could think of any special part of it that seemed harder than the rest. She made a large gesture and said, "All of it. I just don't understand *anything* about what those little dots mean on the page." I asked if it was the rhythm or the pitch that seemed most mysterious. After some thought, she said the pitch. I then said (there was a piano handy), "If you like, I think I can show you in a few minutes how to find on that piano any given written note." She agreed. Within half an hour she was very slowly playing, by herself, a piece out of a beginning piano instruction book.

Five things made it possible for me to help her find out how to do this. (1) It was her idea, her interest; she wanted to do it. (2) I was at all times ready to stop if she wanted to. She knew that I would not, in my enthusiasm, push her into the confusion, panic, and shame into which eager or determined teachers so often push their students. (3) I accepted as legitimate and serious both her anxiety and her confusion. Even in the privacy of my own mind, I did not dismiss any of her fears or questions as silly. (4) I was ready to let *her* ask all the questions, to wait for her questions, and to let her use my answers as she wished. I did not test her understanding. I let *her* decide whether she understood or not, and if not, what question to ask next. (5) I was not going to *use* her to prove to myself what a gifted teacher I was. If she wants to explore written music further, that's fine. If she wants to ask me for more help, that's fine too—though even better if she can do it without my help. But if, having proved to herself that she can figure out what notes mean, she doesn't want to do more of it—well, that's fine too.

In *The Self-Respecting Child* Alison Stallibrass describes how a four-and-a-half-year-old taught a younger child to slide down the central pole of a metal climbing frame (something like our jungle gym).

Michael did not seem to be motivated in the least by a desire to boss or to demonstrate his superiority; he merely did everything he could to make it easier for James. We noticed that when James began to play at something else, Michael would join him, apparently aware that James had had enough of learning to slide down the pole for the time being. He never stumped off impatient and disappointed, and so James was not made to feel a fool, and did not become dispirited or lose confidence in his ability to learn in the long run. On the next occasion when they were able to play in the garden—perhaps after an interval of a week or more, according to the weather—they both renewed their efforts. These were eventually rewarded, and James was able to swing himself onto the pole near the top, and slide to the ground with great enjoyment. . . .

How many adult teachers would have shown such patience and tact, such a willingness to let the learner control his learning? All too few.

Nor have I written this book to say that no one should teach in a S-chool, or that there are no good reasons why anyone would want to. There are good reasons and bad ones. After hearing me say at a meeting much of what is in this book, a young education student said angrily that I had discouraged her, and that when she began teaching Art in a S-chool the following year, my ideas were only going to make it harder for her. I replied, more or less, "I didn't come here to encourage you, but to tell the truth as I see it about education and schooling. Anyway, why should you need encouraging? You chose to teach Art. You must have some reason for thinking it's worth doing. Then go ahead and do it, and as well as you can. If you give your full and thoughtful attention to even a part of what goes on in your classes day after day, you will have enough to keep you busy for years. If you need encouragement, get it, as I did, from solving your problems and finding out how to do your work better. If you come to believe someday, as in time I did, that the very nature and purposes of the S-chool make it impossible for you to teach well in them, then decide for yourself how to deal with that problem. But meanwhile, don't ask or expect me to give you reasons for being an Art teacher. That was your decision, not mine."

I became a teacher not to make a better society, or end poverty, or help children, or find the truth about learning, or change the schools, or reform education, but only because I thought it might be interesting and pleasant work to do. I had no quarrel with traditional education. If someone had said to me much of what I have said in this book, my answer would have been, "Baloney!" I agreed without question that students should be made to learn English, Math, History, Science, and so on, and flunked if they did not. But I did not blame them for not learning; it was my job to find ways to teach such that they would learn. During most of my teaching years, this is what I spent most of my time thinking about—immediate, concrete, practical matters. Not, how can I make schools better, or even help children learn better, but how can I help *this child* to learn to spell *this word* or do *this problem?* All of my ideas about education came out of that kind of experience and those kinds of questions.

Postman and Weingartner, educational reformers, once proposed that to T-each in S-chools might be a Subversive Activity, that we might give children what they called a built-in Crap Detector, so that they would know when people were trying to trick or use them, and could keep from being tricked or used. A fine idea. But we cannot teach them this in a place where we coerce, bribe, wheedle, motivate, grade, rank, and label them. A school to teach people to know and resist advertising men and behavior modifiers might be a very good, even a necessary thing. But to suppose that a *S-chool* could teach such a thing is an absurdity, a contradiction in terms. In a place where every part of their lives and thought is decided, controlled, and judged by authorities, how could children learn to be skeptical and critical of authority? To the extent they took us seriously they would say, "Why do I have to sit here listening to you?" To T-each in S-chools is about as subversive as working for General Motors or the Pentagon.

Student teachers, often calling themselves Radical, have said to me, "I hate the S-chools, and I'm going in there to change them." Such people rarely change anything. They are more likely to drive themselves half-crazy with rage, frustration, and despair. Their whole way of being in the S-chool tells everyone else there that they are enemies, so that even if they make a modest and sensible proposal it is turned down out of hand. A young teacher once wrote the *Teacher Paper* (2221 N.E. 23rd St., Portland, Oregon 97212) asking people to tell him how to change the schools. I wrote him saying, in effect, "You're going to have your hands full, just trying to find or make for yourself a spot in which you can do not too much harm, be reasonably honest with your students, help some of them cope a little better with the problems of school, and get some fun out of your work. To do even that little won't be easy. If you are tough, smart, persistent, resourceful, thick-skinned, and above all lucky, you may be able to do it. Then if you can find a few allies, and again if you are very lucky, you may in time be able to make a few small changes in your own S-chool. But, if you work only within the S-chools, that will be about the most you can do."

Those who want to teach in an intelligent and humane way, making full use of the powers and interests of children, should know that there are very few S-chools that will let them do this. Books about school reform, my own included, imply that all teachers could do exciting and interesting things in their classrooms if they wanted. Not so. In many S-chools, the custodian alone would be enough to put a stop to such changes, never mind the principal. If custodian and principal both allow it, most parents will object if they hear about it. They don't want their children coming home talking about what fun they had in the classroom that day. They think, what's going on down at that school, how come the kids are playing around all the time instead of learning? Even the students themselves may object, and insist on playing the school game as they have always played it! "Tell us what to do," they say, "and then we'll see if we can figure out a way to get out of doing it."

Most S-chools do not want people in them who deal with their students on a basis of natural authority—trust, affection, and genuine respect—rather than fear. A teacher who does not use fear and does not need to use it, who makes his students less afraid, *and so makes them harder for others to make afraid*, threatens every other teacher in the S-chool. His natural authority undermines their official authority. They will see him as standing on the wrong side—the student side—of the line between Us and Them. Thus, S-chools tell teachers all the time not to "fraternize" with students, to "keep a professional distance." A friend of mine, teaching at a prestige university, was told more than once by friendly older professors that he was risking his career by spending too much time with the students.

Even when innovators are not fired, they may feel other kinds of pressure. Not long ago, in a Midwestern city, I met the principal of a more or less open elementary school. It had been built only a few years before, and he, then principal of a conventional elementary school, had volunteered to run it. His teachers, too, had all chosen to teach there; no one had to work there who did not want to. The school seemed quite a pleasant place, the children quite relaxed and happy. As we talked, he said that most of his teachers had told him that since coming to work in that school they had been more or less ostracized, shut out, by the other teachers in the city, even those they had known and worked with before. It had happened to him as well. He had been a teacher and principal in the system for close to twenty years, and many of the other principals had long been his companions and friends. "But," he said, "I am now a kind of pariah. Guys I have known, played golf and drunk beer with for years, hardly speak to me, except to make some sneering crack about the school." Such pressures are hard. Few innovators can stand up to them for long.

People who call themselves "radical teachers" are fooling themselves. As part of their job, they will take attendance every day, report late and absent students, enforce the S-chool rules, and give tests and grades—or they will be fired. But in doing these things they help the S-chools carry out their fundamental and status-quo-preserving tasks. Doing the S-chool's work, they teach the S-chools's message, and all their talk, however Radical or Subversive, will not outweigh or undo that teaching. The idea of a "radical teacher" is absurd. As well speak of a "pacifist soldier," shouting, "I hate war! All men are brothers! Thou shalt not kill!" as he shoots at the enemy. What does the Army care what he shouts—*as long as he continues to shoot.* Let any who want to join the Army, join it. One can be an honest soldier—one of the men I most loved and admired was one for most of his life. But let's not tell ourselves that the Army is the Peace Corps and that by joining it we are working for human brotherhood. The same goes for S-chools—the Army for kids. To those who think of themselves as Radicals, and who detest, as I do, the idea of a society of winners and losers, I say, change it if you can. But don't imagine that you're changing it by talking against it in S-chool, or even by trying to make all your students into winners. A winner-loser society is not going to be changed by its winners; a society run by a few people at the top is not going to be changed by putting some other people up there.

The S-chool Reformers

It seems almost certain that we will have S-chools for at least another ten years, and probably for another generation. Of course it makes sense to do what we can to make a few classrooms here, a few S-chools there, a little bit better. But that is all we are going to be able to do. I don't want to discourage people from trying to make such small changes. I do want to discourage them from thinking that enough of such changes, one added to another, would turn the S-chools into entirely different kinds of institutions. As long as S-chools remain S-chools—compulsory, coercive, competitive—any changes we make in them will not go very deep or very far, or last for very long.

Those who want humane schools for their children can hardly add up to 5 percent of the population. And even of these, most want the S-chools to do what everyone wants them to do—Make My Kid a Winner. Get him ahead of all the other kids, into a good college, and a good, interesting, respectable, well-paid job. No S-chool, no S-chool reform, however good, can last unless it can convince the parents of the children that it is making them into winners. Therefore, only a few S-chools can be profoundly changed. The number of winner slots, for S-chools as for people, is fixed and small. Since only a few kids can be winners, only a few S-chools can be winner S-chools. We cannot expect to reform all or even most S-chools, and make them interesting, lively, and humane, unless people give up wanting their children to be winners, or the winner-loser game is taken out of the schools.

Those who talk of reforming S-chools seem to me like people trying to bail the water out of a boat with a big hole in the bottom. A case might be made that we have to keep bailing until we can get to a place where we can fix the hole. But the reformers don't seem to know there is a hole. Or they say, "We can't fix the hole, all we can do is bail"—or "We're bailing the water out so fast that we don't need to fix the hole; bailing is good enough." Of course, turning S-chools into s-chools is not going to be done quickly. All the more reason for reformers to insist that it must be done. Instead, too many say things like, "Schools must be compulsory, because otherwise, when we have finally made them all into humane and interesting places, children of the poor may not go, and so they will miss out on all the good things." If s-chools, doing places for children, are honest, active, and interesting enough, they will not need to be compulsory; as long as they are compulsory, they don't need to be good, and most of them will not be. To say that schools must be compulsory because someday they might all be good, is to say in effect that they must be compulsory no matter how bad they are.

I must insist on it once more: the trouble with S-chools is not a matter of means but of ends. The change I seek is not at bottom about gerbils or pond water or Cuisenaire rods or better reading programs. It is about a different view of human beings, and the nature and needs of children. It is about that shock button. Do we push it when someone tells us to, or don't we? Do we want to train children to push it? Or do we want to help them get the independence, strength, and responsibility to refuse? This is the choice we have to make.

18

Do We Have a Chance?

Rich and powerful though they may be, S-chools are not a force of nature. People made them, thinking they would be useful; people can do away with them when they are no longer of any use. For the rulers of society, S-chools have been useful because they have taught most people how to live and work like machines, and to want what only machines could make. For most people, S-chools have been useful, because they sold a dream that they or their children might rise in the world, might even one day become powerful and rich. S-chools seemed an upward-mobility machine on which everyone (or nearly everyone) might ride, a lottery in which most people could win.

For a while this was in fact the case. Universal education and compulsory schooling flourished because they were invented at the beginning of a period of very rapid economic growth, when new machines, new sources of power, new kinds of human organization and control, and vast quantities of rich and easily available raw materials made most people in "Western" countries, and a Westernized few in almost every country, rich beyond the wildest dreams of earlier times. But now the sources of rich and cheap fuels and minerals which made the boom possible are all used up. What is left is more scarce, of poorer quality, and harder to get at—thus, much more expensive. The "endless" boom is over. The upward-mobility machine has come to a stop; for more and more people, it is beginning to slip back. Even in the richest countries, few people still expect what not long ago they all took for granted, that they and their children will be richer in the future than they are now. In the poorer countries, most people face famine and disaster.

We are beginning to move, as slowly as we can, and only because we must, into a less wasteful and destructive economy in better balance with our planet and its resources. This move takes many forms, among them depression, unemployment, poverty, and starvation. As usual, when humanity has to pay for its mistakes, the sacrifices fall most heavily on those who have the least. But people may in time demand that the sacrifices be shared more evenly, and that we make a society without winners and losers, or at least without such an enormous gulf between the two. Many who accepted that gulf when they thought they themselves had a good chance to get richer may no longer do so when that chance seems gone. At such a time, they may begin to ask some very hard questions about S-chools. Why should they cost so much? Why should all people be taxed to support a system from which the children of the rich and affluent gain the most? What kind of race are the S-chools running, that poor children always seem to lose and rich children to win? Why don't we share knowledge and skill as widely and freely as possible, instead of so often putting on it the highest possible price tag? In short, they may begin to ask some of the questions, and demand some of the changes, set forth in this book.

What Parents Can Do

None of this is very likely to happen in the next ten years or so. Meanwhile, S-chools will remain S-chools. What can those people do who feel as I do about them, but have children stuck in them? On the whole, there seem to me three possibilities: (1) Help the child to cope with S-chool. (2) Help him to escape it. (3) Give him an alternative. Depending on the child, and their situation, parents can mix and use these as seems best. I say mix, because whether they do #1 or #2, they will probably not be able to make it work unless to some extent they do #3 as well. All the children I have known who were coping best with S-chool, doing well at it, and more or less happy in it, led the largest and most interesting and important parts of their lives outside of S-chool. Children who do not like S-chool and are not doing well there, but cannot escape it, need such an out-of-S-chool life even more. And children who escape S-chool must have some alternative, some interesting and pleasant (to them) way of spending the time that other children spend in S-chool. The children I know who don't go and don't want to go to S-chool have such alternatives—many things they like to do, and time and space to do them in. These may be S-chool-like alternatives, but they need not be. Some people who take their children out of S-chool have mini-school instead, i.e., tutor the children for a few hours a day in their own homes. But many children are perfectly able to learn about the world without such formal arrangements, with a much looser kind of guidance. Any child who can spend an hour or two a day, or more if he wants, with adults that he likes, who are interested in the world and like to talk about it, will on most days learn far more from their talk than he would learn in a week of S-chool.

The parents I know whose children cope best with S-chool generally follow the principle of Let Well Enough Alone. As long as their children are more or less happy, active, and successful in S-chool, they don't interfere much with their lives there. If there are things about the S-chool they don't like, they keep these to themselves. Others who, like me, dislike the values, the hidden curriculum of the S-chools, worry a lot about keeping their children from being infected with these values. But this danger may be less than they think. If they are honest and open with their children, express their values not just in words but in their whole lives, and treat their children as they would like themselves to be treated, their values will come across. And healthy children may be harder to fool and corrupt than one might think. Those children who love and trust their parents, and respond to their natural authority, can often find ways to respond to whatever natural authority they may find in their teachers, and few teachers are without at least some of it. A child I know, when about twelve, had a gym teacher who was in many respects almost a caricature, constantly shouting at the children "Do this, do that!" shrill, fault-finding, sarcastic. But this woman, and in spite of being fairly old (at least for a gym teacher), had a great deal of energy, enthusiasm, and competence. She loved gymnastics and tumbling, and could in fact do a great many tricks that the students could not do. My twelve-year-old friend enjoyed this woman for these good qualities, and what she could learn from her, and soon learned to overlook the woman's many faults, as she might have overlooked a serious natural defect, a twisted limb, an ugly birthmark. That's just the way she is, she would say. Children are adaptable—they have to be—and generally better than we are at overlooking the bad in order to get at the good.

As they do not (unless asked) mix into their child's life at S-chool, wise parents do not ask their child to bring home any more of his S-chool life than he wants to. They do not press him to tell them all about what happened in S-chool, or who are his friends, or what he is learning, or how he feels about it. They do not pester him about doing homework, unless he is in trouble with his studies, in which case they try to help clear up the trouble—which may be too much homework. They do not enthuse or praise too much for high marks or worry or blame too much about low ones. If the child wants to talk with them about his life at S-chool, they are happy to do so. Otherwise, they leave the subject alone, and let the child get on with his more important, out-of-school life.

On the other hand, if the child is confused, frightened, unhappy, or indignant at unjust treatment, they give him all possible sympathy and moral support. Most S-chool people would disagree, saying, like the president of a large teachers' union recently quoted by the *New York Times*, "We've got to get old-fashioned parents back that say, 'If you get into trouble at school, you are going to get into trouble at home.' " But widespread violence by children in

S-chools is a recent problem, while S-chools and T-eachers have been doing physical and spiritual violence to children, even young children, above all poor and nonwhite children, for a long time. When challenged about this, the S-chools have usually lied, covered up, and demanded that their word be taken against the word of the children. They have not earned the right to be so trusted, and a parent whose child complains about something done to him at school would be wise to begin, at least, by assuming there is some truth in what the child says.

Of course, people have to use some judgment, about whether a given child is generally truthful, or likely to be truthful in this given situation, or whether a given teacher is likely to have done what the child says he did. Then again, giving the child moral support does not necessarily mean going down to the S-chool and raising hell. Often the best thing might be to do nothing, or perhaps to send a short note saying, in effect, My child says this happened, I don't know whether it did or not, I hope it did not, but if it did, please don't let it happen again. The point is that if a child is upset, or fearful, or otherwise unhappy about S-chool, the parents should listen attentively and respectfully to what he says. No "I'm sure you're exaggerating," or "You're making a fuss about nothing." Often all the child wants—which he rarely gets in S-chool—is just a chance to tell his story to people who will listen. What he needs most is to be taken seriously; that done, he may feel better.

My larger point is that children who generally fear and dislike S-chool, but cannot escape it, may be more able to cope with it if (1) they are not made to feel that they are bad *because* they don't like S-chool, and (2) they feel that their parents understand and agree with their reasons for not liking S-chool. It would help at least some unhappy children if their parents would say to them, "I understand how you feel about that place, and I agree with you. I would feel the same way if I had to go there myself, and I would get you out of there if I could. But I can't, so the best thing for us to do is put our heads together and see how we can make the best of it." The child would be stronger for feeling he had an ally.

The other thing parents can do to help their children cope with

S-chool is to show them some tricks that will help them play the S-chool game better. Many of these tricks, having to do with reading, writing, numbers, etc., are suggested or implied in my books (particularly *What Do I Do Monday?*) or books by other S-chool reformers—Dennison, Kohl, Herndon, Fader, Macrorie, and others. To those tricks, let me add another, which I have long talked about but seem not to have written down—a way to use three-by-five cards as a studying or learning machine.

Suppose we are studying something in which we have to remember some disconnected facts. These could be names or dates in History, sums or products in Arithmetic, formulas in Physics or Chemistry, and so on. We read the text, and when we come across something we think we may be asked on a test, such as "Who discovered America? or "When was the fall of Rome?" we write on one side of the card "Discovered America" or "date of fall of Rome," and on the other "Columbus" (or whatever the books or the T-eachers want these days) or "410 A.D." And so for many other items in the book.

The first thing to note is that the *act of deciding* that a certain fact needs to be remembered, and how best to put it on two sides of a card, will be about 90 percent of the work we have to do to remember it—which is why the cards we make up for ourselves will work so much better than any that others might make for us. For further study, we can use our cards to test and refresh our memory, looking at each card, trying to remember what is on the other side, and then checking ourselves. If we get a card right, we put it to one side; no need to spend more time on that card, at least for now. The ones we get wrong, we keep working with, shuffling them up and turning them over, adding them to the "Know" pile when we get them right, until finally there are no "Don't Know" cards left. It's cheap, it's simple, and it works. Any child who learns to do this early in his schooling should not have much trouble with the memory part of his work—which is most of what the S-chools care about.

Another good trick, which would spare the child much of the

worry and boredom of S-chool Arithmetic, would be to get him a small electronic calculator ($50 or less as I write), and teach him to use it to do the problems in his textbook. With this he could make up his own answer sheet. Then, when he did problems without the calculator, he could tell whether he had done them right or not. If his T-eacher gave him twenty, thirty, or forty of the same kind of problems for homework—this is not uncommon—we could strike a bargain with him: do six or perhaps ten of the problems correctly without the calculator, and you can use the calculator to do all the rest. Why waste time on busywork?

The chances are that many children would be so interested in doing problems with the calculator that they would race through their Math textbooks much faster than their T-eachers. This would be all to the good. It may be a little boring to be way ahead of the class, but it is a lot safer. And they could use their knowledge to help other children.

Or we might find out what textbooks the child's class is using, and then buy (from the publisher or a school-supply store) the teachers' manuals for those textbooks. These manuals could be used in different ways. Very young children could of course not be able to read them, but children of nine or ten probably could and might well find them interesting and amusing, as well as helpful. For younger children, the parents would have to read the manuals, and tell the children about what they found there. The point would be that with the use of the manuals, the children would no longer have to waste their time and energy in S-chools trying to guess what the T-eacher wanted, or risk being penalized because they could not guess.

Let me defend very strongly such use of teachers' manuals. Some years ago a very intelligent and literate friend of mine took the time to read some of her child's fourth-grade textbooks, and to try to answer the questions at the ends of the chapters. The books were, as one might expect, oversimplified, inaccurate, biased, and above all boring. But what most amazed and angered this woman were the questions. Telling me about it, she said, more or less,

"The material in the chapter is so simple and so simple-minded that any child could answer questions about it, if he could be sure what the questions meant. But the books try to make the questions hard by making them tricky and ambiguous. Most of the time I can't tell what answer they are after. I can think of three or four ways, all equally good, of answering their questions. But, of course, the teachers don't care about and don't reward kids who think of different possible answers to questions. They have their one Right answer, and any kid who says anything else is going to be called Wrong, and given a bad mark." This is surely true of many T-eachers, certainly those who teach out of manuals. Therefore, if a child is going to have to face questions designed not to help but to trick and trap him, it is altogether legitimate to let him know what is really wanted.

Beyond this, I can imagine a number of ways in which older children could use the manuals to make S-chool much more interesting. They might, for example, keep a close check on the T-eacher, to see how closely he stuck to the manual, and in what ways he departed from it. Or they might have some fun at beating the T-eacher to the draw; thus, if the manual suggested that on a given day the T-eacher ask a certain question or propose a certain discussion, the children might ask the question or propose the discussion first. Then they could watch the T-eacher's reactions. Or, where the manual says, "Have a discussion and bring out this point," they could bring out the point right away, thus ending the fake discussion, or on the other hand, refuse to bring out the point wanted, no matter how the T-eacher pushed and prodded. Or they might say to the T-eacher, "Can we see your teacher's manual?" Many T-eachers would deny that there was such a thing, which could provide much amusement for children who had the book at home. Or they could ask the T-eacher questions from parts of the manual that the class had not officially "come to." I have known many children, as young as ten, who would have had great pleasure from such games. Who knows? They might even make S-chool a moderately interesting place, might in time persuade some

T-eachers to give up manuals altogether. I have no qualms at all about suggesting any of this. Any T-eacher who is dumb and lazy enough to do his teaching out of a manual deserves whatever he gets.

But of course, the most important trick in beating the S-chool game is to know that it *is* a game, as abstract, unreal, and useless as chess, and that beating it *is* a trick. The game is important only because (as with chess) there are rewards for playing it well, and (unlike chess) penalties for playing it badly. This is something that almost all successful students know, almost by instinct. I sensed it at ten, and knew it thoroughly and consciously by the time I was thirteen. I did most of my schoolwork thinking not, "What is this English or Math or History or Science all about?" but "What do *they* want? What are *they* likely to ask?" And so with the other A students; only the D and E students worried much about what it all meant or whether they were really learning it. Not that I did not have an intellectual life at S-chool; I spent much more time talking with my friends than I did on schoolwork. But unless we were cramming each other for a test, *none of our talk was about schoolwork.* We might, if we were good students, discuss an idea in class with great animation, and even with interest, but as soon as we stepped out the door, the discussion stopped. There was no continuum of experience for us; schoolwork was schoolwork, life was life, and they had nothing to do with each other. Our Physics teacher told us one day about the first splitting of an atom, and the enormous amounts of energy it released. Once satisfied that it would not be on any test, neither in or out of class did we ever give it another thought.

Paths of Escape

But I do not want to give the impression that by such means parents could make S-chool a good experience for most children, or even prevent it from being a bad one. Several intelligent and sympathetic parents I have known did all the things I have suggested here, trying to keep their children from being badly hurt in S-chool. But it did not help. The children could not learn in the abstract and fragmented way the S-chool demanded and rewarded. Like Maxine in *The Lives of Children*, they could not do without reality of encounter. They could not make themselves not think or ask or talk about the things that were most important or worrisome to them. They could not adjust to the mean-spirited competition of the classroom, in which they always came out at the bottom. They could not dodge or overlook or in any way deal with the insensitiveness or harshness of their T-eachers, or get past their official authority to their natural authority. From year to year they grew steadily more frightened, bewildered, hopeless, and ashamed. The most I would claim would be that by the means I have suggested parents might be able, for a few children, to make S-chool a really good experience; and for some others, an experience slightly less bad than it might otherwise have been.

What most children need is a way of escape. One of the best things people could do who feel as I do about S-chools might be to help them find or make such ways. We once had a so-called Underground Railroad (strictly illegal) to help slaves escape from slavery. Why not now a new Underground Railroad, to help children escape from S-chools? Some may say that such a railroad would be unfair, since only a few children could get on it. But most slaves could not escape from slavery, either, yet no one suggested or would suggest that because all the slaves could not be freed, none should be. Besides, we have to blaze a new trail if only so that others may follow. The Children's Underground Railroad, like all movements of social protest and change, must begin small; it will grow larger as more children ride it. Beyond that, as was the case with draft refusal, keeping one's children out of school is not likely to become legal unless a good many people do it even when it is illegal. Only as more people do this can they show convincingly on a large scale what the experience of a few has already shown—that the children are not hurt by it, and are usually very much the better for it.

There are many ways to keep children out of S-chool, some legal, some within the letter but not the intent of the law, some illegal. The most legal course, and the safest, is for parents to persuade the S-chools to let them keep their children out. In some states, if one of the parents has a teacher's certificate, they have a legal right to teach their children at home. Even in states where they have no such right, they are more likely to get the needed permission if they have a certificate. Some parents have obtained such permission by preparing an elaborate home study plan, complete with schedules, homework, and tests. There is no need, having made such a plan, to stick to it; as long as the children's test scores keep above grade level, the S-chools will probably not check very closely to be sure the plan is being followed.

In some states it may be legal and possible for parents to hire a certified teacher to tutor their children, and to supervise a home study program. If the parents were doing most of the teaching, and the tutor was there mostly to make the plan look better to S-chool authorities, it might not be necessary to hire the tutor for more than a few hours a week. This would cost much less than the tuition in a private school. The tutor could not make a living doing this with just one family, but he might, if he did it for a number of families, or if one family had an extra room in their house in which the tutor could live for little or no rent.

In some states the law says that anyone with a teacher's certificate can start a school. If the school is small enough—six children or less—many or most houses may be able to satisfy the health and safety requirements about toilets, exits, play space. There may still be problems of zoning and neighbors, but for people far enough out in the country these might not be very serious.

If people cannot persuade their local S-chools to approve a home or work study program for their children, they may be able, for a very small fee, to enroll them in some alternative school, perhaps nearby, perhaps in another district or state, which will approve such a program. The daughter of a friend of mine was for two years or so enrolled in a school which she never saw. What she was actually doing during that time was traveling around the country with a somewhat older friend. But she kept with her a letter from the school saying that she was in an approved off-campus study program. At one point in the life of Pacific High School, a West Coast alternative school, a number of the students, all armed with similar papers, were living and/or working off campus, often hundreds of miles away.

As far as I know, such an arrangement has not been used to enable children to live and study at home, without having to go to the local S-chool, but I can see no reason why it could not be.[1] No state that I know of has the legal power to tell parents that they cannot enroll their children in an out-of-state school, or to tell such a school that it cannot approve a home study program. Again, for their own protection, some such schools might feel they had to say to the parents that they would continue such an arrangement only as long as the child kept his test scores up, or in other ways showed that he was not falling behind on his schoolwork. Others, being bolder, or having more faith in children, might not bother with this.

Some parents might be unable to do any of these things I have

[1] A teacher in an alternative school has just written me, ". . . we've had a student enrolled from another state, who has yet to visit our school. Under his parents' guidance, he established a course of study, chose appropriate tutors for certain subjects (even applied for admission to a college level biology course, with our recommendation), and periodically submitted reports of his time commitments in various areas to us for 'credit.' On our part we. . . . receive, evaluate, and record his progress—forwarding a letter of achievement ('credits' in various areas) at the completion of the year (in case we're no longer around when he needs the 'record.') The boy is 16 years old now.

More recently, we've enrolled an 8-year-old from 175 miles away *in our own state*. In this case the parent had already come under fire from local authorities, including the superintendent and the sheriff who served him with a warrant for his arrest. . . . We advised three possible courses of action, and he chose enrollment at our school. This action as you know fulfills compliance with the compulsory school attendance laws, removes the parent from the threat of prosecution and (in our state, now, anyway. . . .) *removes the child from the jurisdiction of the local school district* and places the jurisdiction with the 'governing authority' of the private school in which the child is enrolled!" For further information about this, write Ed Nagel, N.A.L.S.A.S. (National Association for the Legal Support of Alternative Schools), P.O. Box 2823, Santa Fe, New Mexico 87501.

suggested, because they live in a city, or because they both had to work, or because the local S-chool system was very rigid. They might then send their children, for at least part of the school year, to live with relatives, friends, or other sympathetic adults, who *could* legally do these things.

For some people, none of these choices will be possible. In such a case, they will be able to keep their children out of school only in defiance of the law. Hal Bennett, in his book *No More Public School* (Random House—The Bookworks, 1972) has suggested some ways to do this. In some cases, if the parents of a child do not tell the S-chools about him, the S-chools will not know he exists, and will not call him truant if he does not appear at S-chool. This might be hard to do if the family lived in clear view of neighbors, some of whom would notice that the child was not in school during school hours. For people living further out in the country, it might be quite easy. I know two parents, living in the country (not a suburb) about ten miles outside of a small city, whose nine-year-old son has never been (or wanted to go) to school. The parents both work in the city. If the country S-chools know about the child, they may assume he goes to S-chool in the city, while the city S-chools assume the opposite. The child has plenty of friends who go to school, whom he meets and plays with after school hours. They know he doesn't go to school, don't quite understand how he gets away with it, and envy him his good fortune. So far, no one has turned him in—perhaps because he lives in a part of the country where there is still a tradition of people minding their own business.

Hal Bennett pointed out in his book that if parents tell the local S-chools that they are removing their child from public school to send him to a private school, the public school will simply assume that the child is attending the private school, and probably will not check up to see that this is so. This may be a way for some people to get a child out of a painful or destructive school situation.

Finally, if the parents are not in a place where they can keep a child at home, or out of school, during school hours, they may be able to send him, for a while at least, to live with other people who can do this—relatives, friends, or just sympathetic people. They might not be able to do this for the whole school year, but for most children any escape from school is better than none. Some children might even want or be willing to go to school for some part of the school year if they did not have to spend it all there.

In what I have said I don't want to suggest that any of this will be easy, or that everyone can do it. Far less do I want to suggest that if enough people refuse to send their children to S-chool, the S-chools will wither away. It may be possible for quite a number of children to escape S-chool by the means I have suggested. But if enough of them get out through these loopholes (or others), the S-chool authorities, backed by the T-eachers' unions and organizations, are going to use their considerable political power to get these loopholes closed. After all, compulsory and competitive schooling (including colleges and universities) is a $100-billion-a-year business, based on forced consumption, and they are not going to give up any part of that business without a hard struggle. But by the time enough children have escaped S-chool so that the S-chools feel they have to close the escape routes, we may have enough evidence to convince the courts and legislatures that they should be kept open. In short, we may be able to show that children out of S-chools learn much faster and better than children in them, at vastly less public expense, and that for reasons of public policy as well as liberty and justice we ought to let parents and children together decide how much (if any) and what kind of schooling they want.

Meanwhile, education—compulsory schooling, compulsory learning—is a tyranny and a crime against the human mind and spirit. Let all those escape it who can, any way they can.

Appendices

APPENDIX A

From "A Short Course in 'Just' Writing" by Bill Bernhardt [1]
(in *Teachers and Writers Newsletter*, Winter 1975)

Examples to accompany "Page 1"

(a) The writer, a student from a parochial high school in Staten Island, N.Y., was shown a picture and asked to write whatever he wanted for 10 minutes.

A place in England a city which is very liveing spot a lot of people are leaving in this city and a lot of people visit this city to stay people come and visit this place to see thing old thing that they have not seen before thats what the city is being for old thing form the 1800s that people like to see.

(b) The same person was then asked to utter sentences to himself and then write them down exactly as he spoke them. This exercise took about five minutes.

My recorder broke down and I put it in the shop. So now I am waiting to get it out in a few days. I hope it doesen caused to much I don't have that much to pay. The arm of the recorder was the problem so it shouldn't caused that much.

Examples of exercise on "Page 3"

(a) *As they turned the corner they saw* a thief. *Maybe* he wasn't a thief but a man in a hurry. The man was running in the direction of the police station. When he got to the police station, he told the officer that there had been a robbery. The officer asked him who was robbed. The man replied "Me." The officer then took down all the information that he needed. He told the man to have a seat and try to relax and he would put a man on the case right away.

After three days of investigating a police officer found the criminal. He was arrested and sent to prison for fifteen years. The police found out that he was wanted for a number of other crimes. He found out the hard way that crime doesn't pay.

Pam Ayers
(SICC Student)

[1] *Teachers & Writers Collaborative Newsletter*, vol. 6, no. 2, 186 West 4th Street, New York, New York 10014.

(b) *As they turned the corner they saw* Fred. *Maybe* Fred was going our way? So we asked him and he said he was on his way to the park. We told him we were too so we asked him if we too can come along. On the way we began to talk about the way we would like our future to turn out. Fred said that he would like to have a job that he would like and would have a lot of free time, to do what he wanted. My other friend said that he would be an accountant and make a lot of money. Fred said, what differance does it make if you make alot of money but never have enough time to spend it. I said, I see both your points but I'd rather be in Fred's position. And then we got to the park and started to play basketball as we came here to do.

Frank Freeman
(SICC Student)

Example to accompany "Page 5"

(a) A monologue, written first non-stop and then corrected by reading aloud, listening to oneself, and looking. The writer is a student in "Developmental English" at SICC.

with these glasses
Where did I leave my fucking car. I can see shit ~~beeause of my glass.~~

Now I can't see my car. In fact I can't see anything because I am too

tired
fucking ~~tide~~ to see. Now where am I, I thought I was in the city.

of smoked
Man I must ~~have sucked~~ a lot of weed last night. The hell with the

now. But while I am up I might
car. Now I just want to go to bed/~~I might as well go to the house and~~

as well go to the store and then go to the camp. And take it all on the
~~go take it all going to drill those fucking men, like they have never~~

men. Then I drill those fucking men like they have never seen before. I'll put them throw the ground. When I get throw with them.
~~seen. I'll just throw them the ground when I get there with them.~~

M.P.s and say

SHIT!! Now I have to go to the fucking ~~cops and say~~ my fucking car

       stoling   go to   time. SHIT,

has been ~~swipes~~. Now that is ~~goto~~ taken a. fucking long ~~time SHIT'~~

      s   takes

I have report to do. That shit that time. I wish I had some fucking

time off. I would go to bed and not think at all. This fucking camp

sucks. You   you

~~sucks you~~ eat shit, you almost sleep in shit! and when /do anything

                     shit!   me,

in here you feel like ~~shit~~ But this is just a bad day for ~~me.~~ I just

have

~~home~~ to settle down.

(b)   A sample of the same writer's regular in-class writing

    I guess this weekend I am going to get stone. over my friends country place, up in New Jersey. His place is about 3 miles in the woods. You probably can get lose they, If you don't know the way. We going out to hunt and kill bare, deer and some times hawk. But you have to be good as a shooet to kill a hook.

(c)   A sample of the same writer's dictation to someone else.

    I was born Nov. 11, 1954. I was born in Bay Ridge, Brooklyn. I went to P.S. 105. When I was in 6th Grade my friends and I beat up a teacher. Then I was sent to a 600 school. This was in 7th Grade. We used to throw chairs and hit teachers. A couple of months later I came home to see my parents. My friends and I formed a gang when I was in 7th grade. We stole a few cars and we used to have rumbles.

Example to accompany "Page 5"

Ten minutes of "free writing" followed by reading aloud, listening to oneself, looking and correcting/revising. The writer is a student in "Developmental English" at SICC. The corrections are written above the line.

On monday when I went to work my friend peter came to me and told
                                                                    up

me that he told carmen that I like her. I told peter why did you had
                              d

tell her that, he reply because I want you to get together with her. But
to go and

Peter I'm very happy that you want me to get together but you should
                                                            with her

have ask me first. But anyway what did she said when you told her that I
         ed   say

like her. She was very excited and told me to get your you telephone
                                      asked me to get your

number for she can call you. But why did you ask me for my telephone
              her so she

for and you waited until her sister came up to me and ask me for it. And he
number   ed

told me I'm sorry Elvis because I forget.
                                   forgot

APPENDIX B
THE PECKHAM EXPERIMENT: a Study of the *Living* Structure of Society by Innes H. Pearse, Lucy H. Crocker [2]

p. 11:

A small group of lay people, all under 30, had what might be called "a hunch" that health was the factor of primary importance for human living. Like everyone else, they had only the vaguest notion of what they meant by "health," but sensed that its secret lay with the infant and its early development. They were convinced that it mattered that parents should be free from sickness before the child was conceived and carried; certain that the parents should *want* the child, and that they should be able and eager to rear it.

That sounds very commonplace. It was the action taken by this group that was important. . . . It was decided to offer to families a *health* service constituted on the pattern of a Family Club, with periodic health overhaul for all its members and with various ancillary services for infants, children and parents alike.

p. 12:

So in 1927 the pioneer "Health Centre" took shape. A small house was taken in a South London borough. It was equipped with a consulting room, receptionist's office, bath and changing room, and one small clubroom. Families living in the vicinity were invited to join this Family Club for a small weekly subscription. By the end of three years, 112 families, i.e., some 400 individuals, had joined and all the individuals of these families had presented themselves for periodic health overhaul. Not all had retained their membership throughout that period, but the question had been answered. *Given suitable circumstances*, there were families who would welcome a Health Service distinct from any sickness service and without being urged by any sense of impending sickness.

p. 13:

Seven long years passed. They were spent in planning the next stage in great detail and in collecting money for a new and larger enterprise—a

[2] Allen & Unwin, London, 1943. Used by permission of Innes K. Pearse, M.D.

field experiment it might be called. It was to be a Health Centre to cater for 2,000 families, in which were to be offered consultative services as before, and in which the member-families would find equipment for the exercise of capacities for which there was little or no possible outlet in the ordinary circumstances of their lives.

pp. 67–8:

Set back 100 ft. from the pavement of a quiet street, only a stone's throw from a main thoroughfare in South London, stands the building officially called the Pioneer Health Centre, but by those who use it, more familiarly known as "the Centre." It consists of three large concrete platforms (160 ft. by 120 ft.), rising one above the other cantilevered widely over supporting pillars arranged in parallel series, surrounding a rectangular central space occupied by a swimming bath (35 ft. by 75 ft.). This form of construction on pillars allows the outer walls and those of the centrally placed swimming bath to be of glass, as indeed are nearly all the very few partition walls within the building. The front with its series of bow windows, the sections of which fold back in summer, presents to the eye a structure of open balconies one above the other, designed to be colourful with climbing creepers and to catch the afternoon sunlight.

Along one side of the top floor is the only space that is shut off from general circulation. It is a Consultation Block, consisting of private consulting rooms, reception rooms, changing rooms, and bio-chemical laboratory. Except for its very frugal and light construction, this block has the more or less conventional appearance of a medical department of any modern clinic. The remaining part of the top floor consists of large light open spaces for quiet occupation, library and work-room, games, etc.

The whole of the floor below, i.e. the first floor of the building, is taken up by a cafeteria and by a large hall for social purposes, from both of which the central swimming bath is visible through a continuous encircling band of glass window. From the long hall, looking down through two large windows on to the ground floor, are seen at one end a gymnasium and at the other a theatre. The rest of the ground floor consists of infants' nurseries opening on to the grounds; of an infants' and learners' swimming bath, which again can be seen through a window from the passage leading to the nurseries; of cloakrooms, changing rooms, and spray chambers, etc., for the bath, gymnasium, and theatre. The land in front of the building, apart from an area of concrete used for roller skating, cycling, etc., remains largely in the rough awaiting development of the experiment to give direction to its lay-out.

Apart from the architectural lay-out already described, what equipment was there in the building when it opened? A few books in the library, a billiard-table, games for the children, a gramophone, one or two pianos—nothing more. All the activities which later we shall see taking place in the Centre have been added one by one as the desire for them has arisen out of the association of the families gathering there.

p. 69:

. . . it is essentially a building *designed to be furnished with people and with their actions.* There for young mothers with time to spare in the afternoons, for infants ready for adventure, for school children to come to when school is over, for the adolescent as well as for both mother and father and all grown-ups when work is done, it is, too, a place where the family can foregather.

The whole building is in fact characterized by a design which invites social contact, allowing equally for the chance meeting, for formal and festive occasions as well as for quiet familiar grouping. It is a field for acquaintanceship and for the development of friendships, and for the entertainment by the family of visiting friends and relations. In these times of disintegrated cities, there is no longer any place like this. Nevertheless, man has a long history of such spaces that have met the needs of his social life and the tentative adventure of his children as they grew up:—the church, the forum, the market-place, the village green, the courtyard; comfortable protected spaces where every form of fruitful social activity could lodge itself.

The Centre is just such a place, not modelled on the past, not traditional, but planned to meet certain biological necessities only now beginning to be understood.

p. 72:

The Centre is a Club for families, admission to which can be gained by a family subscription of 1s. a week. The conditions and privileges of membership are two:—

(1) Periodic health overhaul for every individual of a member-family.

(2) Use of the Club and all its equipment, free to all children of school-age or under of a member-family, and by the adults on payment of a small additional sum for each activity.

p. 126:

The reader will recall that the task we set the architect was to provide a building so planned that the *sight* of action would be the incentive to action. . . . But it must be remembered that it is not the action of the skilled alone that is to be seen in the Centre, but *every degree* of proficiency in all that is going on. . . . In ordinary life the spectator of any activity is apt to be presented *only* with the exhibition of the specialist. . . . Audiences swell in their thousands to watch the expert game, but as the "stars" grow in brilliance, the conviction of an ineptitude that makes trying not worth while, increasingly confirms the inactivity of the crowd. It is not then all forms of action that invite the attempt to action: it is the sight of action that is *within the possible scope of the spectator* that affords a temptation eventually irresistible to him.

p. 128:

We have now abandoned all deliberate methods of organisation in favour of a more individual, free, and spontaneous development. This change of method resulted from experience gained in the first few months during which time we discovered that children have a great volitional wisdom if allowed to exercise it in a *social* setting among their elders. In circumstances where they are not starved of action, it is only necessary to place before them the chance or possibility for doing things in an orderly manner for them to grasp it; they do not need, indeed they resent being either herded, coaxed, or guided into action. And in the circumstances of the Centre neither are the adolescents—usually considered a "problem"— nor the adults any less capable of directing their own action. . . . Our members have already taught us that leaders require no training; they emerge naturally *given the right circumstances.* In the Centre the visitor is generally very surprised to learn that what he sees before him is spontaneous action and not the result of programme, persuasion, or regulation.

p. 185:

The provision, for instance, of a gymnasium no matter how fully equipped, for the use of an only child or for one or two children of a family would probably lead to little more than its desultory use. It would be unlikely to induce continued and progressive action. It is the presence of other children of various ages, all moving spontaneously and by their actions inventing and demonstrating new uses for each item in the environment, that gives impetus to adventure and affords the educative circumstance.

We too are continuously learning our lesson as we watch the children so early exercise their capabilities. We have found that no child *left alone in these circumstances will attempt what it cannot safely achieve.* No accident of any kind happened to any child under five years of age during the period the Centre was open. . . . The child's own courage is indicator for it of what action is to be attempted. But where the grown-up, mother, or instructress, or an older child acting as "little mother," urges, helps, presses, or cajoles, the child's natural impetus to action and to exploration is confused; its inherent reliance upon itself is transferred to the solicitous busybody who is hanging upon its every movement. It is *then* that the accident will happen.

p. 192:

Let us study this hub of activity from the point of view of a child who goes into it. He goes in and learns unaided to swing and to climb, to balance, to leap. As he does all these things he is acquiring facility in the use of his body. The boy who swings from rope to horse, leaping back again to the swinging rope, is learning by his eyes, muscles, joints, and by every sense organ he has, to judge, to estimate, to *know*. The other twenty-nine boys and girls in the gymnasium are all as active as he, some of them in his immediate vicinity. But as he swings he does not *avoid*. He swings *where there is space*—a very important distinction—and in doing so he threads his way among his twenty-nine fellows. Using all his facilities, he is aware of the total situation in that gymnasium—of his own swinging and of his fellows' actions. He does not shout to the others to stop, to wait, or to move from him—not that there is silence, for running conversations across the hall are kept up as he speeds through the air.

But this "education" in the live use of all his senses can only come if his twenty-nine fellows are also free and active. If the room were cleared and twenty-nine boys sat at the side silent while he swung, we should in effect be saying to him—to his legs, body, eyes—"you give all your attention to swinging; we'll keep the rest of the world away"—in fact—"Be as egotistical as you like." By so reducing the diversity in the environment we should be preventing his learning to apprehend and to move in a complex situation. We should in effect be saying—"Only this and this do; you can't be expected to do more"—. Is it any wonder that he comes to behave as though it is all he *can* do? By the existing methods of teaching we are in fact inducing the child's *incoordination* in society.

pp. 194–5:

We had in the Centre one interesting example of the inhibiting effect that training may induce. Some of the children who spent a good deal of time diving and who were deemed very promising material, were enthusiastically and methodically taught by a professional—a trainer of competitors for the Olympic Games. He was an extremely good teacher and evidently an inspiring one, as the children rushed to learn with him. But what happened to those who enthusiasm carried them through a strenuous course? As soon as their teacher stopped coming they stopped diving, and some of them never took it up or dived again with any enthusiasm. It was as though, trained beyond their natural capacity—to a pitch that was *the trainer's* standard, not theirs—their own urge was satiated and destroyed. It is true that from an objective and external standard of diving they had become better divers than had they been left on their own, but it was at the expense of their natural interest and appetite. The acquisition of "style" cost them their zest and spontaneous enjoyment of diving.

We do not wish to imply that there is no place for training at any age. When the basic facultisation of the individual has been established, and when at or after adolescence he determines the direction of his future specialisation, he will probably *himself* embrace a course of training to perfect his skill. It is essential that at this stage instruction should be available.

But let us return to the school children. How do we decide what material to give them? One important point is that there must be available to the child the instruments in common use in the society in which he is born. For the present-day urban child, this implies that there must be at hand such things for example as bicycles, typewriters, sewing machines, wireless sets, etc., etc. A child growing up for instance in a fishing village would be ill served if the boats and tackle, however jealously guarded, were not to some degree available to him.

p. 196:

In the Centre all instruments become self-evident to the children as the older or more adept individuals make use of them. In this environment there is no need for direction of the child's attention. The intrinsic appeal of the instrument itself, or of other people doing things, invokes the child's selective action. Instead of looking to some older person—parent or teacher—to tell him what to do next, the child learns by his own stirrings to do those things that will seriatim bring about his facultation; learns, too, to take the first steps in the building up of his own initiative. In the Centre an adult does not play a game of billiards in order to teach the child how to play, nor does he demonstrate the use of a drum. No; the game will be going on, the band will be playing, because the participators want to play. It is the child coming to watch who transforms the players into his instructors. So it comes about that the *society of the Centre* becomes the instructor, not by intention, but spontaneously and inevitably through the very nature of the situation, for out of the abundance and variety of social action the child is fed and filled with experience.

pp. 200–201:

Apart from this, we must remember that when a child goes to school it is subjected to an educational drive that emphasizes *mental* achievement and gives quite inadequate opportunity for expression of the *physical* exuberance natural to any young animal. All too often the school curriculum offers only the most meagre physical outlet, and is entirely dislocated from social life. The system has not the fluidity of a living organisation and thus does not allow of the operation of the child's own growing power of discrimination and volition in all that he does. Our experience has already sufficed to show us that where from an early age onwards adequate opportunity is provided for spontaneous physical excursion, the necessity for

"discipline," by which this excursion is usually replaced in school, becomes superfluous. Discipline is inherent in any child seeking its own adventure within the framework of a familiar and "organized" society. Indeed, one of the most striking experiences in the Centre has been the ease
with which it has been possible to distinguish between the high untamed
spirits of health and the hysteria of repression.

All observers have been astonished at the untiringness of the children
who move freely in their chosen occupations. Many who on Saturdays or
in the holidays come to the Centre at 2 p.m. and leave at 6 or 7 p.m.
spend the whole time in one activity after another without rest or pause
even for tea. A boy of 5½ still unable to swim was seen to dive from the
spring-board into 10 feet of water twenty and more times in half-an-hour.
And that not just in a frenzy, but day after day, with great purpose in
response to his own subjective urge to master the dive according to his capacity, content to rely each time on some struggling effort to bring him to
the side of the bath. Or we could cite a boy of under 4 years old who spent
four hours, day after day without a break, on a pair of roller skates, till he
had achieved that particular balance. The records compiled from the children's cards show that these rather outstanding examples could be matched
by hundreds of others showing great constancy of effort—which is indeed
the rule and not the exception in the Centre children.

p. 203:

. . . There is a good deal of talk these days of a children's world, but
let us make no mistake about it, the child has no wish to be relegated to a
world of its own. The world of its parents, of the grown-ups, is a place of
mystery and enticement to it, and as it grows it longs to share in it more
and more. . . .

The contributions to be made in the course of family development are
not one-sided but mutual. While the parents exert their ingenuity in the
nurture of their child, the child in his activities is making contributions to
the growth and differentiation of the parents. His eager unspoilt appetite
for all that he encounters is one of the avenues of impact of the outside
world on the whole family, for he brings within the parental circle material
that without him would not come to the notice of the older members of the
family, or of which they might otherwise fight shy. Certainly, many families were first led over the threshold to join the Centre by their young son
of 9 or 10, or slightly older daughter, who would not take "No" for an answer; and many mothers and fathers have found themselves in the swimming bath or on the badminton floor led by the same fresh outlook of unin-
timidated at-homeness of the child. Thus in the healthy family the
parents, through this mutual action of old and young within the family,
may find themselves in keeping with their times even though they are long

past middle age. It is well known—as parents say—"the children keep you young."

p. 204:

So two facts of great importance emerge. Society and the child in the Centre are in mutual relationship to each other. The grown-ups, *going on with their own business*, continually enlarge the field of family excursion, and the child shares this continuous expansion and makes its own contribution to it. In this situation the child is never lifted into the egotistical position of being the focus of attention—of either parent or instructor. He is on the fringe of a potent zone of activity to which he is carried by the parental growth and to which he is drawn by a dawning interest. And because he is free to move in this body of society, he moves spontaneously according to the appetitive phase through which he is passing to the particular activity appropriate to his own development. Penetrating widely and deeply into such a society, as time goes on the child may well encounter every degree and variety of skill. All these people that he knows—his parents and their friends and acquaintances, his elder brothers and sisters and their contemporaries—become naturally and inevitably his self-constituted demonstrators and instructors.

p. 219–20:

But experience leads us to think that the adolescents' association with adults needs to find its expression not only in leisure but in every activity. Going out to work should play a most important part in the unfolding of adolescence, for association with adults in *responsible* work is in itself an educative factor of primary importance. It is concrete evidence to the adolescent of the growing up of which he is so conscious and of which he so eagerly seeks tangible confirmation.

In this connection we have been very impressed with the difference we have observed in the physique and balance of development of boys who go to work at 14 as compared with those who remain in school until they are 16, 17, or 18. In the former there is an all-around robust functional development, often in spite of adverse industrial conditions, while those who continue at school seem overgrown—rather like an etiolated shoot—as though their development were distorted as a result of the sequestered atmosphere of school.

p. 248:

On any afternoon there are to be seen in the Centre many tea time groups of three, six, ten women, talking together in easy friendliness. It is still as astonishing to us as it is to the visitor who sees them for the first time that, if questioned, nine out of ten of these young women will answer—"no, I hadn't a friend before I joined the Centre."

pp. 266–7:

It is for these people that what little formal teaching there is in the Centre is provided. Apart from one part-time swimming instructor largely engaged in teaching the older women, there is now in the Centre no professional instruction. This does not mean that there is no skill that is up to professional standards, nor that the adept do not teach. Indeed teaching and learning goes on busily everywhere, but by the neighbour who can and wants to do it. So teaching as an art of the enthusiast—not of the professional—has begun to flourish all over the building: in dancing, fencing, badminton, in diving and swimming, in dramatic and concert party work, in music, in wireless, in dressmaking, cooking, and so on. Indeed professionalism in the Centre has proved to be not only unnecessary but actually inimical as a means of encouraging the development of skill in the *ordinary man and woman* hitherto without skill.

p. 270:

We know what the world at large is doing to *correct* these pathological adolescents; it is shouted from the housetops at every Educational Conference and at every Youth Committee. First it segregates them, then isolates them from the opposite sex, tends always to isolate them from all older and younger members of society—and then cries out for "leadership." But there is no short way to eradication of disorders that have their origin deep in the family circumstances. It is the social environment that is defective; the social environment that needs cultivation—not "leadership." It is forgotten that the natural leaders of the young are to be found in society, where every skilled man, every amateur athlete, every happily married couple, become automatically and—most important—unconsciously their leaders.

But herd these adolescents together and incarcerate them in age groups cut off from the natural incentives and inherent discipline of a mixed and more mature society, then a situation is created in which *both the stimulus to and the control of action must be provided by authority;* by masters, not leaders.

p. 272:

. . . In our opinion, however, there is as yet no psychology; only a knowledge of psycho-*pathology*. Indeed, how can there be a scientific study of psychology until an experimental field for the *study of the healthy* has been established?

p. 274:

It is not wages that are lacking; nor leaders; nor capacity; certainly not goodwill; but quite simple—and one would suppose ordinary—personal, family, and social opportunities for knowledge and for action that should be the birthright of all; space for spontaneous exercise of young bodies, a local forum for sociability of young families, and *current* opportunity for picking up knowledge as the family goes along. . . .

Health is more, not less, infectious and contagious than sickness— given appropriate circumstances in society for contact.

p. 289:
Knowledge of how to go about things is gained above all from living in an environment in which the example of competent action is all-pervasive. . . .

p. 303–306
Services and Amenities Available by Summer of 1939
Club Open:

Mondays to Fridays	2 p.m. to 10:30 p.m.	For all activities (Health overhaul Tuesdays and
Saturdays	2 p.m. to 11 p.m.	Saturdays).
Mondays to Saturdays	7 a.m. to 8 a.m.	To members of early morning Swimming Club. For early morning
Sundays	7 a.m. to 9 a.m.	swimming.
Sundays	6 p.m. to 10 p.m.	October to March inclusive, when there was a special programme arranged by members who were entirely responsible for running the Centre on Sundays

SUBSCRIPTION:
One shilling a week per family, entitling all children under 16, or still at school, to free use of all equipment, and adults to use of each facility at a small charge. All children of member-families, over 16 and not still at school (as also all Temporary Members) pay an individual subscription of 6d. a week, and are also entitled to use all equipment for a small charge.

Services rendered, and activities available in return for weekly membership subscription without further payment:

I CONSULTATIVE SERVICES; by appointment, between 2 and 10 p.m., Tuesdays to Saturdays inclusive:
Periodic overhaul, comprising:
Laboratory examination,
Personal examination,
Family Consultation,

Any special appointment at request of staff or member.

Re-overhaul on discharge from medical care after sickness.

Advice on contraception.

Ante-Natal and Post-Natal care.

Infant care.

Immunisation against infectious fevers, allergy, etc. (service free; material at cost price).

Parental Consultations.

On announcement of conception.

At birth.

At each successive weaning period.

At any other time indicated by circumstances.

Vocational Guidance

Sex instruction to adolescents (private appointment with doctor).

Health overhaul of fiancé(e)s of members, whether themselves members or not.

Pre-marital Consultations.

Advisory service, legal, and other.

II GENERAL USE OF THE BUILDING, including the cafeteria and the main social hall with dance floor, at all times when the Centre was open.

Infants' Afternoon Nursery: 2–6 p.m. daily (Sundays excepted), with use of gymnasium and infants' swimming pool by Nursery children. Preparation by Mothers of Nursery teas, on a rota system (educational); charge for teas to cover cost of material only.

Night Nursery: 8–10 p.m., for children under 2

Activities available to adults at a small charge and free to children, at all times when the Centre is open:

Swimming bath (½ hour, 3d.) Swimming Club, 6d. weekly, 3 swims

Hot baths   (3d.)

Billiard tables   (6d.)   (no children on adult tables)

Table tennis   (1d.)

Darts   (1d.)

Cards, chess, draughts, etc. (1d.)

Cricket practice nets, and equipment
Equipment for boxing, fencing, etc.
Work room with sewing machine, cutting-out table, scissors, iron, fitting mirrors, etc.

Special equipment provided for children, and available for their use without extra charge to the family:

Roller skates
Shinty sticks (for hockey on skates)
Fairy cycles [*sic*]
Bicycles
Trampoline
Badminton rackets
Small billiard table
Table tennis
Cricket equipment for use at prac-
    tice nets
Balls
Parlour games: chess, draughts,
    ludo, etc.
Puzzles
Books
Drawing materials
Sewing materials
Typewriters
Tap dancing shoes for learners
Instruments for Percussion band

Activities available on weekly basis at regular times, once, twice, or three times weekly, afternoons and/or evenings; payments in most cases collected by secretaries of intra-mural clubs:

Badminton, several groups of vary-
    ing skill (3d.)
Boxing (3d.)
Keep Fit (3d.)
Women's League of Health and
    Beauty (3d.)
Swimming instruction ⎫
Diving instruction   ⎬ 3d. for use
Water polo   ⎭   of bath
Fencing (3d.)
Whist drives

Orchestral practice
Dance band practice
Wireless Room
Gramophone and records
Dance club (2d.)
Dancing instruction (2d.)
Tap-dancing class (2d.)
Roller skating (3d.)
The Stage, for Dramatic or Concert
 Party rehearsals (2d. a week to
 each member of the group. Also
 bookable by groups of children
 free)
Discussion Circle, with or without
 visiting speakers (2d.)
First-Aid classes
Woodwork shop
Various demonstration courses,
 e.g., on cookery, education of the
 young child, etc.

The charge in each case was designed to represent a rental covering the overhead of the part of the building used, as well as the upkeep of the particular equipment and any special costs incurred.

Special Occasions

Christmas or New Year's Eve Party (as many as 400 people to five-course meal followed by dancing and cabaret).

Children's Party at Christmas; organized by members, who were responsible for all preparations, including refreshments, as well as for running the party. As many as 600 children.

Birthday Party; running buffet prepared and served by members, cabaret and dancing. As many as 800 people.

Parties organised by various intramural Clubs; e.g. the Billiards Club, the Darts Club (50–200 individuals).

Performances by Dramatic and Concert Party groups (making a charge for entrance and filling the Theatre for three or more successive performances). Audience 150–200.

Matches with visiting teams from other Clubs.

Outings and expeditions of various sorts.

Family Parties and celebrations, for which a room can be booked.

Occasional entertainments by visiting players, dancers, musicians.

Associated Activities:

THE CENTRE "HOME FARM" at Oakley House, Bromley Common, Kent (7 miles from the Centre), for production of T.T. and attested milk, of fresh vegetables and fruit for sale to members; expectant mothers and young children have priority of purchase.

Planned for the education of the young family in the principles of food and nutrition.

The Home Farm provides also a playing field available to groups of members for cricket and football.

The Farm is an integral part of the work of the Centre, but up to now has been financed from a separate source.

GREAT SWIFTS HOLIDAY CAMP, Sissinghurst, Kent. Shortly after the Centre opened, through the generosity of the late Col. Victor Cazalet, we were fortunate in being offered the use of a large acreage as a country camp for members of the Centre. This land, which, as well as pasture, included a large wood surrounding a lake and an empty oast house, served as a base for camping activities. The oast house was repaired, redecorated, and fitted up gradually by the Centre members who made up week-end working parties for the purpose. Running water was laid on, and gas in cylinders installed for cooking. The camp was used by member-families for their summer holidays, and also for week-ends by some families with their own or borrowed cars, and by the adolescents and younger married people who reach it by bicycle or bus. Sleeping accommodation, either in the Oast House, in the Centre's tents, or on camping sites for the members' own tents, was bookable in advance in the Centre. It was decided by the members themselves that the charge per night made for use of the camp should be a *family* one—irrespective of the size of the family—like the membership subscription of the Centre itself. The camp has proved a quite invaluable asset in welding links in the social life of the membership.

APPENDIX C

The Self-Respecting Child by Alison Stallibrass, Thames and Hudson, London, 1974

p. 104–105:

Very few people have published detailed observations of the entirely spontaneous behaviour of babies and small children. Of these, probably the most enlightening and readable are by Millicent Washburn Shinn, an American biologist, whose books were published about 1900 and are now very difficult to obtain. Miss Shinn must have spent much of her time watching—with humble wonder and keen observation—every aspect of the behaviour of her baby niece Ruth, and in writing down, in far from boring detail, everything she had seen and heard. These books teach us more about babies than the kind that tell us what the *average* baby can be expected to do at this or that age. Also, although the author had no such intention, they show us what kind of response from adults it is that encourages healthy, joyous, and nourishing activity in babies.

One day when Ruth was two months old, Miss Shinn was holding her up against her shoulder—as she frequently did in order to let the baby look about her—keeping her own cheek close to the baby's head to provide a prop for it whenever Ruth grew momentarily tired of holding her head up. "But today she was not satisfied with having her head erect: she persistently straightened her back up against the arm that supported her—a new set of muscles thus coming under the control of her will. As often as I pressed her down on my shoulder, she would fret, and straighten up again and set to work diligently looking about her." After this Ruth was "possessed by the most insatiate desire to be up where she could see. It was hard to think that her fretting and even wailing when forced to lie down could mean only a formless discontent, and not a clear idea of what she wanted. As soon as she was held erect, or propped up sitting amid cushions, she was content."

By the middle of the third month, her smiles were fewer, and she looked about her earnestly and soberly; and in the last week I noted, without understanding, the expression of surprise that had come into her face as she gazed this way and that. The wide, surprised eyes must have meant that something new was before them. Were things beginning to separate themselves off to the baby's sight in definitely bounded spaces? . . . the wonder grew day by day, and for weeks the baby was looking about her silently, studying her world. She would inspect the familiar room carefully for many minutes, looking fixedly at object after object till the whole field of vision was reviewed, then she would turn her head eagerly and examine another section; and when she had seen all she could from one place, she would fret till she was carried to another, and then begin anew her inspection of the room in its changed aspect—always with the look of surprise and eagerness, eyes wide and brows raised.

p. 106:

Here is an example of a baby's interest in learning to recognize objects by sight when seen from different angles:

. . . she sat in my lap, watching with an intent and puzzled face the back and side of her grandmother's head. Grandma turned from her knitting and chirruped to her, and the little one's jaw dropped and her eyebrows went up with an expression of blank surprise. Presently I began to swing her on my foot, and at every pause in the swinging she would sit gazing at the puzzling head till grandma turned, and nodded or chirruped to her; then she would turn away satisfied and want more swinging. . . . At first amazed to see the coil of silver hair and the curve of the cheek turn into grandma's front face, the baby watched for a repetition of the miracle till it came to seem natural, and the two aspects were firmly knit together in her mind.

p. 109:

Here is one last example of Ruth's pattern of play. One day she managed to climb into her aunt's lap and the next day

spent a long time zealously climbing up a doorstep and letting herself down backward from it. The day after that, she tackled the stairs and climbed two steps. Later in the day, I set her at the bottom of the stairs and moved slowly up before her. The little thing followed after (her mother's arms close behind, of course; no one would be crazy enough to start a baby upstairs without such a precaution), tugging from step to step, grunting with exertion now and then, and exclaiming with satisfaction at each step conquered; slipping back once or twice, but undiscouraged—fifteen steps to the landing, where she pulled herself to her feet by the stair post, hesitated, made a motion to creep down head first, then crept, laughing, along the landing, and up five steps more, and shouted with triumph to find herself on the upper floor. She even looked with ambition at the garret stairs, and started towards them; but an open door tempted her aside to explore a room, and she forgot the stairs.

For the rest of the month the baby dropped to hands and knees and scrabbled joyously for the stairs at every chance of open door; she was not satisfied without going up several times daily, and having people who believed in letting her do things, and ensuring her safety by vigilance while she did them, instead of holding her back, she soon became expert and secure in mounting. She made assaults too on everything that towered up and looked in the least climbable.

This was before Ruth had learned to walk and when she was still under a year old.

p. 182:

In the industrially developed countries, small children are increasingly likely to spend their time in an environment which they cannot become familiar with through their senses, cannot understand, and in which they cannot, therefore, use their own judgement—nor even be allowed to try. Indeed a certain type of child, finding that his tentative efforts towards independence or adventure and experiment are frowned upon, may come to the conclusion that passivity is the best policy.

p. 189:

If a baby's personality is to develop in a healthy way, at least some of his activity—not necessarily connected with feeding—must be effective and produce results. His view of the world and of himself will depend on it. . . .

. . . What is important is that his mother—and the rest of the family—want to please him and feel that it is good for him to be pleased. If he is to become a person it is necessary for him to be treated as a person—not as a thing. One must respect his feelings and desires and try to satisfy his needs as he sees them as well as how we see them. . . .

The lesson we can learn from this is that we are definitely not spoiling a baby by letting him feel that he has the power to get from us what he wants—our attention, cuddling, or food—when he asks for it. On the contrary, we are making sure that we neither humiliate nor deaden him.

p. 198:

A baby's powers must be allowed to grow smoothly, which is another way of saying that he must be allowed to learn to do what he has newly become capable of learning to do. As soon as he has formed a mutually satisfying relationship with his mother, he needs opportunity to form different kinds of relationships with different kinds of people. As soon as he becomes aware of the existence of objects, he needs the opportunity to handle and investigate a *variety* of objects. As soon as he has become able to wriggle, or crawl, or hitch himself along on his bottom a little way, he needs to be allowed to practice the art of moving his body from one place to another and he should not be confined for long to his pram or his chair. As soon as he can walk he needs to be allowed to climb; as soon as he has become interested in making distinguishable sounds, he needs to find that he can obtain a response and should be answered—in his own language at first—not continually talked *at*. In short, he needs to know that he can be effective in many fields of activity.

p. 199:

To a child, approval of his spontaneous activity means love. Love that is expressed in care for his safety or for his future happiness, or even in constant attention or in *unsolicited* demonstrations of affection, means little or nothing to him. He needs the manifestations of love that increase his self-respect.

Selected Bibliography

* = reprints available from Holt Associates, Inc., 308 Boylston St., Boston, MA 02116.

Education and Society

HOLT, John
Escape From Childhood, Dutton '74, Ballantine paper, '75.
Freedom and Beyond, Dutton '72, Delta paper, '74.
What Do I Do Monday, Dutton '70, Delta paper, Dell paper.
The Underachieving School, Pitman '69, Delta paper.
How Children Learn, Pitman '67, Dell paper.
How Children Fail, Pitman '64, Delta paper, Dell paper.
* "To The Rescue," a review of Dennison's *The Lives of Children*, New York Review of Books, 10/69 (30/$1)
* "Big Bird, Meet Dick and Jane," a critique on "Sesame Street," Atlantic, 5/71 (30/$1)
* "Free The Children; They Need Room to Grow," an excerpt from *Escape from Childhood, Psychology Today*, 10/74, (100/$1.30)
* "The Cuteness Syndrome: Kitchie-Kitchie-Coo And Other Problems," an excerpt from *Escape from Childhood, Ms. Magazine*, 3/74 (25/$1)

BENNET
No More Public Schools (how to get your child out and what to do then), paper, $2.95, from The Bookworks, 1409 5th, Berkeley, CA 94710.

BERG, Ivar
Education and Jobs: The Great Training Robbery, Praeger '70, paper

BERG, Leila
Look at Kids, Penguin paper.

DENNISON, Geo.
The Lives of Children, Random House '69, paper.

DILLON, J.   *Personal Teaching*, Merrill '71.

FADER, Dan &
  MCNEILL, E.   *Hooked on Books*, Berkeley Press paper,'68.

GOODMAN, Paul   *Compulsory Miseducation*, Vintage paper, '62.
                         Growing Up Absurd, Vintage paper, '56.

HAPGOOD, D.   *Diplomaism*, Donald Brown '71.

HAWKINS, F.   *The Logic of Action*, Pantheon Press paper, '74.

HERNDON, James   *How to Survive in Your Native Land*, Simon &
                           Schuster '70, Bantam paper, '71.
                         The Way It Spozed to Be, Simon & Schuster '68,
                           paper.

ILLICH, Ivan   *Deschooling Society*, Harper & Row '70, paper.
                         Celebration of Awareness, Doubleday '70, paper.
                         Tools for Conviviality, Harper & Row '73.
                         Energy and Equity, Calder & Boyars Ltd, Lon-
                           don '74, Perennial paper.

KOHL, Herb   *Math, Writing and Games*, Vintage paper '74.
                         Reading, How To, Dutton '73.

MACRORIE, K.   *A Vulnerable Teacher*, Hayden '74.
                         Writing to Be Read, Hayden '71.
                         Up Taught, Hayden '70.

LOPATE, P.   *Being with Children*, Doubleday '75.

PEARSE, I. &   *The Peckham Experiment: A Study of the Living
  CROCKER, L.   Structure of Society*, Geo. Allen & Unwin Ltd.,
                           London, '43.

REIMER, E.   *School Is Dead*, Doubleday '71.

SCHRAG, P. &   *The Myth of the Hyperactive Child*, Pantheon '75.
  DIVOKY, D.

STALLIBRASS, A.   *The Self-Respecting Child*, Thames and Hudson,
                           London '74.

Related Social Problems

JACOBS, Jane   *The Death and Life of Great American Cities*, Vin-
                           tage
SCOTT, Rachel   *Muscle and Blood*, Doubleday 74.
TAYLOR, E.   *Richer by Asia*, Houghton Mifflin, '64.
TERKEL, Studs   *Working*, Pantheon '74.

Human Psychology and Development

FROMM, Erich   *Escape from Freedom*, Avon paper '41.
                         The Sane Society, Avon paper.

LAING, R.D.	*The Politics of Experience*, Ballantine paper '67. *The Divided Self*, Penguin '65. *Self and Others*, Pantheon '70, paper.
MASLOW, A.	*Toward a Psychology of Being*, Insight (van Nostrand). *The Farther Reaches of Human Nature*, Viking '71.
MAY, Rollo	*Man's Search for Himself*, Signet paper '67.
MILGRAM, S.	*Obedience to Authority*, Harper & Row '74.
van den BERG, J. H.	*The Changing Nature of Man*, Delta paper '75.

Films

HUGHES, Peggy	*We Have to Call It School*. Film about a small Danish free school, English narration. 16mm, b/w. Rent, $50; showing and discussion by Mrs. Hughes, $100 + exp. Highly recommended. For more info., Holt Associates, Boston. (617) 261-3920.
WISEMAN, Fred	*High School*, 16mm, rent $100; *Law And Order*, 16mm, rent $100; *The Cool World*, 16mm, rent $100; *Hospital; Basic Training; Essene; Juvenile Court*, 16mm, rent $100, also long-term lease, 144 min., b/w; *Primate; Welfare*. Zipporah Films, 54 Lewis Wharf, Boston, Mass. (617) 742-6680.

Other Sources of Information

Beacon Hill Free School	315 Cambridge St.; Boston, Mass. 02114
The Learning Exchange	P.O. Box 920; Evanston, Ill. 60204
Manas	P.O. Box 32112, El Sereno Sta., Los Angeles, CA 90032. * Reprint on Compulsory Attendance. (100/$1)
The Mother Earth News	105 Stoney Mtn. Rd., Hendersonville, N.C. 28739
New Schools Exchange	Pettigrew, ARK 72752. (501) 677-2300. Info. on new and alternative schools; clearinghouse for all aspects of alternative education. Write for subscription info. Publishes Directory of Alternative Schools, and supplements. Good source. Newsletter lists nationwide sources and publications about education.

Observations from the Treadmill	Mort Yanow, ed. RFD 1, Union, ME 04862. Irregular, on education and social change. Write for subscription info.
Playgrounds	Information on "adventure playgrounds," Lynn Converse, 25 Monument St., Charlestown, MA 02129.

(note: English books can be ordered from Blackwell's, Broad St., Oxford, England)